John Donne,
Petrarchist

john donne, petrarchist

*Italianate Conceits and Love
Theory in*

The Songs and Sonets

by Donald L. Guss
WAYNE STATE UNIVERSITY

WAYNE STATE UNIVERSITY PRESS
DETROIT, 1966

To my wife

acknowledgements

Like the academic community at large, I owe a great debt to the unfailing wisdom and charity of Helen C. White— a debt I proudly acknowledge.

I am proud to have had the help of the late Ruth Wallerstein, a gracious and brilliant lady. For decades, many of the finest of Renaissance studies have acknowledged her inspiration; I hope that it is perceptible in my work.

And I am glad to thank my friend Ralph Nash for his advice and encouragement. But I am ashamed to remember how often at lunch, in the elevator, and wherever they could not avoid me, I have taken from him and Alfred Schwarz their ideas and their patience.

This book was begun in Italy, in 1957, on a Fulbright Fellowship. It has since been supported in part by fellowships and grants from the Huntington Library, the Folger Shakespeare Library, the Rutgers University Research Fund, and—most generously—the Wayne State University Research Fund.

Parts of the book have already been published, in somewhat different form, as essays: "Donne's Conceit and Petrarchan Wit," *Publications of the Modern Language Association*, LXXVIII (1963), 308-314; "Donne's Petrarchism," *Journal of English and Germanic Philology*, LXIV (1965), 17-28; and "Wyatt's Petrarchism: An Instance of Creative Imitation in the Renaissance," *Huntington Library Quarterly*, XXIX (1965), 1-15. They are reprinted with the permission of the publishers.

contents

9

1

The Enigma and the Clew

Donne's love poetry has been a cultural force in our time. Like that of Shelley and Byron a century ago, it has inspired sighing girls with longing, and intense young men with ardor. It has provided poets with a model, aestheticians with an exemplar, and dark critics with a mine of phantom blasphemy and pornography.

In becoming contemporary, Donne's poetry has become puzzling. Modern critics find it hard to know whether "The Autumnall" is a somber meditation on death or a learned joke; whether "The Apparition" is savagely contemptuous or elegantly amused; and whether "Aire and Angels" is an attack on women or a celebration of perfect love. Nor is the confusion limited to Donne's difficult poems and impossible critics. Almost any lyric of Donne may now with some justice be thought to be either metaphysical or epigrammatic in thought, gay or sombre in tone, and sociological or intimate in provenance. And the most civilized of his critics will describe him as essentially related to Anacreon, St. Augustine, Alciati, St. Ignatius, Marino, and Cavalcanti [1]—that is, to the most diverse aspects of Western culture, and the least reconcilable elements of the human mind.

The critical problem, then, is somehow to make clear which of many readings of Donne's poems are historically probable. One way to do this is to define Donne's audience, for undeclared assumptions about Donne's audience have guided his critics. Dryden, assuming that Donne means to be gallant to polite ladies, was struck by the inappropriateness of his conceits. Johnson, assuming that

11

Donne writes to please gentlemanly and educated readers, was offended by what seemed Donne's indecorous cavorting and over-eager desire to dazzle. Nineteenth-century critics, assuming that Donne writes from an overflow of feeling, marvelled at his complex soul and profound preoccupations. And many modern critics, assuming that Donne generalizes for a skeptical and intellectual audience, discuss his sharp comments upon life and learning. As such examples indicate, interpretations of Donne are closely related to assumptions about his audience. But though explicit statements of such assumptions may be illuminating, extra-textual research has uncovered little or nothing about Donne's actual readers or his attitude to them;[2] therefore the central problems, though they can be rephrased, cannot be solved through an analysis of Donne's relation to his audience.

What Donne meant his readers to feel may be more fruitfully sought through a study of the tradition in which he wrote. For a poetical tradition, which gives an author rules and techniques, gives his readers a set of attitudes. For example, if Shylock and Edmund are thought of as belonging to a tradition of developmental character analysis, they evoke one reaction; if they are thought of as traditional stage villains, they evoke another. If Milton's Satan is thought of in terms of Romantic Prometheanism, he becomes entirely different from what he is in terms of traditional Christianity. When Donne's conceits are considered in relation to classical literature, they seem laboriously ingenious; in relation to medieval analogy, they seem less original and more philosophic.[3] Historical criticism has rectified misinterpretations of Shakespeare and Milton by placing their works in the traditions to which they belong; it offers the best road to an understanding of Donne.

In fact, most critics of Donne have consciously looked at his poetry in the light of tradition. Until recently, they have concentrated on Donne's departures from poetical norms, so that his originality is a critical locus as familiar as Jonson's art and Shakespeare's nature. But his violation of tradition has been variously interpreted: as innovation (Carew), ignorance (Dryden), wilfulness (Johnson), eccentricity (Coleridge), and iconoclasm (Cleanth Brooks). Thus, though Donne's novelty has until recently been the pivot of critical theories, the general agreement was merely superficial. Dryden blamed Donne for being without the acquirements essential to polite conversation in a Restoration drawing room. Johnson criticized Donne for violating an eighteenth-century taste—which he thought eternal—for sound sense weightily expressed. Brooks praised Donne for attacking Victorian discretion and piety. In consort these critics say that Donne is outside a pattern—but each has his own idea of what pattern, the drawing room, the study, or the family circle. Thus, among the older critics there were sharp disagreements about the nature of Donne's originality. Furthermore, their authority has been vitiated by modern discoveries suggesting that until the late thirties scholars had so little background material available to them, that their estimates of seventeenth-century originality were bound to be naive.

Currently, critical attention has turned with a vengeance to the traditional elements in Donne's verse. The oddest of his images have been accounted for by seventeenth-century theories, and assimilated to ancient analogues. Where thirty years ago a typical scholarly article defined Donne's unique qualities, today such an article finds parallels to his conceits in everything from Hebrew theologians and Arab metaphysicians to courtly tapestries and popular proverbs. The fruits of such studies have been interesting, and their assumptions are invaluable; for to know the tradition in which the *Songs and Sonets* fall would be to know the expectations upon which they relied, and therefore the effects they were meant to have. But modern scholars have in fact failed to provide a convincing explanation of Donne's poetic.

Studies of Donne's background have generally found literary theories which justify his practice; or collected analogues of his images; or explicated his poems by reference to non-literary Renaissance documents. Though each approach has been valuable, none has gotten to the heart of Donne; for none has discovered background material that is clearly and immediately relevant to Donne's poems.

Studies of literary criticism too often seek theories that justify *a discordia concors.* They thereby commit themselves to ahistorical criteria: in defining metaphysical poetry as a *discordia concors* they assume the adequacy of Johnson's sense of disproportion; and they bring together literary principles which seventeenth-century thinkers would have found most diverse—for example, an elegant search for original conceits, with a devout reading of the book of the creatures. Without a more historically based choice of categories, they cannot discover what literary theory Donne himself might have endorsed; they cannot distinguish between his principles and those which are merely vaguely similar.

Studies of Donne's analogues tend to be collections of miscellaneous parallels. Finding that Donne compares lovers to a compass, for example, they list as many instances as possible of early symbolic uses of the compass, or even of the circle; and they argue that Donne's compass includes all the significations previously associated with the instrument, or at least one set of such meanings. Where such studies rely on the notion that Renaissance readers saw symbols everywhere, they are on weak ground; for it is unlikely that Donne's readers would have expected any secular work—particularly a love lyric—to be read allegorically.[4] If they did, they would almost certainly have been innocent of the notion that a term always bears all of its symbolic meanings: a *mundus symbolicus,* like a dictionary, lists meanings that are alternative rather than simultaneous.[5] On the other hand, where lists of parallels to Donne's conceits assume, in an Empsonian way, that any word always reverberates with all its possible meanings, the lists do nothing to discriminate between those meanings which are explicit and essential, and those which are merely delicate nuances.

Explications of Donne's poems in the light of Renaissance writings have similarly failed to distinguish the directly relevant from the peripheral. Certainly, poets and their readers are men; their feelings about poetry are not entirely isolated from their other feelings, and a knowledge of their theology, metaphysics, and art bears upon their poetry. But in the light of Rosemond Tuve's forceful arguments [6] it is illegitimate to assume, and probably impossible to prove, that Donne, like T. S. Eliot, means to exploit all the reminiscences that his culture provides. Most explicators of Donne have been unconscionably vague about the necessary procedural differences between explicating a poem developed by association and archetypal pattern, and explicating a poem developed logically. Where the principles of explication are so ill-defined, allusions to Renaissance tracts seem random. No one would seriously argue that "The Canonization" ("For Godsake hold your tongue") is about religious orders practicing silence, or "The Sunne Rising" ("Busie old foole, unruly Sunne") about astronomers who disagreed whether the sun moves. But readings as improbable have been maintained, for explicators have failed to define convincingly a standard of relevance.

All three sorts of historical studies illuminate Donne's poetry by considering it within its time. All make it harder naively to associate Donne's compass with a twentieth-century grammar school, or to assume that Samuel Johnson is Donne's ideal audience. But all have been weak in distinguishing general background material from elements directly relevant to the poems. It is my theory that such a distinction could be made if Donne's verses were set in a poetical tradition; for such a tradition is the set of resources upon which a poet directly draws. For example, it is interesting to wonder whether Milton's invocations to his muse are signs of a Catholic temperament, but any discussion of his invocations must be founded on the tradition of the epic invocation—it is that which is central.[7] Defining the tradition used by a poet is the most precise tool we have for distinguishing the immediate from the peripheral in his art.

Some critics have considered Donne as a poet entirely outside of tradition, basing their theories on a hostility towards elegance and a sympathy for frankness. There, they have said, were the Petrarchan poets, languishing in various uncomfortable postures expressive of devotion. And then, suddenly, there was Donne—intellectually inquisitive, sexually eager, and marvellously complicated. There were the Petrarchists, carefully ornamental and studiously trite; and then there was Donne, colloquial, fervent, and brilliant. There were the Petrarchists, half-cured and perfectly well-bred; and then, happily, there was Donne, brutal, vibrant, and alive. This picture of Donne has more than a grain of truth—it has a world of responsiveness.

But in elaborating his response as a historical theory, the critic has tended to oppose Donne to the Petrarchists in a sort of ideological warfare, as though the Petrarchists were freshmen, naive and confident in the bourgeois beliefs of their families, and Donne a heroic sophomore, wittily revealing the way things really are. The problem here as elsewhere is a failure to distinguish the peripheral from the primary meanings of a poem: a failure to differentiate Donne's temperamental individuality from iconoclasm, or Petrarchan clichés from propaganda.

In sum, most treatments of Donne have not clearly shown that the elements with which they are concerned, like universal analogy or the Spenserian style, are directly, immediately, and centrally involved in Donne's poetry. It seems likely that a clearer view may be obtained by studying Donne in relation to strictly poetical traditions, relegating cultural milieu to the background and maintaining a sensible view of what a tradition is. In this book I propose to relate the *Songs and Sonets* to the dominant poetical tradition of Donne's time—that is, to Petrarchism.[8]

In this context, Petrarchism must not be too closely associated —though it be vaguely connected—with Victorian manners, courtly refinements, or literary decay. In one sense Petrarchism is an elaboration of politeness. But in another, and more proper, sense, it is the mainstream of Italian literature.[9] As a primary channel through which Italian influence reached transalpine Europe, it is a main aspect of the Renaissance. And it is a rich and subtle convention. The Petrarchists imitate Petrarch as creatively as Racine imitates Greek drama. Limited by their times, guided by their philosophies of life and art, and directed by their individual geniuses; seeking in Petrarch sometimes poetic inspiration, sometimes standards of taste, and sometimes a vocabulary of gallantry, the Petrarchists form a tradition which endured from the Middle Ages through the Counter-Reformation, which reached from Petrarch's religious meditation to Serafino's witty compliment, and which influenced poets from England to Hungary.[10] The richness of Petrarchism explains the richness of Donne. In the course of its development, Petrarchism digested elements of scholastic logic, Augustinian moralization, and

Neoplatonic theorizing—of lascivious naturalism, Anacreontic wit, and pastoral affectation. It was a mode of expressing the major intellectual movements of the Renaissance; and it was adapted by each important Petrarchist to a new culture, and often to a picturesque personality. It offered Donne examples of the most diverse ideas and attitudes expressed in a conventional language and form.

Despite its richness, Petrarchism remains readily recognizable. It is thus like the epic tradition. To allude to the epic, a writer did not need to adopt a pre-established philosophical attitude or literary style—on such grounds, there are vast differences among the *Iliad,* the *Aeneid, Paradise Lost,* and the *Dunciad.* What the imitative poets did adopt is a general mood (of grandeur); formal devices (like the catalogue); recurrent details (like the seven folds of a shield); and characteristic figures of speech (like allusions to rosy-fingered Aurora). The tradition is not absolutely inherent in any one or two elements, but it is distinctly recognizable. Petrarchism, partly because of its affiliations with popular songs and partly because the early Renaissance is not thoroughly formalistic, is not so discrete as the epic tradition. But the Renaissance poet could call up its context by such things as a general sense of love's dignity and a tendency to exalted sentiment; by themes like the aging lover and the obdurate lady, and details like the radiance of the lady's eyes; and, above all, by conceits like the lady-murderess, the tear-flood, and the sigh-tempest. Though a poet might use a Petrarchan theme or conceit incidentally, what I mean to demonstrate is that Donne's Petrarchism is as essential, though as original, as Milton's use of the epic convention.

One result of this demonstration will be to explain Donne's differences from the Spenserians. For although Elizabethan rhetorics have names for Donne's tropes—as they do for those of Martial, Byron, and Dylan Thomas—Donne's manner is clearly different from Spenser's. Yet the historical nature of the difference is elusive. If Donne's style is occasioned by the baroque *zeitgeist,* it is strange that Serafino (d. 1500) anticipates his radical image (and his conjunction of love with death), while Marino, Donne's contemporary, continues to practice melodiousness, pictorialism, and allegory. If

Donne's metaphysical logic stems from Ramism, it is odd that the logical, metaphysical sermon-style was bitterly attacked by the Ramists. And if Donne's conceit derives from universal analogy, it is hard to see why he was reputed an original wit—and harder yet to distinguish him from Spenser, whose allegory has the same root.[11] In short, the baroque, Ramism, and universal analogy fail to explain Donne's stylistic innovations.

Petrarchism, however, does explain them. For there are two modes of Petrarchism. One, which I call humanistic, aims at universal truths, eternal emotions, and neoclassical decorousness: it is elegant, idyllic, and sentimental. This form of Petrarchism spread throughout Europe with the mid-sixteenth-century Bemboist anthologies. In England and France, its neoclassical bias was reinforced by a tendency to treat Petrarchism as a noble cultural import on a par with Latin and Greek forms—as another classical genre. Before Donne, humanistic Petrarchism dominates the English lyric.

Donne, however, writes in the other Petrarchan mode—that characterized by fantastic arguments, emotional extravagance, and peregrine comparisons. Transalpine poets knew this strain both as an element in Petrarch's own lyrics, and as developed by Serafino, the Neapolitan anthologies, Tasso, and Guarino. In the sixteenth century they generally assimilated such Petrarchism to humanistic standards. At the end of the sixteenth and beginning of the seventeenth centuries, however, the unregulated emotions and indiscriminate wit of extravagant Petrarchism became fashionable throughout Europe, helping to produce Gongorism, *préciosité,* and Marinism.[12] Donne's stylistic departure from the Spenserians results largely from his being the first great English lyricist to write in the extravagant Petrarchan mode.

Extravagant Petrarchism is Donne's poetic tradition; it is the context to which his lyrics belong. My purpose is to indicate, in the light of this tradition, how Donne is to be read. To do so, I gloss Donne's tropes by reference to analogous Petrarchan conceits. I compare his qualities to those of poets in the same tradition. And I define Donne's historical situation in relation to the general Petrarchan background. Now, the validity of my argument depends on three criteria. It must establish a historical probability that Donne is a Petrarchist and a critical probability that his poems make sense as Petrarchism. In applying these criteria, my reader need use only his reason. But I ask for his faith in applying the third criterion. For I frequently compare conceits and passages characteristic of Donne with passages characteristic of several Italian poets and styles. My method makes sense only if the Italian passages I cite are indeed characteristic of major stylistic movements. Unless my reader has reason to believe that they are not, I ask him to trust that they are.

I claim that Donne writes in a Petrarchan style, not that I have discovered specific models for his lyrics. Indeed, it is virtually impossible to discover the Petrarchists' sources, for they imitate and translate each other as well as common models. It may seem odd, therefore, that I limit my discussion of Petrarchism almost entirely to Italy. But Donne almost certainly knew many of the Italian poets discussed here. He read Italian and regularly inscribed in his books an Italian line from one of Petrarch's lyrics. He read several major Italian authors, developed Italianate love theories, and imitated at least one lyric of Guarino's.[13] Furthermore, no Renaissance literary current can be understood without a full study of the Italians; Petrarchism especially is an Italianate movement; and, to the student of Donne, Italian Petrarchism is interesting for sidelights it casts upon Cavalcanti, Marino, and others. Italian Petrarchists were surely not the only Petrarchists whose works Donne knew. But they are of the greatest European importance in a period when literature is European; and they suffice to identify the tradition in which Donne wrote. If Donne did not know the poems I cite, he knew others very like them.

Having thus justified my method, I may well anticipate my conclusions. I do not mean to deny Donne's originality; but, assuming poetry, like language itself, to be conventional, I mean to discover the tradition in which Donne writes, so that his originality may be properly perceived. Extravagant Petrarchism is the realm of affected sentiment and wit, of hyperbole, complication, and conceit, where outflying philosophy and enormous emotions are generated

19

by ordinary people and commonplace events—where the death of a girl destroys the world, and a lock of hair maintains life in a body. It is, above all else, a super-civilized language, whose extreme sentiments and high-flown conceits are merely polite, and sometimes careless. Donne makes that civilized, ceremonious extravagance meaningful. He makes its affected postures flexible, its esoteric doctrines significant, and its fatuous sentiments passionate. By recognizing the conventional quality of Donne's conceits, one can discover his true value as one of England's greatest poets, and Europe's greatest Petrarchists.

II

The Petrarchan Legions in Italy

For four and a half centuries now, major Petrarchists have been attacked from two directions. By neoclassicists, they have been accused of over-ingenuity, indecorously exaggerated sentiment, and violations of common sense. By others, they have been condemned for imitativeness, conventionalized feelings, and a concern with language rather than meaning.[1] Undoubtedly guilty of both charges, the Petrarchists have never since been esteemed as they were in the sixteenth century. It is no wonder that, distinguishing them from Donne, Douglas Bush refers to "the legion of Petrarchan sonneteers, whose protestations seldom move us." [2]

Nevertheless, Petrarchism is an essential element of Renaissance literature. It dominates the lyric, and permeates Renaissance comedy, tragedy, elegy, pastoral, and chivalric romance. Indeed, Petrarchism is so central to the age that many critics have treated it as though it were the Renaissance. The rejection of Petrarchism by seventeenth-century French critics signaled the repudiation of the Renaissance and the initiation of a neoclassical era.[3] For moderns, "Petrarchism-Spenserianism" signifies the general tendencies of elevated Renaissance literature: literary imitation, classical properties, formal rhetoric, an aristocratic bias, and a dependence upon commonplaces. And many critics seek the limits of the Renaissance in the transitional area between Petrarchism and Marinism, representing respectively Renaissance and Baroque. Such instances are reminders that Petrarchism is a crucial and characteristic expression of the Renaissance.

The critic, therefore, must apply to Petrarchism the principles he applies to such modes as the chivalric epic and the Ovidian elegy; and he must accord it a similar respect. Primarily, he must recognize in Petrarchism an aristocratic literary form, operating in an international—chiefly Italianate—context, and employing conscious literary imitation; and he must not condemn the lyrics before he understands them within these self-confessed limitations. Reputable critics today do not expect Spenser or Milton to look in their hearts and write, or to be concerned with folkways and local color; nor do they pretend that the *Fairie Queene* and *Paradise Lost* had no precedents other than the *Mirror for Magistrates* and the *Davideis*. Yet Petrarchan poetry is considered to be bad because it is imitative and elegant, and Donne is thought to be anti-Petrarchan because he is unlike Surrey and Watson. The historical critic, who makes old literature accessible by defining its premises, must interpret Petrarchism within its Renaissance context.

Few English-speaking critics have recognized the absurdity involved in asking Renaissance lyricists to use a language such as men speak, and to write from a spontaneous overflow of powerful feelings. But Wyatt's Petrarchan poems have been shown to be both personal and valuable.[4] Sidney's and Spenser's are widely admired. And a number of themes whose charm was once attributed to their anti-Petrarchism—for example, the poet's assertion that he writes from his heart, and his declaration of independence from a cold lady—are now understood to be Petrarchan.[5] Though its proper direction is yet to be recognized, there are signs of a revaluation of English Petrarchism.

Italian scholars have gone further: they have reversed nineteenth-century judgments and restored Petrarchism to a post of honor. Furthermore, they have defined and firmly established the four basic principles to be accepted in any approach to Petrarchism. First, as Elwert and Ulivi show, Petrarchan imitation is intended to surpass, not merely to reproduce, its models. Second, as Marzot and Alonso demonstrate, Petrarchism is an evolving, not a static mode, encompassing extremes as divergent as Wordsworth's romanticism and Baudelaire's. Third, as Baldacci proves, even the most imitative Petrarchan school, Bemboism, is distinctly different from Petrarch in its artistic standards and world-view. Fourth, as Vinciguerra says, Petrarchism defined for a peninsula without national identity the language of Italian poetry—a language which retained its preeminence into the twentieth century.[6] With the recognition of these principles, there has been a renewed critical appreciation of Petrarchan poetry. Even Croce finds true poetry in many conventional Petrarchists; and even Chariteo—who had been scorned since the early sixteenth century—has now his expositor and defender.[7] A recent anthology of Italian Renaissance poetry recognizes in Petrarchism a general value and frequent greatness. The most recent history of Italian literature goes further, to declare that Petrarchism was a great accomplishment of the golden age of Italian literature.[8] In general Italian scholars, understanding the limits of Petrarchan aspirations, now value Petrarchan achievements.

There is not yet, however, a history of Petrarchism expressing the results of modern studies, nor has there been a systematic application of modern principles to pre-Bemboist Petrarchism. It is therefore difficult to sketch a history of Italian Petrarchism, and at the same time to convince English-speaking readers of the validity of the new approach. Nonetheless, I shall provide in this chapter a preliminary sketch, asking the reader's trust at points where I contradict the Romantic clichés, and, where brevity requires omission, omitting what is least relevant to the study of Donne.

The Petrarchan tradition is composed of many schools. Each school accepts the central elements of the tradition and develops them in a distinct way. A primary element of the tradition is the Petrarchan attitudes: amorous devotion, dependence, adoration, dolor, and despair. The air with which these postures are assumed varies from helpless emotionalism to sophisticated and frankly superficial compliment.

Another chief element of Petrarchism is its collection of conceits: its fires of passion, tempests of sighs, dying and resurrected lovers, and pictures of ladies engraved on lovers' hearts. The conceits are developed with various degrees of literalness: some poems use them purely as passionate hyperboles, and others pretend that they are literally true, the fires burning houses and the sighs moving ships.

A third element of Petrarchism is its collection of commonplaces of amorous philosophy: for example, the two-in-oneness of lovers, the distinction between base and spiritual love, and the Neoplatonic amorous ladder. Furthermore, in the fifteenth century some trite conceits are given philosophical status by Ficino: for example, death for unreturned love, and the four-in-oneness of lovers. The philosophical commonplaces, like the conceits, are accepted with various degrees of literalness: sometimes they serve primarily to reveal the lover's devotion and belief in love; at other times, they serve as scientific principles upon which are based definitions, distinctions, and conclusions.

Finally, there are stock Petrarchan situations, such as the initiation of love, the parting of lovers, and the despairing poet complaining of his lady's hardness. These situations are conceived with various degrees of particularity. Some poems treat the situations in the most generalized way; others modify a generalized treatment by some particular indications, as by noting, in a poem of parting, the route of the traveller; and some make the themes purely occasional. In conclusion, one might note that there are two poles of Petrarchism: at one extreme, there are occasional poems, sophisticated poses, literal imagery, and logical philosophizing; and at the other, generalized situations, pure sentimentalizing, emotional hyperboles, and dramatically treated thought.

Though Petrarch himself drew on a rich, mature, and living poetic tradition, a brief description of Petrarchism may well begin with Petrarch's *Canzoniere,* the first and greatest of Petrarchan collections. The *Canzoniere* is composed of three hundred and sixty-six components in various verse forms, chiefly sonnets. In the Renaissance as today most editions divided the *Canzoniere* into two parts, the first dealing with events during Laura's lifetime, and the second treating events after her death. Though it includes political, familiar, and religious themes, the dominant theme of the *Canzoniere* is, of course, Petrarch's love of Laura.

The composition of the *Canzoniere* was a continuing process,

stretching across five decades. Some of the lyrics were written before Petrarch thought of a collection, and perhaps before he thought
of Laura; others were written specifically to give the collection
unity—for example, to provide introductions, transitions, and indications of passing time. Some lyrics were tailored to a place in the
whole. Most are only generally relevant, having no more specific a
function than to treat of the joys and sorrows of love.

The union of discrete lyrics in a narrative is one of the most
influential and creative aspects of Petrarch's lyric activity. In one
sense, he was anticipated by earlier poets. The collected lyrics of
Provençal poets were generally prefaced by brief lives invented to
provide a context for the lyrics; [9] and these gave the collection a
kind of biographical unity. In Italian, Guittone's canzoniere tells a
distinct story; and, with the aid of prose, so does Dante's *Vita
Nuova*. But Petrarch's collection, covering so long a time span, re-
cords both his maturation and his reflections upon his life. For
English readers, its effect can perhaps best be indicated by analogy
with Wordsworth. Suppose that Wordsworth had not written the
Prelude but had instead collected his short poems and attempted to
reveal the growth of his mind by arranging those poems, revising
some and adding some others. Suppose as well that Wordsworth
did not often repudiate an old poem whether or not it fit the major
outlines of his work; and that he continued his sequence almost to
his death, revealing his progress from a wild love of nature to a
stricter love of God. Such a supposed sequence suggests the kind of
unity that the *Canzoniere* has. Its story is composed of Petrarch's
feelings during the life and after the death of his beloved lady, and
of Petrarch's progress from amour to repentance and prayer, as he
discovers that the rest and fulfillment he desires cannot be found in
this world. All the poems are the richer for this story; but most of
them affect us primarily as discrete lyrics.

Some of Petrarch's lyrics, then, are those of a young cavalier,
and some are those of an aging cleric. Some are purely gallant;
some are poems of gallantry rewritten by an older Petrarch whose
style was subdued and whose conscience was acute; and some are
introspective and meditative, though given an amorous cast to suit

the collection. Probably the central voice is that of dignified intimacy, of elevated confession; and the central figure that of a lover wandering through a familiar countryside, indulging himself by finding in the streams signs of his tears, in the breeze signs of his sighs, and everywhere tokens of the beauty of Laura or the shortness of life.

In treating these elements, the *Canzoniere* brings together the currents of Latin literature, Romance literature, and Augustinian meditation. Petrarch emulates the linguistic achievement of Augustan Rome, the cultivated sensibilities of Provence, and the self-analysis and Christian eloquence of St. Augustine. Petrarch's union of Latin and Romance germinated many elements of the Renaissance. His Augustinianism too was influential, pointing from scholasticism to Platonic idealization and from generalization to introspection. None of Petrarch's followers, however, treated all three currents as intimately and reverently as he did.

Petrarch's Latinity—which made him a patron saint of the humanists—pervades his *Canzoniere*. It is not that his lyrics are each modelled on classical sources, though some of his themes are Latin (e.g. the poet outside his lady's door), and though his conceits generally have analogues in Latin works (as they do in the *Greek Anthology* and in Provençal lyrics). Nor does Petrarch's Latinity lie primarily in the secularity of his world, in his conception of love as a fatal passion, or in his tendency to pastoral—although these are central to the *Canzoniere,* and definitely colored by Roman literature. Chiefly, Petrarch's Latinity resides in the vast number of phrases translated, of lines recollected from the Augustans.[10] And it resides in the general conformity of his language to those phrases: his conscious imitation of the linguistic purity, generality, and elevation of the Augustans, and of the urbanity and witty phrasing of Ovid.

The Provençal element in the *Canzoniere* is also pervasive.[11] Occasionally, Petrarch seeks metrical difficulties and conscious obscurity; often, he uses subtle discriminations, complicated conceits, allegories, debates, and Provençal images, like the revivified phoenix and the salamander in the flames. Even more centrally, Petrarch's lyrics are generally based on complaints, excuses, lists of impossi-

bilities, and other Provençal forms, radically modified. And his entire sequence rests on the notion that gentility is the highest quality, that love is genteel, and that his own nobility makes his story
marvellous. It is Provençal chivalry, more than Roman aristocracy,
which colors Petrarch's sensibility, authorizing his reverence of elegance and his commitment to hyper-refined feelings.

Petrarch's Augustinianism, explicit in his *Secretum*, is, as Umberto Bosco has shown,[12] a major aspect of the *Canzoniere*. It resides in Petrarch's confessional introspection; in his knowledge that
the will is radically corrupt; and in his deep dissatisfaction with the
mutable, his restless complaints against the inadequacy of the world,
and his consequent turning to God. Indeed, the plot of the *Canzoniere*—an unhappy love, the death of human beauty, and repentance—is, as Petrarch sees it, itself Augustinian.

Latinity, Romanticism, and Augustinianism are, of course, not
discrete in the *Canzoniere*. Petrarch's self-analysis echoes the *Confessions,* but it also echoes the amorous psychology of Provençal
lyricists and chivalric romancers. Petrarch's linguistic stylization reflects Roman aulicism, but it reflects as well the Provençal conceit.
And Petrarch's inability to renounce his love is both Augustinian,
showing the will's corruption, and Latinate, revealing a fatal passion. The strands are not easily separable in the *Canzoniere*. But a
critical focus on each is most useful. The essential elements of the
Canzoniere are elegant gallantry and sententious meditation; the
dignified intimacy of an elevated confession; and the dramatic figure
of a lover alone in a familiar countryside, communing with breezes
and with trees, and indulging his sentiments as he contemplates his
love and his life. These elements take their meaning from the way
in which they are presented—from the Latinate, Romance, and
Augustinian colors cast on them.

The *Canzoniere* joins the medieval with the classic, the secular
with the religious. It fuses thoughtfulness with emotion, gallantry
with piety, word-play with stylistic bareness,[13] and scholasticizing
logic with humanistic rhetoric and polite conceits. Furthermore,
it conceals a profound realism beneath unequalled lyric grace.
Throughout, there is a delicate sensibility isolating and reflecting

27

upon elements of experience; and there is a professional stylization emphasizing each lucent word through puns, conceits, and turns. Although Petrarch's great reputation rested at first on his Latin work and then on his *Trionfi,* it is no wonder that shortly after his death the *Canzoniere* was generally recognized to be one of the greatest bodies of poetry in any modern language.

Petrarch early became the great model of succeeding Italian poets, and he remained so long. The richness of his work, its union of so many elements, and its accommodation of both medieval and Renaissance tendencies, led to the growth of as many kinds of Petrarchists as there are kinds of Christians. For the Petrarchan schools —the chief of which are described below—there are two main alternatives: to employ Petrarch as a guide to experience and morality; or to use him as a handbook of rhetorical methods and conceits. There are other major discriminations to be made—most importantly, perhaps, between those poets who find in Petrarch their artistic ideals and those who find there only usable devices; or between those who imitate the major outlines of Petrarch's story, and those who imitate only his elegant and indirect expressions. But the truly vital distinction—the one which includes most of the others— is, again, that between using Petrarch as a guide to life and using him as a rhetorical handbook.

The first group of Petrarchists of international import are Chariteo, Tebaldeo, Serafino, and their imitators, poets called *quattrocentisti* because they were preeminent at the end of the fifteenth century, though some of them wrote later. I reserve a more extensive description of their poetry for a later chapter. Meanwhile it may be said that the poles of this school were Chariteo, an aulic humanist, and Serafino, an improviser at court. In general, the *quattrocentisti* employ Petrarch's *Canzoniere* as a collection of conceits useful for ceremonious politeness and an elevation of court events. Despite a veneer of courtly Neoplatonism or, alternatively, of classical stoicism, their outlook is not philosophic or even meditative. The purpose of Chariteo is to adapt Petrarchan rhetoric to ceremony and praise. The purpose of Serafino is to accomplish ordinary social gestures in novel and ingenious ways: for example, to console a lady who slips on ice by asserting that the water, frozen by her chastity, would have melted had she felt the poet's passion; or to apologize for not writing an epitaph requested by a lady, by explaining that the poet himself died for love of her. The *quattrocentisti* thus adapt Petrarchism to the needs of an extravagant and emphatically secular society; their Petrarchism is an art of ceremony, gallantry, and conceit, of clever trifling and courtly make-believe.

The so-called Bemboist phase of Petrarchism, dominant in the first half of the sixteenth century, reached transalpine Europe through two anthologies of great international influence, *Rime diverse, Libro primo,* and *Delle rime, Libro secondo.* Bemboism is a classicizing movement. It culminates three developments, the Petrarchan commentary, the Neoplatonic love treatise, and the discussion of imitation in the vernacular. The Petrarchan commentary—whether an explication, a set of footnotes, or a treatise on Petrarch's philosophy—elevated Petrarch's learning and rhetoric, treating his poems as the humanists treated those of Horace, Plautus, and other Romans. The love treatise—which generally depended more on Petrarch than on Plato—gave intellectual authority to Petrarch's statements about love. And the discussion of imitation culminated with Bembo's victorious assertion of the doctrine that Petrarch is the one author to follow in Italian verse, as Cicero is in Latin prose. The result of all three developments was that Petrarch became a classic to be studied as a model of rhetoric, a compendium of philosophic maxims, and an exemplar of the Italian lyric.

One aspect of Bemboist imitation is linguistic. It was believed that as a proper imitation of Virgil and Ovid would yield a pure Latin, so a proper imitation of Petrarch would yield a pure Italian— a most ambitious aim in a land without national identity, where Latin was the official language and where governmental divisions corresponded to dialectic differences. In his prose, Bembo insisted that Petrarch be the model of Italian verse. Following his lead, grammarians like Dolce and Liburnio sought to establish the rules of the Italian language by reference to Petrarch. And many editions of Petrarch—for example, Lanfranco's, Alunno's, Fausto's, and Dolce's

—included elaborate linguistic apparatus, such as alphabetical lists of Petrarch's nouns, each noun followed by all the epithets which Petrarch applies to it. The imitation of Petrarch, which seems so unimaginative today, was an attempt—and a successful one—to create the language of Italian poetry.

A second aspect of Bemboist imitation is intellectual. Because of the humanistic assumption that the poet is a philosopher, and because of the extensive commentaries upon Petrarch, the Bemboists thought of Petrarch as a philosopher of love. Where Petrarch's poems tend to be dramatic meditations, the Bemboists often write high-minded expositions of such commonplaces as love's elevation of the lover's soul, or the lady's reflection of the Beautiful and the Good. Infrequently in Petrarch but most frequently among his Bemboist imitators, a poem is based on a generalization and examples, or on one or two generalizations and a conclusion. Their expository emphasis results from their belief that Petrarch's generalizations express a systematic philosophy of love.

The third and most important aspect of Bemboist imitation is psychological. Like the classics, Petrarch's *Canzoniere* was assumed to show life in its most general and permanent aspects. Insofar as Petrarch was a model of decorous emotions for the Bemboists, he provided them a pattern not of politeness but of human nature. For example, as Roman comedies showed young men to be amorous and old men to be avaricious, Petrarch showed young men to be idealistically in love, and old men to be sage, humble, and pious. Seeking universally human nature in Petrarch, the Bemboists simplified the outline of his story, limited the kinds of events they admitted, and generalized the sentiments. Furthermore, in making Petrarch a classic, many of the Bemboists treated his beloved countryside as an idyllic setting. In short, they emphasized the Petrarchan story, and wrote two distinct kinds of lyrics: the youthful, idealistic, and amorous; and the religious and repentant.

Among Bemboists, the conceit is low-keyed. Petrarch's conceits have a dramatic function: they are in part the private images of a highly conscious mind which has long played upon the same elements of experience. Nonetheless, Petrarch's conjunction of fires with floods and heats with colds is emphatically neat and stylized. The *quattrocentisti* ignore the conceit's dramatic element and exaggerate its neatness. Where Petrarch's figures of speech are imaginative names for aspects of his microcosm, theirs operate on a macrocosmic level: their passion and tears become fire and floods outright, burning buildings and drowning ladies. The Bemboists, partly in reaction, bring the Petrarchan conceit close to a generalized and elegant language like Racine's. Neat points arise from their language because it is Petrarch's; but they do not emphasize those points, and their hyperboles and oxymorons are given positively dramatic roles. In none of the three is metaphor entirely inert. But Petrarch uses the secondary aspects of his terms elegantly: once having called his desire "heat," he calls Laura's refusal "cold" because such an expression is both elegant in itself and suited to an Ovidian turn. The *quattrocentisti* use the secondary aspects of their terms almost exclusively: when their ladies freeze a lake through their cold, the *quattrocentisti* are talking not about chaste ladies but about frozen lakes. The Bemboists follow Petrarch, but in a language in which "burning" and "freezing" are the only polite ways of referring to desire and chastity. In summary, then, the Bemboists use Petrarch as a source of generalized, elegant, and poetic diction; well-accepted love theories; formal modes; and pictures of the simple and permanent aspects of human love.

In the mid-sixteenth century, a new form of Petrarchism gained international prominence through anthologies containing the poems of Angelo di Costanzo, Galeazzo di Tarsia, Annibale Caro, and others. These poets, as critics generally say, threw off Bemboist restrictions. Linguistically, they were innovators, coining words, importing them, and bringing them into poetry from ordinary usage (though their innovations would seem far less radical but for the linguistic puritanism of the Bemboists). Of conceits, too, these poets were innovators. They confined themselves neither to the conceits Petrarch used, like the Bemboists, nor to developments based on such conceits, like the *quattrocentisti*. Indeed, they threw off even the old principles of the conceit. Previously, if desire were a fire it would burn, "burn" being applicable to both desire and fire; but now the fire might grow, heighten, sprout, bloom, or erect itself. (In many ways, the dispute between the Bemboists and the newer school is signaled by Minturno's *Ragione d'alcune cose segnate nella canzone d'Annibal Caro*.) Though critics generally consider the mid-century school a revival of *quattrocentismo,* it seems to owe as much to the cinquecento Della Casa as to Chariteo, and nothing especial to other *quattrocentisti*. In any case, the distinguishing quality of the mid-century school is its freedom in imitating Petrarch, and its all-pervasive attempt at emphasis and the high style. Much of its poetry utilizes a vaguely Petrarchan background for elaborate and hyperbolic, but not essentially amorous, praise. Much of it is a heightening of traditional elements, for example by injecting what was centuries later to be called "gothic" description into the Petrarchan countryside, or gorgeousness into the Petrarchan skies. Throughout, techniques of emphasis—mixed metaphor, hyperbole, and the pathetic fallacy—and a very free imitation of Petrarch are used to create a new sensationalism.

In the last two decades of the sixteenth century, there are many developments within the Petrarchan tradition. The most important are the predominance of the madrigal, and the new Ovidianism. The madrigal leads to neatness, wit, and sentimentality; it is courtly and mannered. The madrigalists often turned to the *quattrocentisti* —whose fame revived at this time throughout Europe—for their conceits; but they were more languishing, more civilized, and less ingenious. The new Ovidianism, meanwhile, had two manifestations: a use of Petrarchan language to express sensual desire for women often cynically portrayed; and a taste for myth, metamorphoses, and sensual tales. Guarino and Tasso, respectively, are the greatest representatives of the Petrarchan madrigal and Ovidian Petrarchism.

To understand Petrarchism one should have at least some idea of the variety of its manifestations: for example, a book in which Petrarch's Laura—revealing the feelings he sometimes attributes to her—answers each of Petrarch's poems, thus forming a dialogue; a book of "honorable" lyrics in which the lady's virtues are decent, wholesome, and bourgeois, and her lover's intention explicitly marriage; and various books in which religious writers adapt Petrarch, poem by poem, to express a love for God.[14] And such works barely suggest the pervasiveness and Protean shapes of Petrarchism. But the summary above will give at least a general impression of Petrarchism.

One aspect of Petrarchism deserves incidental comment. Petrarch sometimes imitated the philosophical love lyric of the *dolce stil novo;* and he sometimes imitated earlier Romance writers in enunciating cryptic rules of love. Later Petrarchists developed a form of wit that relied on logical developments from such rules. Many echoed Ficino and other Neoplatonic philosophers. Nonetheless, Petrarchism is not a metaphysical tradition. The more logical a Petrarchan poem is, the more purely witty it is likely to be. The serious Petrarchists believed in maxims, but not in metaphysical exploration; they sought to define their feelings, not the nature of things. Petrarchism employs definition, deduction, and generalization; but it is not a philosophic lyric.

Two major principles emerge from our survey of Italian Petrarchism. First, Petrarchan imitation was a mode of writing original poetry. The Petrarchists used the *Canzoniere* sometimes as a dictionary, sometimes as a commonplace book, and sometimes as the model of a genre. Each used Petrarch to fit his own needs. Secondly, there are two major kinds of Petrarchists: those who, following Petrarch closely, seek to find through him an interpretation of experience; and those who, using Petrarch freely, seek in him only rhetorical devices for their own ends. These principles illuminate Donne's background.

III

Petrarchism in England: Wyatt and Gascoigne

Inevitably, to assert that Donne is a Petrarchist is to run afoul of the only widely accepted theory about his relation to contemporary poetry: the belief that, as a manly realist, Donne repudiates Elizabethan Petrarchism.[1] This theory prevents a true reading of Donne's poems. And it is involved with so many misconceptions, critical and historical, that it can hardly be answered except through a new understanding of Petrarchan imitation. To achieve such an understanding, to describe the poles of English Petrarchism, and to define the witty, casual, social mode of Petrarchism especially relevant to Donne, I here offer as exemplars Wyatt and Gascoigne. Wyatt represents strict imitation and humanistic Petrarchism, Gascoigne free imitation and social Petrarchism. Neither is less a manly English realist than Donne. And together they reveal the limits of sixteenth-century Petrarchism.

Wyatt is a continental traveller in the courts of the High Renaissance. He is the teacher and model of Surrey, an Elizabethan prototype. And he is a courtier in Castiglione's sense: abroad, he effects his country's policies, and at home he entertains its rulers, and enriches its language and learning.[2] As such facts suggest, Wyatt is a humanist: he reads Plato and Seneca, translates Plutarch, Petrarch, and Alamanni, and believes that there is a close relationship among learning, reason, and morality.[3] His Petrarchism is an attempt to bring to England the beautiful rhetoric and moral wisdom of foreign literature.

Like Spenser's and Milton's, Wyatt's poetry is based on respected literary models and authorized moral views. Wyatt's poetic exemplar, Petrarch, is the father of the new learning, reputed by

Italians to have shown how vernacular literature might equal the classics. And Wyatt's faith in heroic virtue, his mistrust of fortune, and his belief in the moral value of learning are Neo-Stoic.[4] Petrarchan imitation and Neo-Stoic philosophy—two impulses central to humanistic learning in his time—are the heart of Wyatt's Italianate poetry.

At the same time, Wyatt's imitations, like Spenser's and Milton's, are truly original. Often, they are quite faithful to their models.[5] But by repeatedly departing from their models in a few central ways, they achieve Wyatt's own, un-Petrarchan effect.[6] For it is only Petrarch's rhetorical and structural devices which Wyatt adopts; the sense he gives them is his own. Petrarch deals with the position of the ill-rewarded lover, and Wyatt subsumes that position to his sense that he is heroic, virtuous, and ill-treated.[7] He interprets the mistress-servant relationship in terms of distributive justice.[8] He abandons Petrarch's languorous analysis for rhetorical emphasis: he proclaims his merit, reveals the indignities he has suffered, and appeals for judgment. In close and often literal translations, his personal, un-Petrarchan tone is a striking instance of the possibilities of Petrarchan imitation.

Wyatt's transformation of Petrarch is pervasive. For example, in "S' una fede amorosa, un cor non finto," Petrarch summarizes his life as "Un lungo error in cieco laberinto." In "If waker care, if sodayne pale Coulor," Wyatt translates the phrase as "For hope of small, if muche to fere therfore": he ignores the confessional quality of "error" and "cieco" to focus upon a question of rewards. Similarly, in "Rotta è l'alta colonna e 'l verde lauro," Petrarch says:

> Oh nostra vita ch' è sí bella in vista,
>   Com' perde agevolmente in un mattino
>   Quel che 'n molti anni a gran pena s'acquista!

> (Oh this life of ours, how lovely it seems!
>   and how easily, in a single morning, we lose
>   that which costs many years, and much effort, to gain!)

In "The piller pearisht is whearto I lent," Wyatt ignores this characteristic Petrarchan moralization. Instead, introducing perhaps a

Stoic note with the un-Petrarchan "unquyet mynde" (1. 2), he complains of the maliciousness of "happe," "chaunce," and "destenye." [9] Throughout his lyrics, Wyatt's diction reflects the less Augustinian, more Stoic cast of his mind: his "pains" are not merely dolor but efforts expended, deserving reward; his "honesty" is not merely gentility but upright dealing, worthy of honest returns. Throughout, Wyatt's poems reveal themselves to be his, not Petrarch's.

Structurally, too, Wyatt transforms his models. For example, Petrarch's "Or vedi, Amor, che giovenetta donna" is a slight compliment in which Petrarch pictures an innocent Maytime maiden, and appeals to the god Love to avenge the poet on her. The lyric stresses Laura's innocent dignity and Petrarch's awe. Petrarch's basic conceit, his request for revenge, is merely a gallant exaggeration: the lady has done no ill, and her lover is not indignant. In "Behold, love, thy power how she dispiseth," Wyatt reinterprets the lyric's structure, making the desire for vengeance a moral appeal. His lady is neither innocent ("The holy oth, wherof she taketh no cure,/ Broken she hath") nor just ("spitefull withoute cause or mesure"). Where Laura is pure and simple ("E tra duo ta' nemici è sí secura. . . . Si siede e scalza in mezzo i fiori e l'erba"), Wyatt's lady is shameless: "Right at her ease and litle she dredeth." Wyatt's appeal to Love is that of an upright feudal servant begging his lord to right an injury. Thus Wyatt changes the central contrast between the lady's unconscious grace and her lover's timid calculations to an opposition between a faithless lady and her loyal, manly, mistreated lover. His imitation of Petrarch, though direct, is essentially original: it suits Petrarch's rhetoric to Wyatt's own theme, ill-treated virtue.

In "Perdye I saide yt not" Wyatt redirects the rhetoric of "S'i' 'l dissi mai, ch'i' venga in odio a quella." Petrarch protests his truth by listing evils he invokes on himself if he lies; then, in the penultimate stanza, the turn of the poem, he wishes that if he speaks truly Laura would love him as before. Thus, he suits the protestation of truth to gallant courtship. Wyatt changes the turn, and thereby the poem, focusing it on a question of equity:

Yf I be clere fro thought,
  Whye do ye then complaine?
Then ys this thing but sought
  To torne me to more payne.
Then that that ye haue wrought
  Ye must yt now redresse;
Of right therefore ye ought
  Suche Rigor to represse.

What is in Petrarch a list of vows is in Wyatt a definition of the
alternative rewards which, contingent on his merit, should be accorded him; where Petrarch's wish shows the highest good he
knows, Wyatt's is a clear demand that justice be done. Similarly,
to "For Rachell have I seruid,/ (For Lya carid I never)," which is
in Petrarch an undeveloped affirmation of constancy, Wyatt adds:

And as I haue deseruid,
  So graunte me nowe my hire.

Petrarch's lyric, then, is a list of oaths that, modified by gallant
touches, becomes courtship and compliment. Wyatt restructures the
poem and redirects its examples to a clear-cut question of justice.

In "Who so list to hount, I knowe where is an hynde," Wyatt
changes a symbolic narrative to an ironic declamation. Petrarch's
"Una candida cerva sopra l' erba" describes the vision-like appearance of a hind to the poet, and his trance-like pursuit of her.[10]
Petrarch thereby expresses wonder at the beauty and unapproach-
ability of Laura, and amazement at the speed with which his life
has passed in eager and fruitless desire of her. Where Petrarch is
drawn by the hind involuntarily, Wyatt hunts a definite prize.
Where Petrarch enjoys seeing the hind, Wyatt is cruelly wearied by
the hunt. And where Petrarch, deprived of the hind he knows not
how, is left in sorrowful bewilderment at his loss, Wyatt willingly
renounces the quest, perceiving it to be a trap. Essentially, then,
where Petrarch expresses his painful recognition that the world
whose beauty he loves is evanescent, Wyatt objects to the injustice
that has deprived him of his reward. To express his view, Wyatt
changes details, of course: for example, where Petrarch's hind wears
on her neck a statement of God's purpose set in precious stones,

Wyatt's wears, apparently, an iron collar, where a declaration of her earthly bondage has been graven with diamonds. But, more important, Wyatt changes the entire structure of the sonnet. For example, Petrarch's poem begins:

> Una candida cerva sopra l' erba
> Verde m'apparve, con duo corna d'oro
> Fra due riviere, a l'ombra d' un alloro,
> Levando 'l sole, a la stagione acerba.

> (A milk-white hind appeared to me
> on the green grass, with two golden horns,
> between two shores, in the shade of a laurel,
> at the time of the rising sun and at the season of unripeness.)

Wyatt's begins:

> Who so list to hount, I knowe where is an hynde,
> But as for me, helas, I may no more:
> The vayne travaill hath weried me so sore.
> I ame of theim that farthest commeth behinde.

To show his injured but scornful rectitude, Wyatt changes narrative to direct address, pictorial symbolism to irony, and elevated mystery to bitter common sense. For the tapestry-like symbolic scene which isolates Petrarch's experience, Wyatt substitutes a speech set in an ordinary social world. For the shores, the sun, and the season, which symbolize life as a brief passage through a sweet country, Wyatt substitutes a hunter's exhaustion, implying a social context and a desire for earthly success. By such means Wyatt adapts the structure of Petrarch's sonnet to his own theme, the "vayne travaill" he has undergone for a reward that has been taken by others.

Wyatt, then, transforms Petrarch's Provençal lists, Alexandrian myths, and Romance symbols into rhetorical appeals—to Love, to the lady, and to others—that the injustice done the poet be recognized. He transforms Petrarch's conceits as well. For example, in "O bella man che mi destringi 'l core" Petrarch says that his lady's hand, which holds his heart, is bare because the poet has stolen its glove; and he begs Love to let the hand remain bare "to enrich me" by the sight of it. In "O goodely hand" Wyatt, perhaps misunderstanding "per arricchirmi, Amore," [11] says that since the lady's hand holds the poet's heart, it should either squeeze his heart and kill him, or "reche me love againe" (that is, of course, "in return"). Thus Wyatt, balancing Petrarch's heart-holding hand with a heart-offering hand, turns the conceit to his own characteristic request for justice.

In "Goo burnyng sighes vnto the frosen hert" Wyatt changes the direction of the conceits of "Ite, caldi sospiri, al freddo core." Petrarch sends his sighs to his lady: as a personification of amorous pleading, the sighs imply the solitary and meditative world in which signs of passion are Petrarch's intimate companions. Wyatt asks his sighs not only to broach the lady's frozen heart but also to "Take with the payn . . . And eke the flame . . . And leve me then in rest" because the lady's falsity makes it impossible to "assaill her/ With pitefull plaint." Where the phrase "Ite, caldi sospiri" is a parting encouragement to a friend sent on a hopeful errand, "Goo burnyng sighes" is a bitter farewell to a fruitless pain. Similarly, Wyatt changes another sentimental conceit, Petrarch's assertion that by declaring his love he will end his pain, by joy if Laura is kind and by death if she is not. Wyatt introduces these alternatives by a bitter "at lest," thereby revealing not Petrarch's apprehensive resolution, but his own impatience for a clear answer. Again, Wyatt reinterprets the burning-freezing antithesis that runs through Petrarch's sonnet. For Petrarch that antithesis represents the contrast between his ardor and his lady's reserve, between a lover who is "inquieto" and a lady whose state is "pacifico." For Wyatt, however, it signifies the contrast between his truth and his lady's artful cold-bloodedness:

> I must goo worke, I se, by craft and art,
> For trueth and faith in her is laide apart.

Wyatt adapts Petrarch's precious conceits to an emphatic representation of the virtuous man's position in a corrupt world.

Throughout Wyatt's poems, then, love is a relation in which the right-dealing man is open to injury, naked to treachery and malice. It is a sort of fortune, which comes upon him against his will ("Synce loue wyll nedes that I shall love") and rules by "forcyd law and mutabilite" ("Desire, alas, my master and my foo"). In imitating Petrarch, Wyatt expresses his own thoroughly un-Petrarchan outrage and pride.

Wyatt is an important example of that Petrarchism which is aulic and moral. His lyric illuminates Donne's. For, faithful both to its models and to Wyatt himself, it reveals that integrity and individuality are not foreign even to humanistic Petrarchism.

The opposite pole of Petrarchism appears in the love lyrics of George Gascoigne. The serious humanists of Spenser's circle consider Gascoigne to be "a witty gentleman" with "natural promptness" who lacks "learning"—to have "wit," but also "some vanity and more levity," and to want "resolution and constancy." [12] For Gascoigne is careless of Latin learning, strict imitation, and moral philosophy. To him, poetry is partly a craft and partly an elegance of manners; and Petrarchism is a witty mode of social commerce in a hopefully-polite society.

For many modern readers, Gascoigne's lyrics are profoundly realistic. In *The Adventures, Dan Bartholomew of Bathe,* and elsewhere, they form the story of a man who wins the favors of a lewd lady only to be deserted for a new lover. This story—a commonplace from Chaucer's *Troilus and Criseyde* to Lyly's *Euphues*—is treated with striking directness by Gascoigne. His lovers' motives, for example, are notably unelevated: F. J. seeks an easy conquest, and Dan Bartholomew is merely naive. Today, such plotting and motivation in a Renaissance author are often thought to be signs of integrity and even genius. But in fact Gascoigne's lyrics are not meditations upon the meaning of life; they are letters interchanged by lovers at country-house weekends. *The Adventures,* after all, pretends to tell of a contemporary scandal. [13]

In this context, the "realism" of Gascoigne's lyrics is nothing more than unimaginative pragmatism. For the Renaissance as for Dante, [14] love, with arms and religion, is one of the three noble subjects of poetry—an eternal principle of the universe and the human psyche. Gascoigne, however casually, assumes that love is a conscious desire for sexual fulfillment. He seems unaware that it might be anything else. Thus, to illustrate the height of his love in "The

Anatomye of a Lover," he cites its mournful effects upon his limp limbs, which it has left unable "to serve a lovers turne"; and while proclaiming his amorous anguish in "The passion of a Lover," he defines love as a

> . . . fever first I caught by wanton wyll,
> When coles of kind dyd stirre my blood by stealth:
> And gazing eyes, in bewtie put such trust,
> That love enflamd my liver al with lust.[15]

Though "wanton" and "lust" may not bear their specifically sexual senses here, clearly Gascoigne assumes love to be an animal passion [16]—even while professing refined love in an imitation of Petrarch.

As his unelevated conception of love might suggest, Gascoigne's Petrarchism is merely an ingenious method of courtship.[17] For him, poetry is an art of social intercourse which seeks witty novelty above all else. In *Certayne notes of Instruction concerning the making of verse or ryme in English,* he considers invention, the art of avoiding the obvious, to be poetry's chief glory (p. 465). He illustrates poetry's purpose and method so:

> If I should undertake to wryte in prayse of a gentlewoman, I would neither prayse hir christal eye, nor hir cherrie lippe, etc. For these things are *trita & obvia.* But I would either finde some supernaturall cause wherby my penne might walke in the superlative degree, or els I would undertake to aunswere for any imperfection that shee hath, and thereupon rayse the prayse of hir commendacion. Likewise if I should disclose my pretence in love, I would eyther make a straunge discourse of some intollerable passion, or finde occasion to pleade by the example of some historie, or discover my disquiet in shadowes *per Allegoriam,* or use the covertest meane that I could to avoyde the uncomely customes of common writers.
>
> (I, 465-466)

These are the principles of Gascoigne's verse—nowhere more clear, perhaps, than in his "In praise of a gentlewoman who though she were not verye fayre, yet was she as harde favoured as might be," for here Gascoigne displays his abilities by praising that which

41

seems entirely unsuited to praise.[18] His poetry is virtuoso rhetoric applied to specific social purposes.

His titles make explicit the occasional origin of many of his lyrics: "With these verses you shall judge the quicke capacitie of the Lady"; "And for a further proofe of this Dames quicke understand-ing"; "Whiles he sat at the dore of his lodging, devising these verses above rehersed, the same Gentlewoman passed by againe, and cast a longe looke towards him, whereby he left his former invention and wrote thus." His art is the ability to handle any theme, as his titles again indicate: for example, "Gascoignes Memories, written upon this occasion. Hee had (in myddest of his youth). . . And be-ing required by five sundry Gentlemen to write in verse . . . five sundrie sortes of metre uppon five sundrye theames, whiche they delivered unto him"; "This question being propounded by a Dame"; and the titles in the sequence "Certaine verses written to a Gentle-woman," discussed below.

Gascoigne is, then, an improviser whose poems are made for specific occasions. His titles indicate that he desires his readers to be aware of the difficulties under which he labored ("in myddest of his youth"), and of the social eminence of those for whom he wrote. Most of his lyrics propose to accomplish limited aims, the aims of school rhetoric. His art lies in the elegance and novelty with which he accomplishes his aims.

Gascoigne uses Petrarchism as a novel mode of treating amor-ous occasions. For example, the sequence "Certaine verses written to a Gentlewoman whome hee liked very wel" begins with a prose description of eye-exchanges between Gascoigne and a lady, ex-plaining that he wrote verses in a book for her; the verses, a con-ventional description of a lover rendered helpless by his lady's glances, follow. Then there is a prose description of a dinner at-tended by the lady, her husband, the lover who preceded Gascoigne in her favor, and Gascoigne, at which dinner Gascoigne and the lady are said to have recited riddles mocking the previous lover; the riddles follow. Then there is a prose explanation that, after he was her lover, Gascoigne found a love letter from another man, and afterwards a lemon, in his lady's pocket; and his verses and hers on the discovery, verses punning on "lemon" and "leman," conclude the sequence. What is most significant is that the major lyric here, the verses Gascoigne wrote in her book, is Petrarchan. Here are the final two of its four stanzas:

> Thus in thy lookes my love and life have hold,
> And with such life my death drawes on a pace:
> And for such death no medcine can be told,
> But loking still upon thy lovely face,
> Wherin are painted pitie, peace, and grace,
> Then though thy lokes should cause me for to dye,
> Needes must I looke, bicause I live therby.
>
> Since then thy lookes my lyfe have so in thrall,
> As I can like none other lookes but thine:
> Lo here I yeelde my lyfe, my love, and all
> Into thy hands, and all things else resigne,
> But libertie to gaze upon thyne eyen.
> Which when I doe, then think it were thy part,
> To looke again, and linke with me in hart.

These stanzas may be based upon a sonnet of Petrarch, such as "Mirando 'l sol de' begli occhi sereno." But Gascoigne's imitation is very free. Like his riddle and his pun upon "lemon," his Petrarchan thralldom, living deaths, and killing glances ("lookes") are merely clever devices for meeting social situations. In his last couplet Gascoigne is as forward as the lady would wish; for, unlike Wyatt, he finds nothing at all in the Petrarchan situation. In the light of his prose, Gascoigne's Petrarchism can be appreciated only as an ingenious means of avoiding "the uncomely customes of common writers" while disclosing "my pretence in love."

"To the same gentlewoman because she challenged the Aucthour for holding downe his head alwaies, and for that hee looked not uppon hir in wonted manner" recalls Petrarch's "Io temo sí de' begli occhi l'assalto":

> I am so afraid of the attack of the lovely eyes
> in which Love harbors—and my death is with him—
> that I flee them as a child the rod;
> and long it is since first I leapt away from them.

43

From that time on, there can be no place so difficult of access
    or so high, that my will won't rise to it
    so as to avoid that which would shatter my senses,
    leaving me, as it is wont, a frozen stone.
Therefore if I was slow to return to you,
    avoiding the proximity of that which destroys me,
    perhaps my fault was not unworthy of excuse.
And I say further, that to turn against that which I fled,
    and so much to shake off my fear,
    was no slight labor of my faith.

Gascoigne's prose explains that, because he has been avoiding her, a discarded mistress has asked him why he does not look at her as he once did; then, in an English sonnet, he declares that the radiance of her eyes is too great for him, who has once felt their heat, to encounter willingly again. Evidently, Gascoigne uses Petrarch for openly insincere gallantry.[19] And there is nothing aulic in his imitation:

You must not wonder though you thinke it straunge,
    To see me holde my lowring head so lowe:
And that myne eyes take no delyght to raunge,
About the gleames which on your face doe growe.
The mouse which once hath broken out of trappe,
Is sildome tysed with the trustlesse bayte,
But lyes aloofe for feare of more mishappe,
And feedeth styll in doubte of deepe deceipte.
The skorched flye which once hath scapt the flame,
Wyll hardlye come to playe againe with fyre.
Whereby I learne that greevous is the game,
Which followes fansie dazled by desire.
So that I wynke or else holde downe my head,
Because your blazing eyes my bale have bred.
            Si fortunatus infoelix.

Gascoigne's imitation is much freer than Wyatt's. It does not pretend to eloquence, learning, or moral doctrine. In a vulgar situation, Gascoigne uses Petrarchan rhetoric as a merely flippant, clever, and polite way of dealing with social situations.

"The passion of a Lover" and "A straunge passion of a Lover" are imitations of Petrarch's "Pace non trovo e non ho da far guerra."

Unlike Wyatt, who translates the poem, Gascoigne has no intention of being faithful to his model. He finds in Petrarch a rhetorical device, the list of paradoxes, and he employs that device freely. "The passion" uses it as a means of *copia*, rephrasing the same statements as quotations, as questions, and as answers; the final stanza of "A straunge passion" uses it with fine, tuneful simplicity to distinguish Gascoigne's apparent joy from his inner despair, and the pleasures he wishes his lady from the sorrows he suffers. In both, Gascoigne insists that though his passions "seeme strange, yet are they trew," for to him the Petrarchan hyperbole is always "a strange discourse of some intollerable passion" asserted as truth, so as to "disclose my pretence in love." To him, Petrarch's *Canzoniere* is a storehouse of elegant inventions suited to a variety of amorous purposes and occasions.

Wyatt and Gascoigne, then, represent the poles of Petrarchism in English. Wyatt is a serious commentator on life, Gascoigne a pragmatic versifier immersed in week-end affairs. Wyatt is a humanistic imitator, Gascoigne an eclectic rhetorician barely discriminating among Petrarchan conceits, Alexandrine myths, allegories, and lists of exempla. Wyatt writes about a few central, generalized situations, and Gascoigne verse that is occasional, or located within a narrative. Both take Petrarchism far from Petrarch, Wyatt towards neoclassical moralization and learned formalism, Gascoigne towards *vers de société* and superficial elegance. Neither Wyatt nor Gascoigne is an active influence upon Donne. But they illuminate his literary situation, suggesting the adaptability of Petrarchism to various personalities, moral outlooks, and social situations.[20] In a sense, Wyatt and Gascoigne are the extremes of Petrarchism, and Donne the mean: for Donne elevates Gascoigne's witty, free-wheeling, social Petrarchism to an integrity beyond that of Wyatt's.

IV

Discovering Donne's Petrarchism

$\mathcal{D}$onne's poetry follows no model and few literary rules.[1] Therefore, he has seemed to critics to be independent, eccentric, original, or realistic. Unfortunately, however, such adjectives evoke a Romantic context, suggesting that Donne is a young rebel fighting for primitive truths against tradition and complacency. In fact Donne's originality, like that of Gascoigne, is primarily a conscious novelty in conceit and manner, as Carew says.

The nineteenth-century respect for naive vision and spontaneous writing finds no parallel in the Renaissance. Seeing poetry to be verbal and intellectual, and knowing language and thought to improve with education, Renaissance critics believe poetry to be the fruit—not the antithesis—of civilization. In a Renaissance context, the difference between Spenser and Donne is not that the first, blinded by custom, writes what he has been told, and that the second, clear-eyed and undaunted, writes what he feels. It is that the one writes as a careful, learned artist, and the other as a careless, accomplished wit. Neither, that is, seeks to cleanse his soul from custom: both, in fact, strive for culture. But Spenser's culture, is that of the academy, and Donne's that of the court: Spenser seeks erudition and Donne *sprezzatura,* or brilliant ease.

It is not Petrarchism, the poetry of the past, from which Donne departs so radically, but rather neoclassicism, the poetry of the future. Witty writers, whose poetry is memorable conversation, imitate by borrowing from a rich store of ingenious inventions and clever conceits. For neoclassicists, however, imitation is a discipline. They consider poetry a laboriously learned art, and they use classical materials and forms. Donne stands opposed to neoclassicists on all three points: he writes as a wit, he prefers Romance to classical models, and he imitates not to mold himself and his art but to increase his store of devices.

It is not at all clear that Donne advocated any principles for the poetry of his time: he made no poetic manifesto, and his own choices do not necessarily condemn all alternatives. But the neoclassicists did have a critical program, and a critical concern with Donne. As they saw it, the critical battle line was drawn between the neoclassicists on one side, and the metaphysicals and witty Petrarchists on the other. Representing the great body of neoclassical opinion, Walsh fires a double blast at Donne and Petrarch, accusing them equally of a taste for conceit, point, and far-fetched simile, and of a failure to represent the passions in a natural, persuasive, and lively way.[2] Joseph Warton attacks Petrarch because his "sentiments even of love, are metaphysical and far fetched." And an anonymous contemporary of Warton's blames current stylistic extravagances on two parallel influences: that of Petrarch, with other Italians; and that of the metaphysical poets, with Sidney.[3] In general, neoclassicists consider Petrarchist and metaphysical to be allied against simplicity, nature, and reason. That view is shared by Samuel Johnson, who wrote the classic definition of metaphysical poetry. In his *Life* of Waller, after showing Waller to be relatively free of metaphysical excesses Johnson approves of him insofar as he is "less hyperbolical than . . . some other poets. Waller is not always at the last gasp; he does not die of a frown, nor live upon a smile." In context it is clear that the other poets are Donne and the metaphysicals; but the description suggests that they are Petrarchists.[4] Clearly, for Johnson as for Walsh, Warton, and others, whatever difference there may be between metaphysical and Petrarchist is less important than what they share: hyperbole, eccentricity, and extravagance.

Dudley North (Donne's contemporary),[5] Walsh, Dryden, and Johnson see Donne's faults to be strained thoughts, bombastic sentiments, and learning indecorously intruded in poems addressed to ladies, and they attribute the same faults to the Petrarchists. Italian neoclassicists agree. Bemboism is a neoclassical attempt to fit the vernacular lyric to classical standards of taste by purging it of the excesses fostered by Serafino and others. The Bemboists' arguments are precisely those which English neoclassicists turned against Donne. They are thus summarized by Angelo Colotio, who attempts to refute them, in his sixteenth-century defense of Serafino:

> they claim that it is indecorous for the lutanist to have spoken not merely of natural things, but also to have lifted his soul to speak of destiny and fate, though singing for ladies. . . . Then another crowd of fools argue that the construction of his verses is arid and compressed. . . . Others would want more sobriety in his metaphors, arguing that he is too audacious in figures of speech, and often uses over-extended metaphors . . . but to them it should be replied that such was the usage of Dante and Petrarch. . . . Many others argue that in many places his figures of speech are too concise and compact . . . the tumid veins and overly extended muscles of his arguments appear on the surface . . . he was impetuously exorbitant in his exaggerations. . . .[6]

Except by a superior power of generalization, Samuel Johnson hardly departs from these Bemboist clichés in his famous definition of metaphysical poetry.

In the early Renaissance, Petrarch's place is parallel to that of Virgil, and neoclassicists seek to bring Petrarchism back to its pristine purity. In the Enlightenment, neoclassicists choose more strictly classical models, and Petrarch himself is widely charged with the faults attributed to Serafino and Donne. Here, for example, is François-Benoit Hoffman's attack upon Petrarch:

> la recherche des idées alambiquées, des subtilités indignes d'un grand poète, et des traits d'un mauvais esprit [i.e., sallies of tasteless wit]. . . . pensées fausses, . . . des jeus de mots, des subtilités et des conceptions puériles. . . . que dirai-je d'un poète qui dialogue avec son âme et qui cause avec ses pensées; . . . qui fait des pointes dans le sentiment. . . .[7]

Hoffman correctly sees in Petrarch those elements by which Johnson—and many nineteenth-century critics—define Donne. In the eighteenth century Donne's extravagance of manner was not generally distinguished from that of the Petrarchists.

For modern critics, it is evident that the *Songs and Sonets* are one of the greatest collections of love lyrics since Petrarch's, and perhaps the collection most faithful to the texture of experience. It therefore seems unlikely that Donne should be a Petrarchist, when Petrarchism suggests conformity to a fatuous decorum. However, as recent studies have shown, Petrarchan poetry is much better than it seems to those who do not read it. And, as Wyatt and Gascoigne illustrate, the Petrarchan mode is capable of various significant uses and independent developments. In short, though modern Romantics see Petrarchism as timid conformity, it appeared differently to Donne.

To Donne, two mature lyric traditions offered their resources, the classical and the Romance. Donne's originality in respect to the Petrarchists has been attributed to his classical inclinations:[8] and indeed Donne echoes the Greek epigram,[9] the Ovidian elegy, and, in his epigrams, Martial. But classical poetry was for the Renaissance an art of generality, reason, and simplicity. It was an art of the surface, and Donne imitates it when dealing with externals— with amorous manners. Romance poetry, on the other hand, is an art of the interior: of personal feeling, fantasy, and elaboration. It translates social events into sentimental drama through introspection, hyperbole, and conceit. It adds metaphysics to compliment, subtlety to *savoir faire,* and introspection to casual poise. Clearly, it is Romance poetry which Donne needed, and which he uses.

Petrarchism provides Donne his subject, themes, and images. The subject of Petrarchism is love conceived as a noble way of life, and the lover as an aristocrat of feeling. In the Greek epigram and in Ovid, love's mastery over the poet is occasional and extravagant: immoral, or at least frivolous. But Petrarchism is a convention in which love is spiritual superiority and in which a sensible, moral, and elderly man may choose love as a way of life. Donne wrote several libertine epigrams. But in his greatest love poems—for example, "The Canonization," "The Anniversarie," and "The Relique"— Donne's subject is Petrarchan love.[10]

Like his subject, Donne's themes are Petrarchan. The themes shared by most Petrarchan collections, perhaps, are the proem, the initiation of love, the complaint against the lady's obduracy, the expression of sorrow at parting, the remonstrance against the god

Love, the elegy on the lady's death, and the renunciation of love. Other common themes are the lady's eyes, her hair, her illness, the dream, the token, the anniversary of love, and the definition of love. Outside of the proem (which belongs only to sequential collections), the lady's hair, and her eyes, Donne uses all these themes: [11] few of the *Songs and Sonets,* indeed, are on un-Petrarchan themes. The themes of classic poetry—the poet at his lady's door, *carpe diem,* and so on—are, on the other hand, conspicuously absent from his lyrics.

Thus, in subject and theme Donne's lyrics follow the Petrarchists in a general way, as his satires follow the Romans and his epithalamia the Elizabethans. That is, Donne's form is sometimes specifically Petrarchan—a list of impossibilities, a dialogue with his heart, or a curse. Generally, his lyrics reflect Petrarchism's focus upon the lover, its use of hyperbole, metaphysics, and conceit, its apostrophes, prayers, and mythical narratives, and its conception of love and of the lyric.

Such Petrarchan elements are essential, but evasive. The most readily demonstrable Petrarchan element in Donne's lyric is his language. Donne owes little to the fading rose, setting sun, and Alexandrian Cupid of classical verse; but his language is saturated with the images of Petrarchism—with deaths for love, sun-darkening ladies, pictures on hearts, ships of love, floods of tears, and miraculous ladies.[12] Like Gascoigne, Donne uses the Petrarchan language freely; but he uses it, in the *Songs and Sonets,* almost exclusively.

Donne repudiates, of course, many Petrarchan attitudes. In "To the Countesse of Huntington: That unripe side of earth," he says (11. 55-76) that Petrarchan love is the least efficient manner in which to win a woman; that love exists only where it is returned; and that he, though capable of fidelity, is especially incapable of loving a woman who does not return his feeling. Such beliefs permeate the *Songs and Sonets,* in some places as a disdain like Suckling's for the ineptness of mute young sinners, and in others as a firm faith that love is returned affection. But Wyatt and Gascoigne are no more pale, fond lovers than Donne; and he is no less a Petrarchist than they.

For Petrarchism is a poetic manner, not a moral doctrine. Though critics have seen Donne as a culture hero liberating his people from a servile, foreign poetical yoke, in fact there is every reason to think of Donne as a Petrarchist. Indeed, the editor of Donne's lyrics seems to have so thought of him: for he arranges the love poems in a Petrarchan order, beginning with the initiation of love and concluding with its renunciation; [13] and he entitles the lyrics *Songs and Sonets,* naming the two characteristic verse forms of the Petrarchan sequence.

If it is strange to think of Donne as a Petrarchist, that is because modern English-speaking critics often forget the Petrarchism of Gascoigne: an affected language adaptable to all sentiments and circumstances. Like Gascoigne, Donne employs Petrarchism as a repository of fashionable conceits and mannerisms.

In doing so, Donne follows the majority of Renaissance poets. The Renaissance lyric lacks a full critical formulation; for classical prose provided none, and humanists preferred to erect none which would work against vernacular Petrarchism. The critics, therefore, discussed lyrical style, not form. There are suggestions of formal definition in the divisions commonly found in Renaissance editions among sonnets, strambotti, ballets, etc.; but these divisions are primarily metrical. And while humanistic poets achieved formal definition through strict literary imitation, humanists dominated no national lyric for more than a few decades. Therefore, in the long run both critic and poet treat Petrarchism not as a genre, but as a general manner—that is, as a set of stylistic resources and effects.

That Donne too uses Petrarchism in this way has been obscured by scholars who picture him overthrowing the Petrarchan Establishment. Their notion, however, implies that Petrarchism is a brief interlude between Sidney and Donne (after all, the *Songs and Sonets* are virtually contemporaneous with the *Fairie Queene*), while simultaneously identifying it with the bourgeoisie, the Establishment, and Mrs. Grundy. Actually, Petrarchism dominates the English lyric at least through the time of Cowley's *Mistress;* and in the mid-eighteenth century, as novels abundantly show, the *beau monde* remains peopled by ladies whose killing glances eclipse the sun, and by swains who peruse the images on their hearts, and die for love. Seen in the large, English Petrarchism moves from a brief period of humanistic translation, to a longer period of free adaptation of Petrarchan mannerisms. And Donne initiates the second period.

Many critics would conclude from this that Donne is a bad poet: that his influence was malign, and his poetry trivial. But Donne's minor followers were often good poets, as H. M. Richmond's *The School of Love* (Princeton, 1964) shows; and in any case Donne's influence has been exaggerated to accord with his value. As for Donne's own verse, it is undoubtedly affected and elegant. Donne is much like Gascoigne, who excuses himself to a lady whom he has avoided by explaining that the glory of her eyes is too bright for him to bear. Donne declares that a lock of hair given him by a lady will maintain his body when he has died for love ("The Funerall"), and be worshipped as a relic when his bones are discovered ("The Relique"). He depends on affected hyperbole and extravagant compliment—on sun-eclipsing eyes, ladies richer than both the Indies, and death for love. To paraphrase Johnson on Waller, he is always at the last gasp, dying from parting and dissected by a frown. Donne makes the poetry of affectation great, just as Shakespeare makes the popular theater great. Donne gives it a new flexibility and often a deep significance. But, especially in the context of modern criticism, it is necessary to stress the principle that Donne's mode is that of complimentary Petrarchism.

In all probability, the majority of the *Songs and Sonets* were written in the 1590's, before Donne was thirty years old. At that time he was, according to Richard Baker, "not dissolute, but very neat; a great visitor of ladies, a great frequenter of plays, a great writer of conceited verses." [14] Baker's statement implies that Donne's verses belong to the world of soirées and theater parties; and in fact their conceits are rooted in an extravagant language of compliment—a language preserved in *Euphues,* in drama, and in epistles (including many of Donne's own verse letters and *Letters to Severall Persons of Honour*). This language reflects the influence of poetic conceit and rhetoric upon courtly conversation and ceremony.

There was a conscious effort to make the grace of poets available to fashionable people for daily occasions: Italian treatises were written for the purpose,[15] and so, in large part, was *The New Academy of Complements* (London, 1669). Poets wrote for court occasions; and courtiers wrote verses. Thus was created the nexus of polite society, fashionable affectation, and applauded ingenuity which is the context of Donne's verses.

The achievement of Donne within the Petrarchan manner may be illustrated by "The Apparition." Here the lady lying, worse than alone, with a lover who shrinks from her further embraces; the poet who threatens a fearsome revenge—these seem radically different from gentle Laura and her humble Petrarch. Yet Donne is dying of unrequited love, denouncing his lady as his murderess, and looking for vindication to the after-life. He is, in short, assuming an extravagantly Petrarchan manner:

> When by thy scorne, O murdresse I am dead,
>   And that thou thinkst thee free
> From all solicitation from mee,
> Then shall my ghost come to thy bed,
> And thee, fain'd vestall, in worse armes shall see;
> Then thy sicke taper will begin to winke,
> And he, whose thou art then, being tyr'd before,
> Will, if thou stirre, or pinch to wake him, thinke
>   Thou call'st for more,
> And in false sleepe will from thee shrinke,
> And then poore Aspen wretch, neglected thou
> Bath'd in a cold quicksilver sweat wilt lye
>   A veryer ghost then I;
> What I will say, I will not tell thee now,
> Lest that preserve thee'; and since my love is spent,
> I'had rather thou shouldst painfully repent,
> Then by my threatnings rest still innocent.

Essentially, "The Apparition" expresses a lover's anger at his lady's refusal. What Petrarchism contributes to its manner can be seen by the difference between Donne's lyric and Antonio da S. Croce del Valdarno's "Venir tipossa el diavolo allo letto":

> May the devil go to bed with you,
> since I'm not welcome there;
> may he break a couple of your ribs,
> and the rest of your body, made by God;
> may he drag you over mountains and through valleys,
> and chop your head clean off.[16]

Clearly, "The Apparition" is very distant from this simple curse. Its difference is the result of the Petrarchan tradition, through which Antonio's theme was refined. To treat with elegance the theme Antonio treats crudely, the Petrarchists used three conceits: death through unrequited love; supernatural punishment of obdurate ladies; and the rejected lover's desire for vengeance. It is these three conceits which place "The Apparition" in the Petrarchan tradition, as a vehement love-complaint refined by conceit, hyperbole, and extravagance.

The situation of "The Apparition" is based on the premise that lovers die from their ladies' scorn—a Petrarchan cliché.[17] The lover's death and its consequences are elaborated by many Petrarchan poets besides Donne. In "Chiare, fresche e dolci acque," Petrarch imagines Laura weeping over his grave. Serafino often develops the theme: with less sentiment and more wit, he emphasizes the ordinary concomitants of more usual deaths, imagining the lover's mourners, his funeral procession, and his final convulsions.[18] Thus, the consequences of death-for-love are a common theme of the witty Petrarchists.

As in "The Apparition," so in many acknowledgedly Petrarchan poems the conceit that the lady will be punished appears. Early Romance writers said that hard-hearted ladies would suffer in the after-life; the Petrarchists wittily said that the lady would suffer as a murderess because she killed her lover. The fifteenth-century Neopolitan court poets, for example, say that the lady will be publicly shamed because she will be unable to dispose of her lover's corpse; and that the poet, when he is dead for love, will at least have the consolation of seeing his lady punished in hell for her cruelty.[19] This theme was spread throughout Europe by imitations of Chariteo's magniloquent, refined, and witty "Voi, Donna, e io per segni manifesti." Chariteo says that when he and his lady are sent to hell, he for his presumption in loving her and she for her cruelty to him, he will enjoy her beauty though she may suffer from the unwelcome sight of him. This sonnet, because of its macabre elements, has, like Donne's lyrics, been mistakenly likened to Baudelaire.[20] Like "The Apparition," it is an elaborate treatment of the conventional theme that the cold lady will suffer for the death of her rejected lover.

Unlike Chariteo, who is tender and respectful, Donne expresses delight at the lady's anticipated torments. Like death for love and the punishment of hard-hearted ladies, the lover's desire for vengeance is a conventional theme. Petrarch often expresses such a desire in a complimentary way. "Far potess' io vendetta di colei," for example, is thus summarized by the commentators in *Il Petrarca* (Lyone, 1564):

> Here the poet wishes that he could avenge himself on Madonna Laura, who destroys him so that he cannot sleep. And he adds that his soul, which is chased by death from its residence in the poet's heart, freed by sleep, may go to Madonna Laura, who menaces it; then Petrarch says that he is amazed that Laura is not awakened by his soul as it speaks with her, weeps, and embraces her.

Although the commentator's syntax is unclear, in this sonnet it is literally sleep, and only metaphorically—and in a grammatical modifier—death, which frees the soul from its body; and Petrarch's revenge consists of kissing and fondling his lady. The lover's desire for vengeance is however associated clearly with his death in Riccho's "Ogni statuto che qua giu si lege":

> Every law on earth
>   condemns to death him who kills and steals.
> And you have killed me, and care nothing
>   for policemen and ruling magistrates.
> You have stolen my heart, disregarding the laws
>   which govern the common people, the lords, and nature.
> Indeed, manifestly you have no fear
>   of heaven, which guides and governs this earthly vale.
> But know, lady, that God's justice
>   is not dead: and at last torments

and pain you will suffer, unless you help me.
However, I want you to repent of your sins
and return me to life with a loving look,
for penitence makes amends for every crime.

Serafino is even more threatening when he warns his lady not to reject him in "S' io per te moro e calo nell' inferno":

If I die for you and go to hell,
all my sufferings will cry for vengeance;
I shall compose a legal brief of accusations against you
and give it to the infernal furies.
You will be condemned to eternal fire
and immediately made to plummet down to me;
and though you may live a while more in song and festival,
yet my ghost will always be before you.

For the amorous haunting, as for so many conceits of the witty Petrarchists, there is classic as well as Petrarchan precedent. In the *Aeneid,* IV, 384-87, Dido bids Aeneas go (in C. Day Lewis' translation [Oxford, 1952]):

I'll dog you, from far, with the death-fires;
And when cold death has parted my soul from my body, my spectre
Will be wherever you are. You shall pay for the evil you've
done me.
The tale of your punishment will come to me down in the shades.

In "Epistola V: Tu sei disposto pur crudel lassarmi," 11. 97-112, where a Dido-figure writes to her departing lover, Serafino assimilates the Virgilian theme to the detailed and literal elaboration of metaphors which is the manner of the *quattrocentisti:*

But you cannot go so quickly
as to escape my ghost, which will track you down
and remain forever beside you, visible
And bleeding, exactly as I was
when, with cruel hand, I killed myself.
It will be next to you whether you sleep or wake,
Not to harm you—for I couldn't—
but so that one day you may regret your errors,
so that one day you may understand my sufferings,

56

As you hear me howl wildly,
    lamenting repeatedly because of you
    and reproaching you in all my outcries.
And, although my simple, foolish soul
    may be out of its weary, worn body,
    do not hope that it will be untied from you on that account:
For a true love is not weakened even by death.

Based as they are on the suicide of an innocent, deserted lady these lines may not recall "The Apparition." But Serafino adapts the theme to the Petrarchan situation of a mistreated lover and cruel lady—and so anticipates Donne—in Strambotti 103 and 104, "E se gli ver che lalma tormentare" and "E se glie ver chel spirto vada a torno":

And if it is true that the soul must be tormented
    in the very place in which it sinned,
    I hope to abide within your body,
    since it is through your cruelty that I die damned.
And with my own hand I want to tear apart
    that false heart that has been so hard to me,
    until I kill you, for my revenge:
for every sin meets its just reward at last.

And if it is true that one's ghost wanders about
    when his soul is untied from his body,
    know that I shall always be about you,
    and never weary of warring upon you—
so much so that you will always curse the day
    that you refused to content me upon earth.
And thus I hope to possess you some time,
    and, alive or dead, to have you in my hand.

These strambotti, which may be the source of "The Apparition," place Donne's lyric squarely in the Petrarchan tradition. Donne is not here more realistic, more baroque, more manly, or, indeed, more rebellious than his Petrarchan predecessors: his complaint against his lady and his conjunction of love with death are rooted in Petrarchan clichés;[21] and his picture of the afterlife follows Chariteo and Serafino.

There is, interestingly, an anti-Petrarchan analogue of "The

Apparition." In "Capitolo secondo alla detta: Tu sei disposta pur, ch' io mora affatto,"[22] Francesco Berni says that his lady would rather see him die shrieking like a cat, than content him. He says that if he dies he will enter her body, devouring her guts and flopping about in her belly as though that indeed were the matter in dispute between them. Then he shrewdly threatens that if she does not make up her mind by evening, he will kill himself to begin his revenge. Berni's humour lies in treating a well-known Petrarchan theme with buffoonery: in the grossness of his diction, the vulgarity of his conceptions, and the peasant-like shrewdness of his threats. Evidently, Donne is closer to Serafino's sophistication than to Berni's buffoonery.

Its Petrarchan analogues show how misplaced has been the critical emphasis upon the symbolism of haunting in "The Apparition." The image in itself is neither personal nor original, and reflects no new ordering of the elements of experience. "The Apparition" is not a symbolist poem. Nor is it exposition. Read as statement, it makes no sense: if Donne is no longer in love, as he asserts, then he cannot die for love, as he intends. In fact, "The Apparition" is a deliciously pointed use of elaborate Petrarchan politeness. Donne has been rejected by a lady whom he desires. He does not, like Wyatt, pretend to virtue, declaim against immorality, and so expose himself to ridicule. Instead, he responds with delicacy to his social situation. He pretends to adore his lady absolutely, and to die for her. His pretense leads to the melodrama of mock-threat, which means nothing but which expresses indirectly Donne's irritation. Then Donne hints like King Hamlet of horrid secrets, and, vowing revenge, commits himself to malignant silence. Socially, "The Apparition" is a triumph. Faced by her dying and vengeful lover, the lady has nothing left to say.

Its Petrarchan analogues show too the originality of "The Apparition." Donne, more than any other Petrarchist, makes melodramatic the scene of the haunting and the feelings of the unprepared and unsupported lady as she suffers a horrible visitation. He realizes in the figure of the lover that play of jealousy and anguish which might lead him to hope for a post-mortem vengeance. Here

—and in general—Donne gives the Petrarchan image a dramatic rather than a rhetorical vitality.

Further, Donne gives the conceit a complexity of insinuation, a flexibility, and a liveliness at every point, that make it different in kind from its Petrarchan analogues. For most Petrarchists, the problem is to find a witty conceit and a proper attitude. Once their basic conceit is clear, their poems hold few surprises—and those are generally the unannounced appearance of some other Petrarchan cliché, which surprises by its aptness: by the fact that it changes neither conceit nor attitude. Donne's conceit is completely clear by the end of his fourth line, and yet his lyric becomes more interesting as it continues. First, there are the dramatic details of the scene: the "sicke taper," the "Aspen wretch neglected," and the "quicksilver sweat." Then, there is the way Donne's feelings appear: for example, in "fain'd vestall," "worse armes," and "my love is spent." Finally, there is the overall complexity of the relation between the pseudo-drama of the haunting and the immediate intention of Donne. The very fulness with which the scene of the haunting is developed indicates a sophistication on the part of the poet. Among the Italian Petrarchists, there is often sophistication beneath a sentimental veneer. But here the sophistication is part of the poem's mystery and its charm. Donne has not merely found a proper manner through which to address his lady; he has given that manner so great a complexity of intention that it remains piquant and enigmatic still.

Because of the novelty of the idea that "The Apparition" derives from a Petrarchan social manner, it may be worth describing its effect by analogy. Donne may be thought of as a mean between Gascoigne and Pope, who both use Petrarchism to deal with social situations. Gascoigne's Petrarchism is a fashionable vocabulary, ostentatiously fine and distinctly inappropriate to his commonplace mind. Pope's Petrarchism is impersonal and general, an element of the idyllic or heroic style: where Gascoigne's lyrics show him busily involved in life, Pope's verses show him to be a commentator, with nothing to do but to look about him, and to die. Imagine, however, a lyric in which Pope describes himself as a combatant in that battle of killing glances and dying swains which climaxes "The Rape of the Lock," and imagine him flattering his beloved so:

> Bright as the sun, your eyes the gazers strike;
> And, like the sun, they shine on all alike.

The combination here of personal involvement with poise, and of elaborate politeness with accurate evaluation, would place such a lyric in the line of "The Apparition."

In short, "The Apparition" makes meaningful the polite extravagances of Petrarchan sentimentality. Petrarchists handling similar themes generally simplify their material to bring out only one sentiment; and although such a theme is necessarily sophisticated they commit themselves entirely to its sentiment. Donne makes the visionary melodrama more self-sufficient, more complex, more fully dramatic, and at the same time imbues it with a sense of the complexity of the poet's motives for sentimental extravagance.

What Donne gains from Petrarchism can be suggested by contrasting "The Flea" and "The Apparition," both conceited poems directed to reluctant ladies. The conceit of "The Flea," though it has literary antecedents,[23] has no ready-made social context. It therefore invites the reader to apply his own standards of propriety, and probably to find its cleverness either vulgar or, at best, academic. Through Petrarchism "The Apparition," on the other hand, evokes the poise and propriety of a courtly culture. It says exactly what Donne wants to say with a flourish of neatness, fancy, and wit. Thus, the Petrarchan manner affords Donne poise and grace; and he gives it a new force.

V

Donne's Logic and Petrarchan Wit

Oonne's Petrarchism, in "The Apparition," is an exaggerated manner: a pretense that conventional hyperboles are literally true. It is this manner which is the key to Donne's more problematic poems.

Though Donne's language presents few semantic problems, it is today often impenetrable. For example, in "The Funerall" Donne says that a lock of his lady's hair will be more effective than his own spinal cord in keeping his body together. He argues that where his spine comes *down* from *his* brain, her hair comes *up* from *her* brain; and that, up being better than down, and her brain better than his, her hair will do the better job:

> For if the sinewie thread my braine lets fall
> Through every part,
> Can tye those parts, and make mee one of all;
> These haires which upward grew, and strength and art
> Have from a better braine,
> Can better do'it.

Today, the intent of this argument is puzzling. Is it literal and medical? Is it allegorical? Is it literal, but irrational—perhaps parody, or perhaps Baudelairian fantasy? Or is it not a statement at all, but a polite gesture, like a bow? In short, *how* does "The Funerall" mean—through denotation or connotation, allegory or symbol, exposition or gesture? The argument of "The Funerall" is enigmatic; and almost all of Donne's love poems depend on similar arguments.

Essentially, the question concerns Donne's attitude. It would remain acute even if the nature of Donne's semantics were clear.

For example, let us assume that the diction of "The Funerall" is denotative and literal, and that its argument is frankly irrational. Is Donne, then, mocking, and, if so, what is he mocking? Is he pensively revealing a private fantasy? Is he malicious or benign, poised or furious? Though critics have their opinions, an informed scholar must be in doubt about what Donne means by "The Funerall"—and therefore about what "The Funerall" means.

In the context of Petrarchism, however, "The Funerall" is quite clear. Many Petrarchan poets attribute miraculous powers to their ladies' eyes, clothes, pets, books, and gifts. For the *quattrocentisti* especially, the lady's gift—whether a lock of hair or an apple, a ring or an artichoke—is a favorite theme. Their usual method of developing the theme is to amass arguments, with as much logical rigor as possible, to show the powers or significance of the gift. Their exposition, no matter how extended, means nothing in itself: it is intended only as a gallant gesture. Similarly, Donne's definition of the powers of his lady's hair is a mere hyperbole.[1] He himself considers it to demonstrate only his devotion: " 'twas humility/ To afford to it [the lock of hair] all that a Soule can doe." In short, Donne's argumentative rigor, like that of the *quattrocentisti,* is a means of emphasizing his exaggeratedly gallant pose.

But, unlike that of the *quattrocentisti,* Donne's gallantry is ironic. He speaks of the lock of hair with reverence: it must be neither touched nor questioned; it is a mystery and a holy sign, a manifestation of divine things; it is a relic which, if discovered, might lead to idolatry. Yet, in conclusion, turning from those who bury him to his lady, Donne says,

> since you would save none of mee, I bury some of you.

Here the nature of Donne's manner is clear. A reasonable man does not humbly die for love while worshipping a lock of his lady's hair. The *quattrocentisti* pretend to do so; and their poems remain mere pretense, polite exaggeration. Donne adopts their manner, but not their merely polite intentions. Through their sophisticated pose, he reveals a sophisticated awareness.

In many of his lyrics, Donne's arguments are straightforward and even philosophic. But no adequate approach to Donne can ignore his logic of gallantry, and his sophisticated Petrarchan manner. These can best be understood through an understanding of the witty Petrarchists.

The witty Petrarchists adapt the convention, with its eschatological and ontological concerns, to a world like that of the Restoration drama.[2] They make Petrarch's contemplation of beauty more sensual, his pleadings more practical, and his sentiments more mundane. And they sophisticate his conceits: Petrarch's sighs reverberate in the valleys, but Serafino's impede the birds; Laura shines more brightly than the sun, but Tasso's lady purifies seawater better; Petrarch's tears bathe his breast, but Guarino's form an ocean in which his lady lives like a siren.[3] The witty Petrarchists offered Donne a tradition of unclassical wit employing psychology and dialectic, expressing passion and politeness, and aiming at hermeticism and triviality—a tradition characterized by peregrine comparisons, extravagant hyperboles, and epigrammatic statement.

The witty Petrarchists could hardly have been unknown to Donne. They were enormously popular in Donne's time.[4] Their wit formed the tone of courtly conversation; their poems were extensively translated and imitated. No neat young man about town, no great frequenter of the ladies, and above all no man of literary interests could have avoided at least an indirect acquaintance with their poems. Donne's acquaintance was probably direct: he knew Italian, and he imitated Guarino at least once. Close comparisons between the conceits of the *Songs and Sonets* and those of the witty Petrarchists show it to be probable that Donne borrowed from them, and certain that his wit is in their manner.

The witty Petrarchists may be subdivided into three groups. First, there are the court poets of the late quattrocento and early cinquecento—Tebaldeo, Chariteo, Serafino, and their followers. Second, there are the literati represented in two influential anthologies, *I fiori delle rime de' poeti illustri* (Venice, 1579) and *Rime di diversi illustri signori napoletani, Libro Quinto* (Venice, 1552). Finally, there are the late sixteenth-century poets, chiefly Tasso and Guarino. For the development of the "metaphysical" conceit, the second group is transitional, and I shall consider Donne's wit chiefly in relation to the *quattrocentisti,* and to Tasso and Guarino.

The *quattrocentisti* (the name is only vaguely chronological) —Tebaldeo, Chariteo, Serafino, Sasso, Cei, Accolti, and others—use Petrarchism as a means of giving mythological dignity to court life. Through a clever logic of imagery, they translate trivial affairs into Petrarchan terms. For example, Petrarch says that his love turns him to a stone. When Serafino sees a statue of Cupid in a garden, he claims that the god has been made stone by the lady. Petrarch talks about the prison and the chains of love. When Accolti sees a chain in a lady's garden wall, he says it is there for her lovers. Petrarch calls Laura's glances, blows. When he sees a lady looking in a mirror, Serafino wonders why her glances do not break the glass.[5] Repeatedly, the *quattrocentisti* take Petrarch's sentimental hyperboles as facts, and then either claim that some ordinary event has been caused by them, or wonder why it has not. Thus they invest ordinary affairs with grace and fancy.

Sometimes their logic is used for social purposes. For example, Tebaldeo wants to apologize for having failed to help extinguish a fire at a lady's house. Petrarch talks of the fires of love; and Tebaldeo explains that he wanted to avoid adding his flames to those which were already burning the house. Serafino wants to excuse himself from writing an epitaph requested by a lady. Petrarch claims to die for love; and Serafino says that it is he who is dead, and who therefore needs an epitaph to be written for him. Accolti wants to thank a lady for an artichoke. Petrarch says that love inspires hope, but gives no fruit; and Accolti says that the artichoke, like the lady, gives little fruit, though its green inspires hope.[6] Thus these poets use Petrarchism for an elaborate courtesy.

As these examples show, it is not the statements but the basic metaphors of the *quattrocentisti* which are emotionally important. For example, Accolti does not mean that artichokes really make him hopeful—he means merely to discuss the artichoke in terms which imply the lady's beauty and his love. The connection between the actual occasion and the Petrarchan terms—that is, between the poem's sentiments and its statements—is left to pure ingenuity. The

more elaborate quattrocentist poems apply the greatest possible number of arguments to connect Petrarchan worship with the subject at
hand. For example, a lady objects because Serafino squeezes her
hand while dancing with her. He excuses himself on the following
grounds: the hand he squeezes squeezes his heart (Petrarch says
both that his heart is in Laura's hand, and that it is constricted);
the lady cannot be pained by the pressure since she is stone (Laura,
according to Petrarch, is stone); it must have been his heat that
made her uncomfortable, she being so cold (Petrarch is afire and
Laura frozen); and, finally, the contraction of his hand was a muscular spasm caused by his death (Petrarch says that he dies for
love).[7] Thus Serafino multiplies the apparent relevancy of Petrarchism to his situation by a series of pretended causes. Other poets use
the *topos* of likeness rather than that of causality for a similar purpose, sometimes approaching emblematic interpretation thereby. For
example, Accolti argues in "Della Duchessa di Urbino sculpita: Io
che son sculpita in marmo humido e basso" that a statue of the lady
is like the lady: the statue is a fountain, and the lady evokes amorous tears; the statue and lady are both hard, cold, white, and amazing; and both evoke amorous desires without satisfying them. Thus,
by such *topoi* as pretended causes and likeness the *quattrocentisti*
cleverly complicate their translation of mundane affairs into the
mythology of Petrarchism.

Although their techniques are best suited to verse written for
social occasions, the *quattrocentisti* often treat the general situation
of the Petrarchan lover. Chariteo, especially—a ceremonial humanist rather than a polite improviser—deduces from Petrarchan metaphor not social incidents, but the dramatic pattern of Petrarchan
love. For example, two standard Petrarchan situations are the lady's
avoidance of the poet, and her illness. Chariteo deduces these situations from two Petrarchan metaphors, the lady-goddess and the sun-
like lady. He explains that it could not have been fear that caused
his lady to avoid him since, being celestial, she does not fear, but
that, being heavenly, she did not deign to look on a mortal being.
And he prays that God keep his lady Luna alive so that no more
than one sun and one moon should be in heaven.[8] Thus Chariteo

uses the logic of *quattrocentismo* to explain and analyze Petrarchan situations by Petrarchan metaphors.

Serafino carries the logic even further from Petrarch's sentimental rhetoric. He shifts the emphasis from the poet's emotional circumstances to the literal implications of his metaphors. For example, where Petrarch exaggerates the quantity of his tears and sighs, Serafino offers to provide beseiged men with water and becalmed sailors with wind (cf. "The Canonization," "What merchants ships have my sighs drown'd?/ Who saies my teares have overflow'd his ground?"). Petrarch expects to die for love, and Serafino elaborately imagines his funeral and the actions of his ghost.[9] Thus Serafino treats Petrarch's sentimental tropes as literal truths, and expatiates on their consequences. By so doing he provides Donne with the basis of the metaphysical conceit.

In this study, I shall confine my consideration of the *quattrocentisti* to Serafino. Serafino was one of the most universally admired of Renaissance poets. When he took Sasso's mistress, Sasso, though condemning his lady's infidelity, celebrated the seraphic ("Seraphino" is "seraph") prowess of his friend. When Serafino died, the most renowned poets of his time paid tribute to his glory. And though Serafino was repudiated by Bembo and his followers, he was translated and imitated by Wyatt and Watson, Guarino and Tasso, Ronsard and Desportes. He was particularly influential in Donne's time, and Marinism, Gongorism, and *préciosité* all owe a great deal to his wit.[10]

A comparison of Donne with Serafino highlights three aspects of Donne's use of metaphor. First, Donne, like Serafino, expresses his feelings not through what he says, but through his assumption that amorous hyperboles are true: for example, in "The Apparition" he does not really mean that he will haunt his lady; but he expresses his love by assuming that he will die, and his anger by assuming that he will haunt his murderess. Second, Donne, like Serafino, pretending that a Petrarchan cliché is literally true, applies to it laws relevant to its literal but not to its metaphorical meaning, and deduces consequences from it. For example, in "The broken heart" he accepts as literally true the Petrarchan statement that the poet has lost his heart; he demonstrates that the heart is not outside the poet; and, invoking the physical law that matter cannot be totally destroyed, he concludes that the heart must be in him still, but broken (the broken heart, obviously, being another cliché taken literally). The same method is used in several other lyrics: for example, "The Legacie" takes literally the exchange of hearts, and "The Will," death for love. Third, Donne, like Serafino, erects similar arguments upon the details of his situation. For example, "The Funerall" is ostensibly about a lock of hair; "A Valediction: of weeping" about tears; "A Jeat Ring sent" about a ring; and "A Valediction: of my name, in the window," about letters scratched in a window pane. These lyrics erect sentimental arguments upon details, as "The broken heart" erects them upon a cliché. All these aspects of Donne's art aim at indirectness, wit, and sophistication in handling sentiment. And they all reflect the art of Serafino and his followers.

"The Apparition," as shown in Chapter IV above, parallels and perhaps even imitates Serafino's Strambotti 103 and 104. Serafino wittily extends conventional conceits. The Petrarchan poet says that he will die for love; Serafino gravely speculates on the actions of his ghost. The Petrarchan lover cries out against his lady's heart; Serafino fiercely threatens to avenge himself on that organ of her body. The Petrarchan lover accuses his lady of cruelty; Serafino condemns her to death. Thus Serafino's conceit results from the pretense that Petrarchan clichés are literally true. Donne's lyric is more dramatic. It portrays vividly the scene of the ghostly confrontation. More important, it realizes the outrage and anguish which a lover who desires revenge after death must feel. "When by thy scorne, O murdresse I am dead" converts to an outcry the first line of Serafino's sequence, "When you have led me to my death" (Stram. 99, "Quando a morte per te sero condutto"); "fain'd vestall" changes Serafino's "false heart" to a jealous exclamation; and Donne's refusal to reveal his future speech discovers in Serafino's prediction of his lady's repentance a triumphant vengefulness. Thus Donne makes Serafino's extravagancies reflect the lover's feelings. But his lyric, like Serafino's, is based on the witty pretense that obdurate ladies do in fact murder their lovers, as Petrarchists say.

Donne's "A Jeat Ring sent," like "The Apparition," may show the influence of Serafino. It is a speech to a ring given a lover by his unfaithful lady. After speculating on the ring's emblematic import, Donne concludes:

> Yet stay with mee since thou art come,
> Circle this fingers top, which did'st her thombe.
> Be justly proud, and gladly safe, that thou dost dwell with me,
> She that, Oh, broke her faith, would soon breake thee.

Serafino's Sonnets 51-54 are all addresses to a black ring given him by a lady. His oft-imitated ring sonnets are, as Joseph Vianey shows, characteristic of Serafino's art and influence.[11] Sonnet 52, "O vago anel, che in su la bianca mano" tells the ring that in leaving the lady it has lost heaven, as the poet has lost his heart; then, noting that the once-bright ring has been made black by the lover's flames, it moralizes upon the instability of fortune and advises the ring to be content with the security of the mean estate. Although Donne congratulates the ring on its escape where Serafino consoles it for its loss,[12] he employs Serafino's mode of wit—sympathizing with the ring as with a companion and pretending that the lady's moral qualities will affect the ring materially. But Serafino's sonnets are merely polite: they compliment a benefactress by pretending that her beauty is great enough to influence a ring. Donne's lyric is dramatic. In it a betrayed lover talks to the ring which he finds himself still wearing, though its giver has cast him off. His unconfessed self-pity leads him to sympathize with the ring, which, like him, has escaped the lady; his ironic fantasies are natural to a betrayed lover contemplating a token of his lady's fidelity. And behind his statement that the ring's cheapness was intended to show that love is cheap, lurks the bitter dramatic question: what, after all, did the lady mean by her gift? Thus, "A Jeat Ring sent" is a dramatic reflection naturally occasioned by a ring; and to show the lover's feelings, Donne uses the art of Serafino, who had developed a witty method of reading amorous fantasies into such mundane subjects as gifts.

"Witchcraft by a picture" also shows similarities to Serafino. Its argument is that Donne's reflection burns in the lady's eye, and drowns in her tears; that she might thereby kill him by witchcraft; but that, drinking her tears with kisses, he saves himself, since the only picture that remains to her, being in her heart, must be free of malice. Conceits based on the reflection of one lover in the tears or eyes of another appear often in Donne. They are anticipated by Serafino's Sonnet 36, "Mentre che amore in me non abitava," where Serafino explains that his lady, who used to enjoy seeing her picture in his eyes, no longer looks kindly on him because his weeping deforms her picture.[13] The minuteness of Donne's image, the analytical quality, is paralleled by Serafino. So is his general method, for, like Serafino, Donne explains motives by pretending that Petrarchan metaphors (blazing eyes and a picture in the heart) interact with material circumstances (tears and reflections). Thus both Donne and Serafino make specious but senseless explanations. Here as elsewhere Donne makes Serafino's sort of argument express a dramatic play of awareness. His concern with his lady's tear reflects both his physical and his emotional situation. His idea that his lady might kill him expresses whimsically his dependence upon her; his proof that he is safe reveals his sense of her innocence and fidelity. But like Serafino Donne exercises deductive logic upon a confusion of material and spiritual facts. To express the tenderness of a lover who sees his beloved weeping at parting, he adopts the Petrarchan manner; to reveal his amorous fancies, he employs fanciful Petrarchan logic.

"A Valediction: of my name, in the window" is another example of Donne's use of Serafino's sort of wit. A series of conceits upon so unpromising a subject as a window, it resembles a sequence of strambotti—as the numbering of its stanzas suggests. Here are the first two stanzas:

> My name engrav'd herein,
> Doth contribute my firmnesse to this glasse,
>   Which, ever since that charme, hath beene
>   As hard, as that which grav'd it, was;
> Thine eye will give it price enough, to mock
>   The diamonds of either rock.

> 'Tis much that Glasse should bee
> As all confessing, and through-shine as I,
> 'Tis more, that it shewes thee to thee,
> And cleare reflects thee to thine eye.
> But all such rules, loves magique can undoe,
> Here you see mee, and I am you.

Stanza 1 proves that by scratching his name on her window Donne has given the lady a diamond: assuming that a diamond is defined by hardness and value, it asserts that the window has taken firmness from Donne, and will take value from the reflection of his lady. So strangely conceived a gift is reminiscent of Serafino. In Sonnet 29, "Lo indegno mio servir per suo restoro," for example, Serafino, obligated to give a lady a gift, offers her the impressions of her face which have been stamped on love's golden arrows as they have hit the portrait of her engraved on his heart. Donne, like Serafino, presents as a gift a merely imaginary consequence of conventional metaphors, literally understood.

Stanza 2 of "A Valediction" proves that the window's transparency and its ability to reflect faces are miraculous. Its argument, a sort of extended zeugma, is based on the pretense that transparency, whether of man or of glass, is always the same, and that a person and his image are identical. Donne's use of the conventional theme of "loves magique" is in Serafino's vein: for example, in Strambotto 77, "Se salamandra in fiamma vive: e poco," Serafino reveals as a great marvel the fact that his icy lady resides in his fiery heart. Donne, like Serafino, expresses wonder at a miracle which is merely fanciful, a literal-minded deduction from tropes.

In Stanza 11, Donne excuses the invective of the preceding stanzas as the raving of a dying man:

> But glasse, and lines must bee,
> No meanes our firme substantiall love to keepe;
> Neere death inflicts this lethargie,
> And this I murmure in my sleepe;
> Impute this idle talke, to that I goe,
> For dying men talke often so.

Similarly, in Sonnet 30, "Cresi venire al ballo, e venni al laccio,"

Serafino, having been reprimanded for squeezing a lady's hand, explains that the contraction of his hand was a spasm caused by his death for love. Donne, like Serafino, excuses himself by pretending that his real actions have been caused by his purely figurative death.

Where Serafino's wit makes myths out of ordinary events, "A Valediction" is a thoroughly dramatic poem. Donne discriminates among his emotions—tenderness, jealousy, and sorrow—and convincingly represents the interplay among them, and the development of his thought as, standing before a window with his beloved, he thinks with pain of their coming parting. In order to reveal the fancies of a sentimental lover in a moving situation, Donne could have found nothing better than the Petrarchan conceit—which is, of course, a rich mine of amorous feeling and fantasy.[14] Donne's is a dramatically motivated train of thought: the gift of the pseudo-diamond reveals the lover's sense that his constancy and his lady's worth make them able to transcend their bitter necessities; and the image of the dying man's babble reflects his sorrowful awareness that he has been talking nonsense, and that he really has to go. Donne's aim, then, is dramatic where Serafino's is merely polite. But for the drama of love, Donne assumes the Petrarchan manner, and adopts Serafino's Petrarchan logic—the pretense that conventional metaphors are literally true, and that they explain his actions and the nature of his environment.

Serafino's example serves to show that there was nothing necessarily iconoclastic about cynical Petrarchism. Incapable of aspiration and grandeur, he nonetheless anticipates Donne in the realistic spirit with which he treats Petrarchan clichés. He mingles passionate hyperboles with boldness, lasciviousness, and an attention to practical affairs; though his metaphors are elegantly sentimental, he is never committed to an idealization of his lady. Essentially, however, Serafino is important to students of Donne as an epigone of Petrarchan logic and the Petrarchan conceit. By deducing consequences from Petrarchan metaphors as though they were literally true Serafino creates a mythical world: a world in which amorous passions affect the weather, in which men die for love and are eaten by worms, and in which ladies' gifts perform miracles. Serafino

71

creates a language in which extensive logic is a mere gesture to show that the poet believes in love. Donne writes of the same mythical world, in the same elaborate logic; but where Serafino uses them for mere compliment, Donne makes them express the lover's feelings and fantasies. Thus Serafino's lyrics anticipate and illuminate the wit of the *Songs and Sonets*.

Guarino's poetry is sentimental and affected. Its passion is fatuous; its wit, complacent. Foreshadowing the verse of the Italian Arcadia, it is overly mannered, overly delicate, and essentially trite. But Guarino is important to Donne because he suits Serafino's fantastic logic to exposition. He subordinates the play upon the literal meaning of metaphors, to sensible ratiocination. Where Serafino's logic of imagery is merely gallant gesture, Guarino's is the embellishment of essentially expository statement. Therefore, where Serafino anticipates Donne's sophisticated indirection and sentimental fantasies, Guarino anticipates his amorous philosophizing.

In Strambotto 106, "O morte: o la: soccori," for example, Serafino wittily employs the traditional theory that lovers die and are resurrected daily. He prays to Death to kill him; Death responds that he in fact does, frequently; the poet, inquiring of his heart, is told that he dies and is reborn repeatedly; and thus the poet remains frustrated in his hope of death.[15] Here as in general, Serafino's intention is revealed chiefly by the premises of his myth, which itself means nothing: to show that he is tormented for love, Serafino invents a myth about his discovery that he is immortal. In Madrigal 37, "Una farfalla cupida, e vagante," Guarino adapts a similarly witty argument to sentimental exposition. To show the extremity of his amorous fervor, Guarino claims that though in the radiance of his lady's eyes he dies like a moth in a flame, he is resurrected like the phoenix. His conjunction of eye's flame with candle's fire, and dying moth with dying phoenix, is witty. But fundamentally Guarino is declaring his faith that love is regenerative despite its torments; and the images he uses add only piquancy, and a certain traditional authority, to a prose statement. In the third stanza of "The Canonization," Donne too shows his heroic faith in love, declaring that where critics claim that he and his lady die like moths in a flame, actually they are resurrected like the phoenix. The obstacles faced by Donne are serious: not merely the flame of a lady's eyes, but age, illness, poverty, and contempt. His situation calls for a more convincing heroism than Guarino's. To express his devotion, Donne attributes to the traditional images an absolute validity, arguing that, like the phoenix, the lovers are one, and hermaphroditic. He assumes the pose of a Petrarchan martyr by adopting Guarino's Petrarchan logic; and he gives logical direction and dramatic urgency to what is in Guarino merely witty phrasing and polite courtship.

Guarino's Madrigal 69, "Era l'anima mia," is a dialogue in which a lady saves her lover's life by declaring, "If you die, Alas! it is not you, but I who die." [16] Again, there is a more vigorous logic in analogues by Donne—for example, in "since thou and I sigh one anothers breath,/ Who e'er sighes most, is cruellest, and hasts the others death" ("A Valediction: of weeping," 11. 26-27). Unlike Guarino's use of "death," which is merely a complication of language, Donne's argument is ostensibly medical: he may even be thinking that "anima," "soul," is etymologically breath, and that love, as he says in "The Extasie," "interinanimates two soules." In "A Valediction" Donne expresses a fervent faith in love as he comforts his lady and appeals to her love for him. To express utter devotion, he assumes a pose like Guarino's, and accepts as a fact the sentimental hyperbole which Guarino develops as neat affectation.

One of the most famous of Donne's images, the compass figure from "A Valediction: forbidding mourning," is a similar renewal of a traditional conceit used by Guarino:

> Our two soules therefore, which are one,
> Though I must goe, endure not yet
> A breach, but an expansion,
> Like gold to ayery thinnesse beate.
>
> If they be two, they are two so
> As stiffe twin compasses are two,
> Thy soule the fixt foot, makes no show
> To move, but doth, if th'other doe.

73

And though it in the center sit,
      Yet when the other far doth rome,
It leanes, and hearkens after it,
      And growes erect, as that comes home.

Such wilt thou be to mee, who must
      Like th'other foot, obliquely runne;
Thy firmnes makes my circle just,
      And makes me end, where I begunne.

Though the compass was frequently used as an emblem of constancy,[17] I know of no parallel so close as Guarino's Madrigals 95 and 96, "Tu parti apena giunto" and "Con voi sempre son io."

[Lady:] You leave though barely come,
      fugitive, cruel man. Will a day ever come
      when your return will conclude your departure?
      Oh sweetest fair—
      if you were not so fairly inclined to wayfaring—
      at least leave your faith fixed,
      and let not your heart flee from me, though your foot flies.

[Lover:] I am ever with you,
      agitated, but fixed,
      and if I steal my lesser part from you, I leave my greater.
      I am like the compass,
      fixing one foot in you as in my center:
      the other endures the circlings of fortune
      but can by no means fail to circle around you.

Guarino is interested chiefly in the piquancy of the situation and the aptness and extravagance of the speakers' sentiments: for example, in the lady's languishing assumption that her lover means to avoid her, and in the precious innocence of her "at least." Donne expresses the overwhelming tenderness evoked by his parting, by his lady's sorrow, and by his intention of comforting her. To reveal his faith in the supremacy of love, he adopts a Petrarchan posture, and attributes philosophic validity to the extravagant statements of such Petrarchists as Guarino.

Guarino's statement is essentially prosaic. In his compass—as in his conjunction of "fixed heart" with "fleeing foot"—the literal meaning of the tropes echoes their intention, but is logically super-erogatory. The lady has asked whether her lover will leave some part of himself with her; he answers her metaphor as well as her meaning. But he does not resolve the contradictions in his statements that he is always with her, mostly with her, and partly with and partly circling about her—the witty coherence of Guarino's images is logically inert. Donne, on the other hand, expresses his extreme devotion by treating similar hyperboles as philosophic principles. He asserts with Petrarchan thinkers that two lovers are one, and remain united though they part.[18] By the material relations among his images—the distinction between stretched gold and spread compasses, for example—he defines the precise nature of an amorous union which transcends separation. Furthermore, through words which apply to both terms of his comparison (e.g., "leanes," "fixt," and "firmnes"), he defines the emotional nature of that union. Thus, here as elsewhere, in order to express a supreme love Donne attributes philosophic validity to the sentimental conceits of madrigalesque Petrarchism.

Where Serafino's extended metaphor is a logical structure and Guarino's a decoration, Torquato Tasso's is a way of picturing love as a glorious enterprise in a world that reverberates to beauty. Donne's amorous poetry is often analogous to Tasso's, but I shall here consider parallels to Tasso (along with parallels to Serafino and Guarino) only in the chivalric imagery of "The Dampe":

> When I am dead, and Doctors know not why,
> > And my friends curiositie
> Will have me cut up to survay each part,
> When they shall finde your Picture in my heart,
> > You thinke a sodaine dampe of love
> > Will through all their senses move,
> And worke on them as mee, and so preferre
> Your murder, to the name of Massacre.
>
> Poore victories! But if you dare be brave,
> > And pleasure in your conquest have,
> First kill th'enormous Gyant, your *Disdaine*,

And let th'enchantresse *Honor,* next be slaine,
    And like a Goth and Vandall rize,
    Deface Records, and Histories
Of your owne arts and triumphs over men,
And without such advantage kill me then.

For I could muster up as well as you
    My Gyants, and my Witches too,
Which are vast *Constancy,* and *Secretnesse,*
But these I neyther looke for, nor professe;
    Kill mee as Woman, let mee die
    As a meere man; doe you but try
Your passive valor, and you shall finde than,
Naked,[19] you'have odds enough of any man.

The first stanza of "The Dampe" treats literally two traditional figures, the lover's death and the picture on his heart. Donne
pretends that amorous death is real enough to occasion an inquest,
and that the image on the heart is material. Both conceits are fore-
shadowed by Serafino: in Strambotto 89, "Quando sero portato in
sepoltura," Serafino describes the funeral procession which will follow him when he has died for love; and in Strambotto 126, "Felice
specchio hor che madonna godi," he says that if his breast were
opened everyone would recognize the image of his lady on his heart
(as, in "The Dampe," everyone does see a similar image). The possibility that the lady's picture may harm whoever sees it (11. 3-6)
is also suggested by Serafino: in Sonnet 35, "Ciascun vol pur saper
che cosa e quella," Serafino says that a locket containing his lady's
picture, and thus both the entire world and the cause of his death,
is dangerous to whoever opens it. Furthermore, Donne's witty explanation of his lady's motives, which assumes that she actually
bases her plans on battles and images which exist only metaphorically, is in the vein of the witty Petrarchists. For example, in Madrigal 7, "Lasso, perché mi fuggi," Guarino says that his lady avoids
him so that he may die, and he tells her that she will fail in this
attempt, for she has his heart, and without a heart he cannot die.
Thus Donne, like the witty Petrarchists, uses old hyperboles not for
their purely expressive functions, but to form fantastic explanations.

The second and third stanzas of "The Dampe" elaborate the conventional Petrarchan conceit that the lady makes war upon the poet. But where Petrarch was content to call his lady a sweet warrior, Donne conceives of a combat involving giants, enchantresses, witches, and other accessories of chivalric romance. Donne's conceit is a variation of one of Tasso's favorite themes. The amorous combat, the lady's use of magic, and her victory through kindness (cf. the final four lines of "The Dampe") appear, for example, in Tasso, *Rime* 113, "Quel generoso mio guerriero interno" (11. 48-60), where Tasso's "magnanimous warrior" (his indignation at the way his lady treats him) complains that his lady-enemy, who

> Seems, amazingly, to be a new and delicate monster,
>   through natural operations or through magical arts
>   transforms both herself and the desires
>   of our soul, which sighs for her.
>   . . . .
>   . . . and the less she is ferocious,
>   the more I feel the strength of her blows,
>   and consent willingly to be wounded.

The lady's use of "arts" for her martial "triumphs over men"—another theme of "The Dampe"—appears in Tasso 105, "S' arma lo Sdegno, e 'n lunga schiera e folta." Here, after describing his pride arming itself, and then the rout of its enemies, Tasso says:

> Beauty that is artfully neglected, gentle gestures,
>   pity that is feigned, and persistent, obdurate scorn,
>   complaints and sweetly enunciated cajoleries,
> And receptions now joyful, now sad, and now solemn—
>   till now these have been the arms of my enemy,
>   and now they are the trophies won by these ardent warriors.

Allies much like Donne's "constancy and secretnesse" appear as Tasso's lieutenants in 446, "Amor, contra costei che 'n treccia e 'n gonna":

> Love, against her who is armed in tresses
>   and a gown, and who encamps and gathers her warriors,
>   among the host of desires one, becoming our queen,
>   guides in our mind full a thousand bold wishes:

all the stars in heaven promise us
the dear, amorous spoils of the unvanquished lady;
and faith and suffering and alert concealment
press upon her, and her fate is sealed.

Though there is no indication that "The Dampe" imitates any particular poem of Tasso's, Donne's use of the martial conceit resembles Tasso's.

"The Dampe" concludes the warrior image with the suggestion that the lady's victory ought to occur in bed—"Naked, you'have odds enough of any man." This conclusion is anticipated in *The Greek Anthology*, 16. 171, which tells an armed statue of Venus that, having defeated Mars when she was naked, she needs no arms against mortals. It is also anticipated by the *pre-secentisti,* who often play with the idea of the clothing necessary for love's warfare (probably in imitation of Petrarch 121, "Or vedi, Amor, che giovenetta donna," which, encouraging Love to attack Laura, observes that he is armed, and she dressed in a mere gown). Tasso, for example, conjoins the lady's lack of armor with the lover's hope of possessing her in 446, "Amor, contra costei che 'n treccia e 'n gonna," and with her victories over men in "Questa leggiadra e gloriosa donna" [20] (Sonnet 195, *Opere . . . Vol. IV: L' Aminta e rime scelte* [Milan, 1824]). Guarino, though speaking of Love rather than of the lady, notes the power of nudity in amorous combats in Madrigal 68, "Quest' è pur il mio cor." And Riccho, in "Horsu Madonna ogni vergogna scaza," tells his lady that she should not be ashamed to content him, since Love himself goes nude. Although it is difficult to determine whether the conceit's origin is Anacreontic or Petrarchan, it is clear that the burst of wit with which "The Dampe" closes, and which is so characteristic of Donne, is in the manner of the *pre-secentisti.*[21]

Like its images, the improbable and sophisticated persuasion of "The Dampe" is pre-secentist. The transformation of an elegant and sentimental, conventional plea ("Sweet warrior, I die for you; be kind") to an unconvincing and fantastic demonstration ("You hope for a martial victory through my death; gain it in bed instead") is a common pre-secentist form. For example, in Sonnet 14,

"Deh perche son da me toe luci tolte?" Serafino persuades his lady to see him again on the ground that a good warrior returns to view the enemy he has defeated; and in 369, "O con le Grazie eletta e con gli Amori," Tasso, presuming the conventional comparison between the lady's charms and the spear of Achilles, argues that the lady should love him for the glory she would gain by demonstrating that she can cure as well as wound (ll. 65-80). In basing a persuasive argument on the obviously fantastic premise that the lady is desirous chiefly of martial glory, "The Dampe" is pre-secentist.

The wit of "The Dampe" results, however, as much from Donne's dramatic imagination as from his pre-secentist logic. In the lyrics of the *pre-secentisti,* the image of love's warfare often implies that the lady wants to flatter her vanity, and that the lover desires to possess her; but the sentiments expressed are Petrarchan. Donne resolves what is apparently a dramatic disparity between the lover's realistic observation and his high-flown sentiments: he abandons the sentimental languor which the image of the lover's death implies. He develops a lover who, in Donne's terms, is capable of both desiring the lady and perceiving her foolish vanity; and he reduces the martial imagery from an expression of the poet's exorbitant sentiments to a playful exaggeration of the lady's foolish fancies. Thus "The Dampe," which instances the emphatically casual air and flagrant good sense that he bequeathed to the Cavalier poets, exemplifies as well Donne's characteristic method—the modification by dramatic development of the conceits of the witty Petrarchists.

The witty Petrarchists are important to Donne in many ways. They anticipate his dramatic form with Arcadian dialogues, and his dramatic material with quotidian subjects. They foreshadow his exalted common sense by using the language of Petrarchan devotion with a keen awareness of feminine manners and a practical concern for their own interests. And they precede him in adapting Neoplatonic analyses to love poetry. Above all, they provide him a logic of imagery suitable to his habits of mind. Joan Webber shows that Donne's sermons multiply the relations of their texts to Donne's own feelings through symbolism, analogy, and argument.[22] In Biblical exegesis, such extended interpretations were traditional. For

Donne's love poetry, the witty Petrarchists provide a similar method of elaboration. Donne commits himself to a basic set of metaphors as he does to a Biblical text; and he employs quattrocentistic logic to make the metaphors yield an expression of his own feelings.

A recognition of Donne's Petrarchan antecedents provides the means of resolving many critical debates. It shows, for example, how Lederer could suggest and Miss Freeman deny [23] that Donne's conceit is basically emblematic: for Donne, like the extravagant Petrarchists, employs much the same subject matter as the amorous emblems [24] and a similarly systematic logic, without maintaining a distinction between picture and meaning. Again, it explains why the well-authorized notion that Donne is like Marino has been forcibly disputed: [25] for Donne is truly like Serafino, whose taste resembles Marino's, but whose conceit is logical where Marino's is descriptive. Finally, the situation of Donne in the tradition of witty Petrarchism explains how he could have reconciled universal analogy with a satiric spirit and an epigrammatic form: for he comes at the end of three centuries of progressive secularization of the *dolce stil novo*.

More importantly, a recognition of his Petrarchan antecedents permits a sound evaluation of Donne's art. For ironic poise Donne adopts their elegant postures; for sentimental fantasies, their fantastic logic; for extreme emotions, their sentimental hyperboles. His comparisons are not weird, his logic is not medieval, and his lyrics are not the perverse and individual researches of an oddly alert mind. Instead, Donne writes the language of the social, and highly sophisticated, courtly Petrarchists. His modern reader, therefore, need not seek in Donne either metaphysical profundities or *symboliste* orgies of imagination. He can instead respond to Donne's sentiment and meaning: smile when he is clever, sigh when he sorrows, and feel exalted by the extremities of his passion and the height of his faith.

VI

Baroque and Précieux Elements in Donne

Onne's hyperboles seem strange today, and his tone is hard to recapture. It is understandable, therefore, that critics have considered him to represent a bygone taste—a baroque spirit.[1] But surely Donne is not to be read in the same way as Marino or Gongora.

For "the baroque," though meaningful when referring to one particular late-Renaissance style, is confusing when used otherwise. It is misleading, for example, if it suggests that literature should be approached through the categories of art history. Certainly, a poet may share intellectual predispositions with a sculptor, or be inspired by a painting. But he can hardly use the techniques of painting in verse, which is neither visual nor spatial. To talk of a poem's chiaroscuro or vertical organization, therefore, is always to fall through the rabbit hole. And such terms are particularly unsuitable to Donne, whose lyrics are not even descriptive.

Again, the baroque is deceptive when it pretends to be a historical cause. Like other phenomena, the baroque style exists without the intervention of a numen. Plants grow without Vegetable Souls; opium causes sleep without aid from Soporific Powers; and poets employ special styles without compulsion by a *zeitgeist*. Literary critics had best avoid fanciful ontology.

Finally, the baroque is a treacherous concept when it suggests that all literature between Renaissance and Enlightenment is essentially the same. To define "baroque" so inclusively requires too general a definition, and too elaborate a set of subdivisions.[2] And, in any event, no poem has been illuminated merely by being located within a century-and-a-half of European literature.

Freed of misconceptions, the question of Donne and the baroque is concerned with the similarities between Donne and poets of a particularly lush Italianate style—Tasso and Marino, for example. What gives this question point is that Donne's conceits have many baroque analogues. But though he has in common with contemporary European imagery both Petrarchism and quattrocentist wit (a distinguishing feature of the baroque in Italy and Spain, and of *préciosité* in France[3]), Donne's style and sensibility are most unlike those of characteristically baroque authors.[4]

For, seen as one mode of late Renaissance literature, the baroque is a virtuoso use of description, personification, and periphrasis to heighten the style and to invest objects with extraordinary emotional importance. Quite different is Donne, who generally prefers a relaxed style,[5] a poised and reasonable tone, a logical (not descriptive) structure, and direct or even homely diction (not periphrasis). Thus, Donne's images are like those of the baroque poets; but they are used differently. Both points may be made by comparing Donne with Tasso, a touchstone of the early baroque.

Tasso is a sentimental and exotic neoclassicist. As a critic, he defends the genre of the chivalric epic, and argues for exorbitant tropes, sounding verse, and Ciceronian gravity: that is, he vindicates the use of classical techniques for a heightened emotionalism. As a lyricist, he is musical, pictorial, and languorous. Thus, Tasso is in many ways at the furthest pole from Donne. Donne exaggerates Petrarch's distinction, definition, and self-awareness, Tasso his contemplative brooding, his delicacy, and his epideictic elaboration. Tasso's art is classical and his tone emotional; Donne abandons the art but preserves the reason of the humanists. The differences between them may be suggested by a consideration of "The Baite."

"The Baite" treats the theme of Marlowe's "Come live with me." Marlowe's poem is a pretty piece of pastoral, whose charm lies in its imitation of the simple, quaint courtship of shepherds. Raleigh's answer is a plain statement of moral truths in the language of pastoral. Herrick's "Come live with me and thou shalt see," with its note of graceful abandon, is about seizing the pleasures of life. All three lyrics adapt the pastoral convention to common-sense ideas and to the common feelings of humanity in a naturalistic world.

The beginning of "The Baite" suggests that the poet is going to vary Marlowe's theme only by substituting the pleasures of streams for those of fields—a characteristically Renaissance variation, as the contemporary fame of Sannazaro's piscatory eclogues shows. But the next four stanzas say that the lady's eyes warm the stream and darken heavenly bodies, that Donne needs no other light than she, and that fish yield themselves to her through love. These exaggerations suggest Tasso:

> There will the river whispering runne
> Warm'd by thy eyes, more then the Sunne.
> And there the'inamor'd fish will stay,
> Begging themselves they may betray.
>
> When thou wilt swimme in that live bath,
> Each fish, which every channell hath,
> Will amorously to thee swimme,
> Gladder to catch thee, then thou him.
>
> If thou, to be so seene, beest loath,
> By Sunne, or Moone, thou darknest both,
> And if my selfe have leave to see,
> I need not their light, having thee.

In 84, "I freddi e muti pesci usati omai," Tasso—like Bembo in "Questa del nostra lito antica sponda"—makes piscatorial a favorite theme of Petrarch, the poet's address to the countryside which has enjoyed his lady's presence:

> Here the cold, mute fish have learned
>   to burn, now, and to speak of love,
>   and you, who quiet your winds and waves, now know
>   how rare beauty sets the heart afire;
> Since now in you are strewn the sweet, joyous rays
>   of that sun whose birth was the honor of this shore,
>   that radiant sun to whom you owe far more
>   than to the other sun arisen from your bosom;

For he, ungrateful, without recalling
  how he is nourished by you, and how received,
  steals the best of you and leaves the salt and sorrow;
But this sun with her serene, divine lights
  refines and purges you, and gives you sweetness and joy,
  rendering you far more than she takes from you.

Donne's lyric and Tasso's are alike in some details and meth-ods—particularly in elaborating literal consequences of the lady's metaphorical radiance. But the lyrics are radically different. Tasso heightens every element he treats: his lady does nothing but shine, his fish nothing but burn and speak; his sea has sorrow, not salt, and his lady divine lights, not eyes. Donne, on the other hand, retains the low elements of his piscatory situation: his lady fishes or swims, and his fish express their love by their movements in the water. Later, Donne speaks of cold fishermen, cut legs, and slimy nets. In short, where Tasso makes a lady's proximity to the sea the occasion for a general, elevated Petrarchan paean, Donne freely in-troduces Petrarchan conceits into a piscatory context.

More importantly, where Tasso's hyperboles are asserted as facts, Donne's are qualified by self-awareness. Throughout "The Baite," there is that sense of the deceptiveness of amorous pleasure which, in Italy, was expressed by a pun on "amo," *hook* and *love*.[6] Though Donne's sands, lines, and hooks are golden, silken, and silver, they are still sands, hooks, and lines: and, as Donne concludes with a sigh,

That fish, that is not catch'd thereby,
Alas, is wiser farre then I.

Where Tasso's whole purpose is to celebrate the absolute perfection of his lady (who even purifies sea-water), Donne's every hyperbole reflects his own foolish passion: for example, he says not that he sees by his lady in the dark, but that, having her, he cares for no celestial light. Through hyperbole Tasso forms an anthem of praise in a world moving voluptuously towards beauty; whereas Donne, even while expressing the most exaggerated passion, recognizes the folly of his love.

More reminiscent of Tasso and *secentismo* than "The Baite" is "Twicknam garden" (11. 15-27), where the supposedly baroque theme of transformation appears:

> Love let mee
> Some senslesse peece of this place bee;
> Make me a mandrake, so I may groane here,
> Or a stone fountaine weeping out my yeare.
>
> Hither with christall vyals, lovers come,
> And take my teares, which are loves wine,
> And try your mistresse Teares at home,
> For all are false, that tast not just like mine;
> Alas, hearts do not in eyes shine,
> Nor can you more judge womans thoughts by teares,
> Then by her shadow, what she weares.
> O perverse sexe, where none is true but shee,
> Who's therefore true, because her truth kills mee.

Donne's conceit here is basically Petrarchan. The idea that the lover is a stone appears frequently in Petrarch—for example, in "Fresco, ombroso, fiorito e verde colle." It is elaborated as a metamorphosis in "Nel dolce tempo de la prima etade," where Petrarch claims that love has transformed him to a stone (1. 80) and a fountain of tears (1. 117). Petrarch's transformations represent his psychological history so as to render it marvellous and exalted, as his commentators recognize.[7] In "Chi non sa ben, com' una fiera Donna," Claudio Tolomei treats Petrarch's theme with that extravagance which, in mid-century Petrarchism, anticipates the baroque. Technically, he increases the difficulty of a Petrarchan form, writing a double sestina with only two rhyme words, "Donna" and "pietra." Thematically, he limits his subject to the stony lady and her petrified lover, omitting Petrarch's psychological narrative. And stylistically he emphasizes praise and the marvellous—for example in these lines:

> O new Circe, oh enchantress-Lady,
> who softened my heart, and now make me a stone,
> . . . if I am made nothing but a voice and a stone,
>
> . . . .

you will be thought to be a pitiless Lady,
a naked voice in a living stone.
. . . .
You tears, that from this stone
    pour forth day and night, go to my Lady,
    whose face shows her to be a lady,
    and who is, within her hard breast, a hard stone.
    Then weeping tell her, "O exalted Lady,
    let your heart break with pity for him, for he is stone."

Be careful, lest before that lady
    as I once, through burning, became a stone,
    you, disturbing the pleasure of my lady,
    may be changed to *crystal,* or hard stone.
    Therefore speak sweetly to that hard stone,
    more bitter than ever yet any other Lady.[8]

With all its exaggeration, Tolomei's lyric is devoted to courtship. Tasso brings the theme closer to the baroque by divorcing it from its persuasive purpose, and inflating its rhetoric further, in Canzone 20, "Perche la vita è breve":

And though my soft breast by the hard strokes
    is not more shattered within,
    that is not because of armor or of magic,
    but because the passion of fear
    seems to transform me to flint.
    Oh marvel! Love wounds the flint:
    yet from the deep wound
    no warm drop of my blood issues.
    Oh my fortune, Oh fate, Oh stars, Oh heaven!
    I am of marble and of ice,
    and the marble burns and throws sparks at the strokes!
    Because of the wound, meanwhile
    (Love knows, for he opened it with his arrows),
    I pour forth tears, and in tearful song
    make my plaint melodious by praising you.[9]

What these baroque lyricists share with Donne is the elaboration, in the mode of Serafino, of the material properties of conventional images. For example, when Tasso's literally soft breast is broken by the metaphorically hard strokes of love, it pours forth

the fountain of his tearful verse; when Donne's wished-for insensi-
tivity makes him metaphorically a stone, his real tears become the
waters of a fountain to be drunk by other lovers. Through an artful
confusion of metaphor with fact, both poets develop in new ways
the Petrarchan conceit of the weeping stone.

In Tasso, however, such imagery tends to oxymorons and
antitheses: soft breast and hard blows, burning marble and sparkling
ice. In Donne it repeatedly turns to moral argument: "hearts do not
in eyes shine"; "perverse sexe, where none is true but shee." More
centrally, in Tasso such imagery amplifies sentiment: it is colored
by apostrophes, wild pictorialism, and references to marvels, blood,
and melodious plaints. In Donne, however, the imagery functions
for polite compliment and a common-sense critique of Neoplatonic
love. Donne is extremely polite, referring to the lady's home as a
"True Paradise," unbenighted and joyful (11. 9-13), and to her as
a paragon of beauty and chastity (1. 26), whose visage and speech
are a panacea for every disease but love (11. 3-4). Affectedly, he
claims that he cannot endure either to part from the lady or to stay
near her; inflamed by love and frustrated by her chastity, he is irri-
tated even by the serene beauty of the lady's estate. But though his
pose is extravagantly sentimental, Donne is clear-headed. He argues
that love of the eyes and ears (1. 3), which for the Neoplatonist,
is "human" love,[10] is unsatisfactory because the lady's graces raise
further desire: the spider love, a snake in the Paradise of the lady's
beauties (st. 1),[11] transubstantiates all. Thus Donne's transformation,
like his death in "The Dampe," is an extravagant affectation with
comic point: it insinuates that only a stone could love as the lady
desires, seeing and hearing but wanting no more. Where Tasso's
metamorphosis reflects irrational longings, Donne's is a sophistication of manner, an exaggerated gesture conveying a most sensible
comment.

Without venturing far out on the dangerous terrain of the
baroque, one may declare in general that Tasso's hyperboles are
asserted as facts and Donne's assumed as gestures; that Tasso's development is sentimental and Donne's logical; and that Tasso's
style is pictorial and emotional, and Donne's dramatic and reason-

able. And Tasso, quite properly, is always reckoned an exemplar of the baroque.

Donne's extravagance is not, then, baroque. Since it so often functions as a sophistication of manner, it may be thought instead to be related to another continental style, *préciosité*. But here again Donne, while using continental conceits, stands apart from continental styles. For the art of *préciosité* is that of elevating the commonplace to the pretty and idyllic; and while Donne transforms the commonplace with irony and transcendencies, he is never merely pretty.

Donne's differences from more precious poets may be seen in "A Feaver." "A Feaver" treats the Petrarchan theme of the lady's illness. In "Amore, natura, e la bell' alma umíle," Petrarch writes of his lady's illness and possible death. Characteristically, he adapts the theme to a reflection upon his own life. He attributes Laura's illness to those things which have frustrated him throughout his life: to Love's malice towards the poet, to Laura's natural delicacy, and to her extreme chastity, which is shy of this vile life. And Petrarch takes occasion from Laura's illness to reflect upon the course of his life, saying that in threatening Petrarch's death (through Laura's), Love follows his custom; and that he now perceives the state of those vain hopes in which he has lived. Though eloquently phrased and extravagantly delicate, Petrarch's sonnet is dramatic: Laura's illness is treated as a historic event which the poet sees in the light of his past, and as a sign of his future.

Tasso treats his lady's illness in Sonnet 26, "I begli occhi ove prima Amor m' apparse." He employs a meditative structure, brooding upon the changed state of his lady in the octave, and breaking out in passionate exclamations in the sestet. Characteristically, he strives for novelty in two ways. First, he sharpens Petrarch's oxymorons by developing conventional language materially: for example, making paradoxes of the fact that his icy lady is beset by a hot fever, and that her brilliant eyes are clouded. Second, he fuses two traditional (and here Petrarchan) themes, that of the lady's fever with that of her infected eyes. (As in "I freddi e muti pesci usati omai," the fusion suggests that his lyric is occasional.)

By these innovations, Tasso approximates both the baroque and Donne. He is different from Donne, however, in his unique concentration upon the lady's beauty and his love. Through that concentration he substitutes for Petrarch's Christian drama a passionate meditation in the world of Renaissance Ovidianism, where the flames of love and the ice of ladies are the only real heat and cold, and where events like illness merely rearrange the relation of desire to beauty:

> The beautiful eyes in which I first saw Love—
>   who circles and shines there as in his own heaven—
>   are now shadowed by a cruel cloud which contends with me
>   for that sweet ray that dazzles and burns me,
> Alas! and that cold breast, which Love's flame
>   could not kindle, is lit now by the fires
>   of an evil, malign fever; and the snow and ice
>   in which it is usually armed now fail to defend it.
> Oh! why might not I suffer in her stead
>   that intense fire, so that she might then
>   feel but one little spark of my flames?
> And surely, Love, every other torch would be
>   a joy and a game, and surely it would seem cold and spent,
>   to one whose heart knows your flames.

In Madrigal 56, "Langue al vostro languir l'anima mia," Guarino treats the lady's fever in a purely precious manner. He prettily translates illness into idyll:

> My soul languishes at your languishing,
>   and I say, "Ah! perhaps it is love's wound
>   that leads her to such boiling pain."
> Oh soul too rebellious to love,
>   how much better would it be for you
>   to feel that dear heat that makes you lovely
>   rather than that which makes you pale!
> Why is my destiny not such that I
>   burned with your fire, and you with mine!

Structurally, Guarino uses many of the dramatic devices by which Petrarch characteristically reveals the processes of his thought: he begins by declaring his emotions, proceeds to relate his meditations, and breaks out in a fervent wish; he speculates on his lady's motives, meditates on antitheses, and reflects on his own condition. But essentially Guarino's madrigal is the application of Petrarch's attitudes to a situation which does not support them: to a pseudo-situation which is in fact merely a witty correspondence between love's heat and a fever. Guarino reacts sentimentally to a witty confusion between metaphor and fact. And he thereby illustrates a new kind of sentimental wit, composed of delicate passions and epigrammatic neatness.

Donne's "A Feaver" is as close as any of his lyrics to Guarino's affected sentimentality, and to preciosity. It expresses an adoration so extreme as to deny its own occasion, the lady's illness. Each of its stanzas is a wittily rounded paradox, hyperbole, or material treatment of metaphor. In short, it approximates the madrigal. Nonetheless, there is no real possibility of confusing Donne with Guarino.

> Oh doe not die, for I shall hate
>   All women so, when thou art gone,
> That thee I shall not celebrate,
>   When I remember, thou wast one.
>
> But yet thou canst not die, I know;
>   To leave this world behinde, is death,
> But when thou from this world wilt goe,
>   The whole world vapors with thy breath.
>
> Or if, when thou, the worlds soule, goest,
>   It stay, tis but thy carkasse then,
> The fairest woman, but thy ghost,
>   But corrupt wormes, the worthyest men.
>
> O wrangling schooles, that search what fire
>   Shall burne this world, had none the wit
> Unto this knowledge to aspire,
>   That this her feaver might be it?
>
> And yet she cannot wast by this,
>   Nor long beare this torturing wrong,
> For much corruption needfull is
>   To fuell such a feaver long.

These burning fits but meteors bee,
    Whose matter in thee is soone spent.
Thy beauty, 'and all parts, which are thee,
    Are unchangeable firmament.

Yet t'was of my minde, seising thee,
    Though it in thee cannot persever.
For I had rather owner bee
    Of thee one houre, then all else ever.

Perhaps to a modern critic the most evident difference between Donne's lyric and Guarino's is that Donne's is logical. His logic here has two aspects. In the first place, the entire structure of "A Feaver" is argumentative: having in stanza 1 asked the lady not to die, in the next three stanzes Donne proves, through the argument from definition, that she cannot die; in stanzas 5 and 6 he proves that she cannot even be feverish long; and in the final stanza he explains how it was possible that she might have been ill. In the second place, Donne's logic is the method he uses for developing each idea. When in lines 6-7 Guarino says that love makes the lady beautiful, he supposes that the lady's beauty is created by her lover (cf. the final stanza of "The Will"). He does not, however, develop this principle logically; instead, he uses it to create an antithesis between two kinds of fire, the fever which makes pale, and love which makes beautiful. With a very different method, in stanza 4, meaning to express hyperbolically his fear for the lady's health, Donne makes his hyperbole a scholastic question. Similarly, in stanza 5, meaning to say that his lady is too pure to be ill, Donne argues from the general principle that disease results from a corruption of matter. And in stanza 6, meaning to express his sense of the lady's sublime perfection, Donne refers to the astronomical distinction between eternal and corruptible celestial matter. Throughout Donne develops every point logically.

More important, Donne's manner is different from Guarino's. Donne's lyric is affected, not dramatic, as comparison with Petrarch makes clear. For example, both poets reconcile the lady's divinity with her illness: but where Petrarch, asserting that his lady is too delicate to desire to remain in an unworthy world, brilliantly reveals the way his mind applies ideas it has always had of Laura to the particular circumstances, Donne, asserting merely that his lady cannot be ill, shows no similar dramatic richness. Again, both poets are amorous egoists: but where Petrarch's statement that his lady's illness is a conspiracy against him reveals an egocentric mind, and a passion like those of Racinian drama, Donne's statement that it is the world, not the lady, which is threatened, is more nearly madrigalesque extravagance. And throughout Donne represents the lover disabusing himself of the notion that the lady can be ill—a theme hardly dramatic, since she is ill, and rationalization is not in question. Thus, "A Feaver" is not a dramatic lyric—not a lyric concerned primarily with the mental processes of a lover whose lady is ill.

But, on the other hand, neither here nor elsewhere is Donne so intent upon being complimentary that his affectations become absurd. Preciosity appears in a pure form in a lyric by the Abbé Cotin on the fever of a great lady, a lyric Molière mocks in *Les femmes savantes,* III, ii:

> Votre prudence est endormie,
>   De traiter magnifiquement
>   Et de loger superbement
>   Votre plus cruelle ennemie.
>   Faites-la sortir, quoi qu'on die,
>   De votre riche appartement,
>   Ou cette ingrate insolemment
>   Attaque votre belle vie.
>   Quoi! sans respecter votre rang,
>   Elle se prend à votre sang,
>   Et nuit et jour vous fait outrage!
>   Si vous la conduisez aux bains,
>   Sans la marchander davantage,
>   Noyez-la de vos propres mains.

Various technical elements distinguish "A Feaver" from "Votre prudence est endormie." For example, in "A Feaver" the basic situation, the lady's illness and recovery, is real; the hyperboles reflect the lover's reaction to these events. In "Votre prudence," the basic

92

situation—the lady's decision about how to treat the fever—is not real, and signifies only the poet's respect for her omnipotence; and yet the poet, adopting the role of adviser, shows no motive for his exaggerated respect. Again, Donne's hyperboles cohere, since they express one set of attitudes; and they fit their occasion, expressing terror at the lady's illness, and exaltation at her recovery. But Cotin's images neither cohere nor fit their subject: sleeping prudence, evicting a guest, bargaining, and strangling are ill-consorted images; and, in reflecting upon their occasion, Cotin's images both insinuate that the lady has been too stupid to dislike her fever, and suggest that she is the sort of prince who invites a guest only to strangle him.

Reserving my critical approach to Donne for a later chapter, I shall not analyze "A Feaver" here. The essential principles are those Molière applies to Cotin's verses. As a social gesture, the Abbé Cotin's lyric is absurd: ridiculous in compliment ("riche appartement," "belle vie"), fatuous in counsel ("Votre prudence est endormie"), and thoroughly inappropriate. It is clearly bad taste to tell a feverish lady to be more alert, and to strangle her fever bare-handedly. It is a similar though less preposterous bad taste which leads Guarino to remind a sick lady that she would be better off if her fever were merely amorous. Such social absurdities are the essence of preciosity. There is nothing, however, unacceptable in Donne's statement that his lady's fever threatens to burn the world. Indeed, it is of the essence of Donne's art that he makes the most extravagantly complimentary and passionate assertions without *gaucherie*. In short, essentially unlike precious poets, he achieves a manner which is transcendent, not ridiculously delicate.

The question of Donne, the baroque, and *préciosité* concerns Donne's manner—in the sense in which *manner,* suggesting *manners,* refers to the almost-social impression which the poet makes upon his readers. Normally, to assert that Donne is baroque is to suggest that he is emotionalistic, intolerant of the confines of relaxed manners and common sense. To assert that he is precious is to suggest that he is extravagantly delicate, treating daily occasions so as to avoid every hint of unpleasantness, and thereby falling into absurdities of conduct and of metaphor. But, though Donne's

themes, techniques, and metaphors—his audience too, presumably—
are not radically different from Tasso's or Guarino's, his style is
clearly distinguished from those traditionally called baroque and
precious by its self-awareness and common sense.

VII

Donne's Realism and the Petrarchan Manner

Onne adapts a courtly, fashionable conceit to the passions of a reasonable man. His hyperboles permit him both irony and enthusiasm. Beneath them, there is a familiarity with and an acceptance of life.

Donne's realism appears in his sharp definition of worldly motives and affairs, as in "The Will." It appears in his refusal to let his will dominate his reason, as in "The Blossome," where he gives up a lady who will not love him fully, and in "Aire and Angels," where he contents himself with the imperfections of woman's love. Furthermore, Donne's posture is often relaxed, as in "The Dampe," and he is willing to accept the limitations of life and love.[1] Though no materialist, Donne accepts things as they are.

Many critics think Donne's realism to be incompatible with his hyperboles. They explain, therefore, either that Donne parodies sentimentality, or that he recognizes the fantastic and centrifugal diversities of life.[2] Such explanations often assume that the *Songs and Sonets* form one long poem in which lyrics with radically different emotions coexist in dissonance.[3] In fact, however, Donne's lyrics are discrete. Their variety reflects different amorous situations: the poet may be emotionally uncommitted ("The Indifferent"), or he may fall in love ("The good-morrow"); his love may be happy ("The Anniversarie") or unhappy ("The Funerall"); he may repudiate love ("Loves Alchymie"), or mourn a dead lady ("The Dissolution"). In Petrarchan sequences, such variety reflects the progressive stages of love. Though the *Songs and Sonets* may not be an autobiographically ordered sequence, they are surely not a symbolic

95

amalgam: Donne's libertinism in one poem does not reflect ironically upon his amorous enthusiasm in another.

Furthermore, there is no reason to think of Petrarchism as an
antithesis to realism. Essentially, Petrarchism is an expressive mode.
Patterns may be imposed upon it: the humanists seek to express
their feelings in universal, traditional forms; the court wits seek
to express theirs in socially preferred ways. But a Petrarchist may
express distinctly individual, or impolitic, or realistic feelings.[4] And,
in fact, the great epigone of realistic Petrarchism is Petrarch himself.

Petrarch's poetry, of course, is unlike Donne's. It is a solitary,
quintessential imagining, its phrases choice and pellucid. Its realism
is an Augustinian sense of the vanity of the world, the folly of desire, and the complexities of the mind.[5] While it is possible to consider Donne too a Christian realist,[6] his *Songs and Sonets* show little of classical rhetoric or Augustinian meditation. But their means
of fusing elegance with realism recall Petrarch's.

Petrarch develops the subjective value of situations.[7] Unlike
many Renaissance lyricists, he is not concerned with the concrete
aspects of courtly occasions.[8] Instead, seeing Laura, or the town in
which she lives, or a river he knew before she died, he recollects the
past, considers the future, and broods upon the meaning of life. The
incident in which his lyric originates becomes merely a stimulus to
passion and introspection, and even Laura is described chiefly as she
is remembered. For Donne, similarly, a name scratched on a window, the gift of a ring, or the parting of lovers is merely a spur to
esoteric meditation. For both, the occasion of a lyric is developed
subjectively. Thus, both poets are elegant, for they immediately
transcend mundane facts. At the same time, they are both realists:
they do not magnify what they know to be unimportant, a tree or
a ring; expressing passions rather than facts, their hyperboles are
no more than adequate.

Further, Petrarch develops the dramatic, not the didactic, value
of generalizations. For example, at the conclusion of "Se co 'l cieco
desir che 'l cor distrugge," Petrarch recognizes that his amorous
hopes have been frustrated:

Et or di quel ch'i'ho letto mi sovene:
Che nanzi al dí de l'ultima partita
Uom beato chiamar non si convene.

(And now I remember what I have often read:
that before the day of his final parting
no man can be called blessed.)

In "Soleasi nel mio cor star bella e viva," after considering the change that Laura's death has made in him, Petrarch says:

Veramente siam noi polvere et ombra,
Veramente la voglia è cieca e 'ngorda,
Veramente fallace è la speranza.

(Truly, we are dust and shadows;
truly, the will is greedy and blind;
and truly a liar is hope.)

Clearly, Petrarch means not to declare that fortune and hope are treacherous, but to express his feelings. His maxims have primarily a dramatic purpose. Similarly, in "The Canonization" it is the faith of the weary, badgered lover which appears in the statement that love is holy; in "The good-morrow," it is the ecstasy of the lover gazing into his lady's eyes, which appears in the declaration that love is eternal. In Donne's lyrics as in Petrarch's, general statements are primarily responses to emotional experience.

Again, Petrarch's conceit is emotionally flexible. It is mannered: that he calls his love a fire and his sorrow a flood of tears reveals Petrarch's aristocratic, affected sentiment. But within the limits of his manner Petrarch's artificial language, antitheses, and oxymorons express a wide range of feelings. For example, in "Sento l'aura mia antica, e i dolci colli," Petrarch, returning to a familiar countryside after Laura's death, feels it to be widowed and barren; he wishes he were dead, so that he might have died still hoping for Laura's love; and he concludes,

Ho servito a signor crudele e scarso;
Ch'arsi quanto 'l mio foco ebbi davante,
Or vo piangendo il suo cenere sparso.

(I have served a fierce, grasping lord:
for I burned when my fire was before me,
and now I am left to weep its scattered embers.)

The flames of passion and the lord Love—conceits to indicate the intensity of desire—here superbly express the desolation of a man who sees his entire life to have been wasted; and the conjunction of wet tears with hot fire provides an ironical summary of Petrarch's life. Petrarch, mastering his manner, suits it to truly dramatic meditation.

Donne's conceit, though less imbued with the poet's history, is similarly expressive. When in "A Valediction: forbidding mourning" Donne asks his lady to die like a saint, his comparison of parting to death is not a display of wit, but the language of a man to whom love is all. Though mannered, it is flexible enough to express a masculine tenderness far from the rhetoric of courtship. Again, when in "The Canonization" Donne asks

What merchants ships have my sighs drown'd?
Who saies my teares have overflow'd his ground?

he is not wittily exaggerating the quantity of his sighs and tears, but bitterly declaring that his abused love is harmless. His conceit expresses dramatically appropriate irony, like Petrarch's statement that after a youth spent in fruitless burning, his age is left to weep the ashes of his fire. Thus, in neither Donne nor Petrarch is the conceited manner a set of artificial sentiments. In both it is expressive of a wide range of thoughts and feelings—and, in one sense, realistic.

Donne, then, like Petrarch, makes an elegant manner reasonable by stressing the interior value of incidents, the dramatic value of generalizations, and the expressive possibilities of conceits. Both his elegance and his realism may be seen, for example, in "The Dissolution":

Shee' is dead; And all which die
To their first Elements resolve;
And wee were mutally Elements to us,
And made of one another.
My body then doth hers involve,

And those things whereof I consist, hereby
In me abundant grow, and burdenous,
      And nourish not, but smother.
  My fire of Passion, sighes of ayre,
Water of teares, and earthly sad despaire,
      Which my materialls bee,
But neere worne out by loves securitie,
Shee, to my losse, doth by her death repaire,
     And I might live long wretched so
But that my fire doth with my fuell grow.
      Now as those Active Kings
  Whose foraine conquest treasure brings,
Receive more, and spend more, and soonest breake:
This (which I am amaz'd that I can speake)
     This death, hath with my store
      My use encreas'd.
And so my soule more earnestly releas'd,
Will outstrip hers; As bullets flowen before
A latter bullet may o'rtake, the pouder being more.

In "The Dissolution" Donne presumes that the united lovers were a little world. He argues that their microcosm decomposed at the lady's death, leaving him overburdened with an excess of uncompounded elements. He concludes that though this great quantity of matter may seem to presage long life, he will die soon, since his sorrow increases as quickly as the fuel (tears and sighs) it consumes. Thus, "The Dissolution" is a characteristically clever set of deductions from a basic conceit.

Its wit, however, is not inappropriate to its theme; for it is made expressive in three ways. First, its situation is internalized. The central fact it proclaims is that "Shee' is dead." This fact is removed from objective circumstances. Treated only as it affects the poet's little world, it becomes subjective.[9]

Second, Donne's generalizations are developed dramatically. Though argumentative in form, "The Dissolution" reflects a movement of feelings: Donne broods upon the difference between his past and his present sorrows (11. 1-8), declares his utter wretchedness (11. 9-14), and hopes that he may die (11. 15-21). His deductions do not pretend to literal truth; they are instead the meditations of a man whose love was so much his entire life, that his lady's death seems to dissolve the world.

Finally, Donne's conceit is expressive. The statement that he is composed of four elements (11. 9-11) is not merely a witty comparison between the materials of love and those of the world, but a revelation that love was all the world to him. The declaration that those materials, never entirely expended before (1. 12), will be so now, and that they are only now become burdensome (11. 6-8), reveals the terrible difference between the sighs of love and those of mourning. The increase of tears, brought on by the dissolution, is Donne's mourning. The capacity of his fire to consume that fuel expresses his belief and his hope that he cannot live long in such distress. In short, throughout its logical development "The Dissolution" expresses sorrow. Its extravagant conceit, revealing as it does the totality of his love, highlights the extremity of Donne's passion.

It is interesting to compare "The Dissolution" with Petrarch's "Quand' io mi volgo in dietro a mirar gli anni":

> When I turn back to view the years
>   that, fleeing, have scattered my thoughts,
>   and extinguished the fire in which, freezing, I burned,
>   and ended my repose full of torments;
> Breaking the faith of the amorous treacheries,
>   and making of all my good a mere two parts,
>   one in heaven and the other below ground,
>   and taking the gain of my losses;
> I shake myself, and find myself so naked
>   that I envy the extremest fate:
>   such heart-sorrow, such fear, have I for myself!
> Oh my star, oh fortune, oh fate, oh death,
>   oh day [on which I first saw Laura] eternally sweet
>   and cruel to me,
>   in how low a state have you put me!

Its affective rhetoric,[10] its oxymorons, and its verbal delicacy make this sonnet most different from "The Dissolution." But, like "The Dissolution," "Quand' io mi volgo" is full of conceits and paradoxes—freezing fires, eternal days, and tormented repose. And, like "The Dissolution," it employs such wit for intensely emotional expression. For example, Petrarch's statement that his freezing fires are extinguished and his amorous treacheries turned faithless is an ironical comment upon the course of his life. Petrarch's hopes were always misleading, his love always tormented; but now that Laura is dead his previous unhappiness seems to have been a joy. Now he is naked and desolate: the fires which, at best, were hot torments, are out; the hopes which were always false have deserted him. Thus, Petrarch's antithesis and oxymorons are the convincing expressions of his desolation. In their use of wit to heighten an extreme emotion, they anticipate Donne.

"The Dissolution" is not properly realistic. But it does employ a fantastic conceit for dramatic meditation, and for a clear recognition of the terrible facts of Donne's situation. It is thus as realistic as Donne usually is: that is, its extended hyperboles are responsive to experience and to unpleasant facts. Its realism is neither anti-Petrarchan nor iconoclastic.

Similar conclusions may be drawn from "A nocturnall upon S. Lucies day." This is a ceremonial poem in remembrance of a beloved lady's death.[11] Because it is the blackest and most death-like day of the year, Donne considers Saint Lucy's day fit to be his beloved saint's eve, and he keeps vigil that night.[12] In verse that is solemn, funereal, and resonant, he performs the rites of mourning.

Donne achieves emotional emphasis by choosing a midnight, midwinter setting, and by twice contrasting his somber desolation to the hope and lust of springtime lovers.[13] But the heart of "A nocturnall," as of "The Dissolution," is a wittily extended conceit.

Donne declares that, because of his lady's death, he is now nothing. In itself, his declaration is a sentimental hyperbole, like Petrarch's declaration that Laura's death killed him.[14] But Donne takes the hyperbole literally and makes it the basis of an extended logical argument. In stanzas 2 through 5, he distinguishes among the degrees of nothingness, and elaborately proves that he is the quintessential nothing. Thus, he exaggerates the hyperbole, and develops it logically.

His witty logic is suited to somber mourning in three ways. First, Donne treats the lady's death subjectively. Second, he develops his generalizations dramatically: the more he insists that he is noth-ing, the more clearly he reveals his grief. Thus Donne limits his exaggerations to his own feelings—where they are no more than adequate.

Third, Donne makes his conceits expressive—for example, in the following lines:

> Oft a flood
> Have wee two wept, and so
> Drownd the whole world, us two; oft did we grow
> To be two Chaosses, when we did show
> Care to ought else; and often absences
> Withdrew our soules, and made us carcasses.
>
> But I am by her death, (which word wrongs her)
> Of the first nothing, the Elixer grown;
> Were I a man, that I were one,
> I needs must know; . . .

Here Donne treats his non-existence almost as a metaphysical prin-ciple. He distinguishes among kinds of non-being: a drowned world, a chaos, a carcass, and essential non-being. He employs technical theories: that an absence of form is non-being; that, since death is a separation of body from soul, and since the lady is her lover's soul, lovers' parting is death; [15] and that there was a primal nothing (i.e., that the world was created *ab nihilo*). He offers a rigid proof, by elimination, that he is nothing. Here he shows that he is not a man: referring to the classic definition of man by his reason (or, perhaps, by self-knowledge), Donne argues that since he does not know he is a man, he is not. Later, with similarly specious argu-ments, Donne proves that he is nothing else. Thus Donne, with characteristic wit, extends and exaggerates a hyperbole.

His exaggeration, however, remains dramatic. For Donne is expressing the absoluteness of his desolation. In doing so, he reveals that the lovers were a complete world, and each other's soul (ll. 1-6 above). Thus, with dramatic appropriateness, as he thinks of his dead lady he remembers how much they meant to each other. Fur-thermore, he compares his past to his present state. With a bittersweet emotion, he remembers the sorrows of love: absence, weeping, and caring for other things. Those sorrows were drownings and deaths to the united lovers. But this is far worse, more absolute: it has left Donne numb, naked of desire and hope. He is now the quintessential nothing. Such, then, is the dramatic content of "A nocturnall," which begins by reading the poet's despair into the landscape, continues with a meditation upon the poet's present, changed state, and concludes with a sentimental extravagance, the poet's dedication of his life to a preparation for death.

In "A nocturnall," Donne is somber about the world, saying that into the earth, "as to the beds feet, life is shrunke,/ Dead and enterr'd." And he is sardonic towards other men:

> You lovers, for whose sake, the lesser Sunne
> At this time to the Goat is runne
> To fetch new lust, and give it you,
> Enjoy your summer all.

To some critics, such melancholy passages seem to be attacks upon naively happy poems. But in fact these lines are primarily descriptions of winter, when vegetation lives chiefly below "th'hydroptique earth," and when the sun enters Capricorn. The descriptions are developed emotionally, not realistically: the world seems dead because of a lady's death; the wanderings of the "lesser Sunne" seem unimportant because of the extinction of her greater glory. There is nothing iconoclastic in such passages: they are extravagantly emotional. All that might properly be meant by calling "A nocturnall" realistic is that it confronts an unpleasant situation, vents bitter emotions, and makes hyperboles expressive.

Similar conclusions may be drawn from "The Blossome." Here, in stanza 1 Donne tells a blossom that, though happy in its ignorance, it will soon be killed by frost. In stanza 2, he tells his heart that, though happy in *its* ignorance, it must soon leave Donne's cold lady to go on a journey. In stanza 3, Donne surmises that his heart will want to stay with the lady; he expects his heart to argue that, going where his body will be cared for, Donne will need no heart. In stanza 4, Donne tells his heart that it may stay, but warns it that no mere heart can win a woman. And in the final stanza he proposes to meet his heart in London in three weeks' time, when he will give it "to another friend, whom wee shall finde/As glad to have my body, as my minde."

Many critics seek Donne's realism in such contrasts as that between "The Blossome" and Petrarch's "Mira quel colle, o stanco mio cor vago":

> Eye that hill well, Oh my weary, longing heart;
>> there we left, yesterday, her who once
>> cared for us a little, pitying our pain,
>> and who now wants to draw a lake from our eyes.
> Return there, for I delight in solitude;
>> see whether there may not yet be a time
>> when our sorrows, which have always increased, will abate,
>> oh partner and prophet of my grief.
> Now you have forgotten yourself,
>> speaking to your heart as though it were with you,
>> wretch full of vain and foolish thoughts!
> For in departing from your supreme desire
>> you left, but your heart remained with her,
>> and hid within her lovely eyes.[16]

"The Blossome" gains from being conjoined with "Mira quel colle." But it would, of course, be foolish to surmise from such a conjunction that Elizabethan England is a Victorian teaparty attended solely by Dickens' more distressingly innocent maidens—although such a conception highlights the vitality and vigor of Donne. In fact, the realism of "The Blossome" derives from a Petrarchan device—the expressive hyperbole.

The central conceit of "The Blossome" is the separated heart. In "Mira quel colle," this conceit is used for introspection as well as gallantry: there is profound self-knowledge in such phrases as "I delight in solitude," "my weary, longing heart," and "prophet of my grief." [17] Elsewhere in Petrarch the conceit from which these phrases arise incidentally, is used to show conflicting motives. For instance, in "Che fai? che pensi? che pur dietro guardi," "Occhi miei, oscurato è 'l nostro sole," and "Anima che diverse cose tante," Petrarch persuades his soul, his eyes, and his feet to turn from Laura to God. In all these poems the poet's speech is firm, but his conceit indicates that his mind wavers.

Donne's use of the separated heart is similar.[18] Incidentally, it leads to an introspective insight: "thou which lov'st to bee/ Subtile to plague thy selfe." Fundamentally, it opposes two conflicting feelings. For Donne loves the lady, but knows unrewarded love to be silly. He turns, therefore, with benign amusement to his foolish heart, warning it of their departure. His heart, with a reason that the reason does not know, says that it will stay, since love transcends absence and bodily deprivation. (Thus, the heart rationalizes the basic conceit of "The Blossome," the separated heart.) But Donne knows that after three weeks in comfort he will no longer care for a lady who loves nothing but his mind; and so he is content to leave his heart and lady, and to go to other pursuits. In short, Donne is divided from his heart; his conceit has introspective meaning.

Donne and his heart speak in a reasonable tone. The heart asks, "If then your body goe, what need you a heart?" There is mundane good sense here, as there is in two of Donne's more famous replies,

> A naked thinking heart, that makes no show,
> Is to a woman, but a kinde of Ghost,

and

> Practise may make her know some other part,
> But take my word, shee doth not know a Heart.

Donne's realism is generally located in such bluff, reasonable lines. But two things are to be noted. First, these remarks are all witty sparks from, and spotlights upon, the conceit of the separated heart. Second, Donne's manliness in relation to his heart results from a fantastic exaggeration of that conceit, which Donne makes a full-blown drama. Thus, Donne's mundane poses and worldly maxims are the fruits of witty extravagance. If realism is to be found in "The Blossome," it is best found in Donne's decision not to desire what he cannot have; and in the expressive and introspective significance he gives to amorous hyperboles.

Sometimes, it is said that Donne alludes to conventional conceits only to attack their sentimental falsification. Sometimes, it is said that he echoes seventeenth-century wit because his is a baroque spirit. But close analysis shows Donne to employ conventional hyperboles as a basis for ingenious wit and emotional expressiveness. His emotions are realistic in at least a limited sense: they do not proclaim Donne a member of a sentimental aristocracy whose intense, esoteric feelings are wonderfully noble. His art, however, is realistic in an entirely different sense: in its adaptation of extravagant poses, striking maxims, and ingenious conceits to dramatic expressiveness. From a literary point of view, therefore, his realism is best defined as a fusion of extravagant wit with eternally moving sentiments—a fusion which shows Donne to be the greatest Renaissance Petrarchist after Petrarch himself.

VIII

A Critical Approach

There is always an area of understanding between a poet and his readers. A convention is such an area, sharply defined. Its clarity permits the poet his quirks and quiddities, offering assurance that his jokes will not be read as metaphysics or his passionate outcries as sociological treatises. To recognize Donne's Petrarchism is to agree with him about his basic intentions.

But Donne's Petrarchism raises sharp critical questions. For the Petrarchist does not contemplate life in its most universal aspect, nor is his point of view unique. His is a public and social convention, which presumes a commonly accepted standard of conduct. He expresses personal feelings through a set of genteel responses to stylized situations. Only indirectly and subtly can he broaden his readers' consciousness. As a Petrarchist, therefore, Donne does not provide what many critics demand of poetry: a broad, radically new conception of life.

The demand that poetry reinterpret experience, however, is ambiguous. It may mean that poetry should be a fresh discovery of the way things really are, stressing facts previously ignored and feelings previously neglected. However, things and feelings are sometimes as they have been thought to be. Like other Renaissance poets Donne, knowing that, is not especially reverent of fact;[1] he is not self-conscious about his individuality. He follows tradition, and traditional idealization. But this does not mean that he ignores experience: for love, the experience which he reflects, is often an idealizing passion.

In another sense, to interpret experience is, like Wordsworth, to discover universal values in one's responses to personal events. Many critics consider such discoveries essential to poetry; and they anatomize poems of various sorts to find within each a personal experience, and a generalization derived from it. But there is no reason that all poetry should be like Wordsworth's in order to be valuable. For poetry may teach by idealization or oratory. It may educate without generalization by exercising its readers' sensibilities. Or, like flowers and sunsets, it may have a value without inculcating one. Doubtless, many good poems discover profound truths in private experience. But not all good poems do, and not all good poems should.

In a third sense, to interpret experience is to record subtle nuances of feeling and imagination. Symbolist critics have read Donne's lyrics as such a record, stressing his fidelity to emotion, his alertness to undiscovered complexities, and his recognition of the multifariousness of experience.[2] But the emotional nuances which Donne catches are more revolutionary in our time than they were in his.[3] And, structurally, his lyrics are not descriptions of delicate, evanescent plays of feeling. They do not define private sensations—reactions to the sadness of rainfall, the sensuality of a rose, or the horror of a city street. Instead, they make public gestures, and produce social effects—comforting or mocking a lady, for example. It is, then, a mistake to reduce Donne's verse to a private flow of sentiments and fancies. Yet it is surely no mistake to respond to the sentiments and fancies which are there.

In asking Donne to be a Romantic,[4] modern critics have yielded to a temptation which "poetry," like "wisdom" and "culture," provokes: they have offered as a definition what is really a ranking of superior and inferior kinds. They have said that poetry is alert to all aspects of experience, and seeks its meaning. The historical critic will define poetry more wisely, and less well. He will see that Donne, like many another poet, is not intent upon extracting a code of values from private experiences; but he will not therefore relinquish the valuable experience of appreciating Donne.

Linguistically, too, Donne's Petrarchism entails critical problems. It suggests that his poetry conveys attitudes, not concepts; and that it is action, not statement. Now, that language may be action is an idea widespread among semanticists and linguists, but too little discussed by critics. Fundamentally, it distinguishes between two uses of language: where what it says is important, language is statement; where what it does is important, language is action. For example, "Good morning," "Thank you," and "How are you?" are verbal actions. So are oaths, toasts, and compliments. And so are those political speeches which are intended to express honest friendliness rather than to inform. In literature, the dialogue of Austen and Dickens is composed largely of characteristic verbal gestures: of linguistic equivalents for Mr. Elton's ingratiating leer, Uriah Heep's lithe wormings, and Jonas Chuzzlewit's nasty grin and knowing poke of the elbow. In short, much language is a verbal equivalent of bowing, leering, kissing babies, or shaking a finger in admonition. Many sentences function primarily to reveal their speakers' attitudes, and to affect their audiences.

It is possible that all poetry is in part gesture: for example, Milton's discussion of his blindness in Book III of *Paradise Lost* is surely no more exposition than it is the heroic gesture of a Christian bard. And some poetry can be understood only as action. For example, Browning's *Prospice* is not a statement about death but an act of courage in the face of death. And Hamlet is not conveying information but playing a trick upon Osric when he says, "Sir, his definement suffers no perdition in you; though, I know, to divide him inventorially would dizzy the arithmetic of memory. . . ." If Hamlet had tripped up Osric's feet or hidden his hat, he would have said as much as he does by parodying Osric's speech: but such actions would have been less discriminating, and less worthy of his nobility. In short, Hamlet's speech is to be read not as a statement but as an action which expresses his feelings and his character. Similarly, much lyric poetry is not statement but action, exploiting all the subtlety of language to strike a pose, or make a gesture. It is the verbal equivalent of throwing a gauntlet, wiping a tear, clasping a hand, or offering a tender embrace.

The witty Petrarchists, especially, are poets of gesture. When Serafino says that a ring given him by a lady has been burnt black by his passion for her, or when Chariteo says that he would have helped douse a fire at a lady's house but for his own amorous flames, these poets are making gestures. Like a smile or a bow, their lyrics convey gracious, sophisticated thanks and apologies. They act, not state. And, with their own subtlety, complexity, and intensity, so do Donne's.

Modern critics have noted that Donne's poems express attitudes rather than concepts. But they have been involved in a cultural argument which was never relevant to Donne, and which is no longer relevant at all. For the early logical positivists, clearing out a philosophic attic, declared that statements are meaningful only insofar as they are verifiable, and that there is little reason to be concerned with unmeaningful sentences. Their attitude seemed to threaten poetry. Therefore I. A. Richards responded by showing that poetry has great psychological utility in inculcating attitudes and values—both excluded from "cognitive language" by the positivists. Richards' defense of poetry is strong; and his concession that poetry cannot make meaningful statements did not trouble critics who believed that the literature of knowledge is antithetical to that of power, and that exposition is necessarily "non-poetry."

Taking Donne as an exemplar, and following Richards, Cleanth Brooks established a method of reading poetry purely for its values and attitudes. Ignoring denotation, he defined a dynamics of connotation through which, he argued, Donne evaluates subjects of general significance. Because semanticists have changed their tack, the questions Richards faced no longer seem vital. But, largely because of his own brilliance, Brooks's reading of Donne has become widespread, and perhaps even standard.

The weakness of Brooks's approach, in relation to Donne, is its attribution of a didactic purpose to poetry. Richards properly argued that poetry has educative value; but Brooks argued that every good poem is structured to achieve an educative purpose, and that it operates through linguistic connotation. Clearly, Donne's poems are not so structured; and if they were they would not have used a sidelong language, for, ignorant of the logical positivists, Donne would have had no more fear of saying "X is good" than did the philosophers of his time. Donne's lyrics are neither structured to improve his readers' values, nor concerned directly with the vital issues of his or any age. But, after all, poetry broadens sensibilities not by didactic insinuation, but by being a deeply felt experience. Donne's poems are such an experience for his readers; and so, without using the means Brooks defines, they achieve the aim he seeks.

One further general point about Donne's Petrarchism may be raised. Read as a symbolist and an antecedent of Eliot, Donne has proven vital to our time. Ought we then to read him in any other way? [5] To the literary historian, who seeks truth, this defense of ahistorical reading has no point; but it is nonetheless not to be immediately dismissed. Several objections to it may be raised, however. For Eliot's poetry will not always be contemporary. Even while it is, Donne's, properly understood, may prove as exciting. And, in any event, it would be an intellectual disaster to have all literature reduced to one mode, and so to forego even the possibility of understanding different things. If poetry is to broaden sensibilities, surely the critic should not be dedicated to narrowing poetry.

Donne's Petrarchism shows his poems to be gestures made from social situations. His compass image, for example, is not a private reflection upon the significance of love, but a gesture of amorous faith made to a lady who mourns at parting—a gesture with expressive value, for, comforting his lady, Donne himself thinks of the stability of his love. "The Apparition," again, is not a meditation upon the meaning of love and death, nor any sort of private fantasy, but an action. Donne has been rejected by a lady whom he desires. His problem is not what to say, but what to do. In response, he adopts a pose that is both languishing and threatening, and so, with sophisticated poise, expresses both his desire and his irritation. In neither "A Valediction: forbidding mourning" nor "The Apparition" does Donne emphasize the particularity of his circumstances or the uniqueness of his sentiments. But in both his response is most individual. In general, as here, Donne's lyrics are gestures with great expressive value.

Indirectly, Donne's lyrics reveal his general values. They may well stimulate the critic to ponder the situation of the seventeenth-century intellectual, or to plunge into a vast obscure of linguistic associations, symbols, and patterns. But Donne is a poet of manner: of attitudes expressed within a social context, through extravagant poses and polite conceits. Methods used to explicate Donne hitherto have mostly been adequate only to private meditations upon the meaning of things. And yet the explication of Donne ought to continue—as Glendower splutters, "It shall, it will; you see it doth." Therefore, it is worth seeking a mode of analysis suited to the poetry of gesture.

Such a method must take account of three aspects of poems. The first is their occasion: for every action must have an occasion. Although ideally the various means of indicating the occasion of a lyric should be defined, I content myself here with dividing the occasions of Donne's lyrics into three categories. Their situation may be general: in "Song: Goe, and catche a falling starre," Donne is talking to someone, but whether to an intimate friend, a naive youth, or a courtly gathering is indeterminate. Their situation may be particular: in "The good-morrow," Donne speaks while gazing into the eyes of a lady immediately after their discovery that they love each other. Or their situation may be mythical: in "The Will," pretending that he will die for love, Donne writes his testament. Where Donne's situation is indefinite, his gesture too must be general; where it is mythical, it has a double effect, since behind the pretended situation there is a real one (in "The Will," the fact that Donne has been rejected). Thus, the situation of Donne's lyrics is real (general or particular), or mythical.

The second aspect of Donne's lyrics is his posture. Acting within a situation, he strikes a dramatic attitude: he may be, for example, angry, enthusiastic, or poised. For an understanding of Donne's lyric, it is well to emphasize three categories here. First, there is Donne's simple posturing: an extravagant pose that shows no complicated awareness. Second, there is his pretended naivety: a sophisticated affectation of amorous adoration. And, third, there is his reasonable manner: a pose which, though heightened and emotional, reveals a broad awareness of life.

The third element of Donne's lyric to consider is the relation between what his statements say, and what they do. Sometimes Donne explicitly argues in defense of his attitudes. At other times his argument is directed to a mythical situation, or it reveals a pretended naivety; and his explicit statements have a more subtle relationship to his intention. These last, subtle expressions have entirely absorbed the attention of the New Critics. But an adequate exposition of any lyric by Donne must consider at least three elements: its situation; its attitude; and the function of its arguments.

These three elements, coming into play in various ways, form in Donne four chief sorts of lyrics. The first is the (un-Petrarchan) epigrammatic poem: one in which the situation is real, the attitude a simple posturing, and the arguments a support for the posture. Donne's epigrammatic lyrics are "Woman's constancy," "The Indifferent," "Goe, and catche a falling starre," "Confined Love," "Communitie," and "The Flea." Most of these lyrics appear to be statements, not gestures: proofs that sexual promiscuity is good. In fact, however, anticipating Suckling, Donne here uses arguments—made more provoking by paradox—only to strike the pose of an insouciant lover who knows women to be unfaithful and who enjoys promiscuity himself. This stance has limited possibilities for Donne. "The Indifferent," for example—stilted, paradoxical, and consciously knowing—is a far cry from the wickedly sensual confession of Ovid, *Amores,* II, 4, which it probably recalls. "The Dampe," on the other hand, where Donne also claims neither to seek nor to profess constancy, is high comedy: its deadly images engraven on hearts and its amorous epidemics, giants, Goths, and witches—its Petrarchism, in short—give it the veneer of a rich civilization. But the point here is that Donne's epigrammatic lyrics demonstrate a stance.

Their structure may be illustrated by "Womans constancy":

Now thou hast lov'd me one whole day,
    To morrow when thou leav'st, what wilt thou say?
Wilt thou then Antedate some new made vow?
    Or say that now
We are not just those persons, which we were?
Or, that oathes made in reverentiall feare

Of Love, and his wrath, any may forsweare?
Or, as true deaths, true maryages untie,
So lovers contracts, images of those,
Binde but till sleep, deaths image, them unloose?
     Or, your owne end to Justifie,
For having purpos'd change, and falsehood; you
Can have no way but falsehood to be true?
Vaine lunatique, against these scapes I could
       Dispute, and conquer, if I would,
       Which I abstaine to doe,
For by to morrow, I may thinke so too.

The relaxed and scornful lover offers the lady various excuses for her coming inconstancy. She may pretend that her next lover has prior rights. She may argue that, having changed during the night (growing new hair, perhaps, and shedding some skin), she and Donne will be different people from those who swore to be true. She may claim that she plighted troth when afraid of Love, and that oaths made under intimidation are not binding. She may argue that, as marriage vows last until death, lovers' vows, a shadow of marriage, last only until sleep, the shadow of death. Or she may say that, having always intended falsehood, she must be false to Donne to be true to herself. Clearly, the logical fertility and rigor here are purely amusing. The arguments are not meant to persuade the reader—Donne assures the lady that he can refute them. Instead, the arguments function to highlight Donne's attitude—to show that he is superior to them, as he is to all naive views and to the lady herself.

The structure of "Womans constancy," then, is epigrammatic. The arguments are explicit and compose a distinct section of the poem (11. 3-13). The poem consists of a flagrantly knowing posture at the opening ("one whole day"); a delightful display of logical agility in the middle; and a surprisingly cavalier gesture suddenly concluding the whole. "Womans constancy," as epigram, represents one extreme of Donne's art. It is better than "The Flea" because of a slight, though telling, structural difference: here Donne is superior to his arguments. Unlike that of "Communitie," its situation is particular. All three poems rely on explicit, paradoxical argumentation, and on a pose that shows no complex consciousness behind it. Their paradoxical, explicit arguments and their limited exploitation of manner mark Donne's epigrammatic (and, generally, his un-Petrarchan) lyrics.

In Donne's Petrarchan poems, there are three chief forms. The first may be represented by "The Legacie":

When I dyed last, and, Deare, I dye
      As often as from thee I goe,
      Though it be but an houre agoe,
And Lovers houres be full eternity,
I can remember yet, that I
      Something did say, and something did bestow;
Though I be dead, which sent mee, I should be
Mine owne executor and Legacie.

I heard mee say, Tell her anon
      That my selfe, (that is you, not I,)
      Did kill me, and when I felt mee dye,
I bid mee send my heart, when I was gone,
But I alas could there finde none,
      When I had ripp'd me, and search'd where hearts
        did lye;
It kill'd mee againe, that I who still was true,
In life, in my last Will should cozen you.

Yet I found something like a heart,
      But colours it, and corners had,
      It was not good, it was not bad,
It was intire to none, and few had part.
As good as could be made by art
      It seem'd; and therefore for our losses sad,
I meant to send this heart in stead of mine,
But oh, no man could hold it, for twas thine.

The intention of "The Legacie" is to reveal Donne's attitude towards a lady whose heart cannot be held, who uses "colours" (i.e., feigning), and who is incapable of love; whose heart "was not good, it was not bad,/ It was intire to none, and few had part." Donne's perception of his lady's shallow and uncommitted soul is not foreign to Petrarchism. In stanzas 92-96, Canto IV, of the *Gerusalemme liberata,* Tasso employs the most sentimental Petrarchan terms to describe the perfidious coquetry of Armida. Her sweet speech and smile, her honorably lowered eyes, and her lovers' ice and fire, smile and plaint, fear and hope are all echoes of Laura's beauty and Petrarch's passion. Yet they show a cold-blooded flirt. And in Tasso's sonnets to Lucrezia Bendido, similar terms have a similar function.[6] But Donne's manner is surely more flexible, more capable of concentrating upon the satiric vision, than that of most Petrarchists.

Nonetheless, "The Legacie" is a Petrarchan poem. Contrary to what modern critics might expect, Donne does not convey his anger by vigorous denunciation. Instead, he turns from the real situation to a mythical, Petrarchan one. Except for the hour-long parting of the lovers, there is no historical event in Donne's story. Donne is not dead, he does not dissect himself, he does not discover his lady's heart in his body. Even allegorically, the events he recounts do not take place: if Donne's lady's heart is so tricksy, he will not find it in his breast. The entire poem is a deduction from conventional tropes. Donne, parting from his lady and sensing that she is untrue, pretends to die for love. Upon that death, he constructs a mock-narrative, in the Petrarchan manner, about post-mortem events. With the conceit that lovers die from the pain of parting, he fuses the exchange of hearts, and the lover's last will and testament. Then, taking these tropes literally, he tells of his effort to bequeath a heart, and of his disappointment when he finds that he has neither his own nor his lady's. Thus, by a logical play upon traditional tropes, he invents a story which expresses, within a polite, Petrarchan context, his disappointment.

In accord with his story, Donne's pose is that of the most extravagant Petrarchan lover. He begins, with rich sentimentality, "When I dyed last, and, Deare, I dye/ As often as from thee I goe." He continues with the most complete adoration. His honest disappointment, his simple doggedness in trying to send at least some heart, and his fixed tenderness in the face of his surprising discovery all reflect earnest devotion. Thus, in order to denounce a lady Donne assumes, with elaborate politeness, a devoted attitude.

Donne's true feelings are revealed partly by his story, where he discovers the nature of his lady's heart. They are revealed, too, in his logic, which fills his seemingly naive statements with significance. Given Donne's purpose, a neoclassicist would define as quickly as possible the events that lead up to Donne's vision of his lady's heart, so as to concentrate upon its nature. Donne, however, takes the contrary course. Reducing the rhetorical point of his poem to a few lines, he complicates and elaborates his initial explanation. He stresses the paradoxes involved in the various identities of the lover as corpse, as executor, and as the lady (who is the poet's very self). He marks the paradox in the fact that it is *"but* an houre" which is *"full* eternity." He follows every idea through a labyrinth. The effect of such indirectness and divagation in the light of Donne's purposed denunciation is to emphasize his detachment and his poise: Donne is by no means furiously impelled to the attack.

Furthermore, Donne's logic indicates the complexities of attitude which his pose as devoted, dying lover seems to ignore. For example, in

> Though it be but an houre agoe,
> And Lovers houres be full eternity,
> I can remember yet, . . .

Donne explains the conventional truth that lovers' hours are long, by the shortness of their constancy. And, without discarding his devoted pose, he insinuates that attitude towards infidelity which he proposes to reveal. Through such incidental by-play, Donne complicates and directs the Petrarchan manner he assumes.

Thus, the form of "The Legacie" is different from that of "Womans constancy," "Communitie," and "The Flea." Instead of explicit argument supporting an extravagant pose, "The Legacie" is based on a sentimental manner and a mythical narrative, behind and through which a wider consciousness appears. In "The Legacie" Donne commits himself to a sentimental posture and, through the logic of Serafino, derives from conventional conceits a plot and a by-play which both have satiric point. He thereby shapes his manner to the indirect insinuations of barbed wit. Formally, "The Legacie" illustrates a second mode of Donne—one which appears, for example, in "The Dampe," "The Funerall," and "The Apparition."

The first mode defined here, then, is that in which Donne's situation is real, the direction of his argument manifest, and his pose exorbitant. The second, that of "The Legacie," is that in which the situation is mythical, the arguments indirect, and the pose pretendedly naive. A third mode is that in which the situation is mythical, the arguments indirect, and the pose reasonable. This mode may be illustrated by "Loves exchange":

> *Love,* any devill else but you,
> Would for a given Soule give something too.
> At Court your fellowes every day,
> Give th'art of Riming, Huntsmanship, or Play,
> For them which were their owne before;
> Onely I have nothing which gave more,
> But am, alas, by being lowly, lower.
>
> I aske no dispensation now
> To falsifie a teare, or sigh, or vow,
> I do not sue from thee to draw
> A *non obstante* on natures law,
> These are prerogatives, they inhere
> In thee and thine; none should forsweare
> Except that hee *Loves* minion were.
>
> Give mee thy weaknesse, make mee blinde,
> Both wayes, as thou and thine, in eies and minde;
> Love, let me never know that this
> Is love, or, that love childish is;
> Let me not know that others know
> That she knowes my paines, least that so
> A tender shame make me mine owne new woe.
>
> If thou give nothing, yet thou 'art just,
> Because I would not thy first motions trust;
> Small townes, which stand stiffe, till great shot
> Enforce them, by warres law *condition* not.
> Such in loves warfare is my case,
> I may not article for grace,
> Having put Love at last to shew this face.

> This face, by which he could command
> And change the Idolatrie of any land,
> This face, which wheresoe'r it comes,
> Can call vow'd men from cloisters, dead from tombes,
> And melt both Poles at once, and store
> Deserts with cities, and make more
> Mynes in the earth, then Quarries were before.
>
> For this, Love is enrag'd with mee,
> Yet kills not. If I must example bee
> To future Rebells; If th' unborne
> Must learne, by my being cut up, and torne;
> Kill, and dissect me, Love; for this
> Torture against thine owne end is,
> Rack't carcasses make ill Anatomies.

Donne's theme here is the folly of passion, one of Petrarch's favorite motives. When Donne says "Onely I have nothing which gave more," and "shame make me mine owne new woe" (i.e., love itself is a woe, and shame of love is a new woe), he is saying what Petrarch often says: for example, "E del mio vaneggiar vergogna è 'l frutto," "And as the fruit of my raving I have nothing but shame" (from "Voi ch'ascoltate in rime sparse il suono"). Indeed, Donne's theme is much that of "Voi ch'ascoltate." Petrarch says

> Ma ben veggio or sí come al popol tutto
> Favola fui gran tempo, onde sovente
> Di me medesmo meco mi vergogno
>
> (But now I know well how I was for a long time a stale story
> in the common mouth, whence now I am often
> myself my own shame).

And here, with additional complications, is Donne:

> Let me not know that others know
> That she knowes my paines, least that so
> A tender shame make me mine owne new woe.

Donne means, then, to express his bitterness and humiliation at the course of his fruitless love. To do so, he again pretends to respond to a mythical situation. His story is conventional: after having long despised love (stanza 4), he is punished by the sight of a beautiful face which makes him fall desperately in love (stanza 5); his lady's hardness leaves him without hope (stanza 1); and so he prays to die, and thus escape the misery of unrewarded love (stanza 6). His lyric is situated in this story: ostensibly, it is an oration to the god Love, who has been punishing Donne. Donne enunciates his complaint (stanza 1), disparages the gift he asks (stanzas 2-3), flatters Love, confessing that he is just (stanzas 4-5), and demonstrates that Love himself will gain by granting Donne's prayer (stanza 6). In "The Legacie" Donne pretends to be concerned with executing a will that was never made; here he pretends to persuade a god who does not exist.

Explicitly, Donne's arguments are directed to his mythical situation. But at every point, Donne exploits conventional metaphors so as to reveal his bitterness. Traditionally, Love is lord of the poet's soul; Donne therefore calls him a devil. Traditionally, love transcends nature;[7] Donne says that his magical power is that of breaking promises. Traditionally, Cupid wears a blindfold; Donne says that lovers must avoid recognizing the nature of love. Traditionally, the person who refuses to love is a rebel; Donne says that his amorous pain is the torture which punishes rebels. At every point, though his arguments are explicitly directed towards Love, his metaphors reveal his angry humiliation.

Though Donne's story is mythical, in "Loves exchange" his posture reveals a broad awareness. Despite his own suffering, Donne recognizes Love's rights and powers; and he admits his own guilt. In less fabulous terms, Donne sees his own position clearly: he sees that he is helplessly in love and, at the same time, that love is childish and his own position shameful. (His vision is very well embodied in the myth of a rebel captured and tortured by Love.) "Loves exchange" is not a brilliant poem. But it serves to illustrate a third mode of Donne's lyric: that in which the situation is mythical, the consciousness complex, and the explicit argument related indirectly to the poet's intention.

A fourth mode of Donne's lyric is that in which his situation is particular, his consciousness complex, and his arguments in direct support of his attitude. Poems of this sort include "The good-morrow," "The Sunne Rising," and "A Valediction: forbidding mourning." I shall not here consider them at length. The chief elements of Donne's art are already clear. Donne, often through the exaggerated postures and extravagant logic of the Petrarchists, uses language as action, not for what it says but for the attitude it presumes. The formal structure of Donne's lyrics depends on whether the situation from which the action arises is general or specific, real or mythical; whether the attitude is expressed explicitly, or implicitly in plot or metaphor; and whether the attitude is simple, ironically naive, or complex. Throughout, Donne's lyrics are not personal meditations upon general truths, in a Romantic mode. They are instead mannered attitudinizing in response to a variety of situations. Usually, their situation is Petrarchan, the situation of a man devoted to love who finds himself rejected, or separated, or triumphant in love; and their contemplation of love is a direct response to such a situation.

Since Donne's lyrics are mannered, expressive, and often sentimental, they ought not to be read as if they were Browning's dramatic monologues. Their rhythms are neither conversational nor unduly harsh.[8] "Loves exchange" may justify Jonson's assertion that Donne deserves hanging for not keeping accent; but "Womans constancy" is singable, and "The Legacie" holds to a rich iambic pattern. In general, Donne's lyrics must be read with a stress upon their metrical values—as Donne's experimentation with stanzaic forms would indicate. For example, though its initial phrase is colloquial "Aire and Angels" does not begin as prose,

Twice or thrice // had I loved thee,

but as iambic verse, with full value accorded to its long *i*'s and *e*:

Twice / or thrice / had I loved thee.

Again, "The Apparition" does not begin

When by thy scorne, / O murdresse // I am dead,

121

but with an iambic pattern strongly maintained against the un-iambic phrasing,

When / by thy scorne, / O murdresse / I am dead.[9]

And "The Canonization," though opening vigorously, does not begin with three prose phrases,

For Godsake / hold your tongue, / and let me love,

but with an iambic pattern given full play in the sentimental outcry of the final phrase,

For Godsake hold your tongue, / and let me love.

Though their phrases are less isomorphic than those of Lyly and Spenser, Donne's lyrics are to be read metrically, not prosaically; they are lyric.[9]

The final question that arises in considering Donne's lyrics as gestures is that of appreciation. Although this question cannot be fully considered without reference to poems which I discuss only later, it may be broached now. One may note, for example, that though they are not symbolic, there is resonant poetry in the phrases which attract Donne's critics: "rags of time," "a Sun dyall in a grave," and "the bracelet of bright haire about the bone." Again, though it is not a new philosophic synthesis which suggests to Donne his gift in "The Legacie," his haunting in "The Apparition," and his prayer in "Loves exchange," yet his inventiveness is delightful. After all, ultimate truths need not be everywhere explicit in good poetry: *As You Like It* is greater than *The Cenci,* and *Absalom and Achitopel* than *Night Thoughts.* Eliot and his followers have taught us to honor wit; in grace to them, we should not insist that wit itself be portentous and solemn.

Essentially, there are three problems involved in appreciating Donne's poetry of gesture. The first is that of responding to a lyric which is not immediate, naive, and sincere, but consciously directed and socially oriented. The second is that of discovering general meaning in such a lyric. Both of these problems may be solved. For Donne's social poise and his irony reflect his sense of what is and what is not important: of what does and what does not deserve a full emotional response. They reveal an ideal of conduct, and of the values which underlie it. This is their irony, and this the sort of moral truth they may be made to teach.

The third problem is that of appreciating a lyric whose ideas are neither unique nor profound. The path to take here is that of the Renaissance itself. For where modern critics often assume that art is radically individual self-expression, Renaissance critics thought that art is the fruit of high civilization. And so it is: the poet's culture is no more dispensable than his individuality. The precision, fancy and poise of Donne's gestures culminate a rich tradition of courtly culture, grace, and intelligence. It would be barbaric to repudiate his grace because it is traditional; it would be dull to reject his wit because it lacks high seriousness. Donne's ideas are not great discoveries, but they are eternally human; his manner is not naïve, but it is complex and individual: and ultimately it is the public, the witty, the courtly quality of his verse which was and is still salutary to an age fed too full of Romanticism.

IX

Renaissance Love Theory

Like his conceit, Donne's philosophy of love is Petrarchan.[1] It can be understood only in the light of Renaissance love theory.[2]

Florentine Neoplatonists consider love to be the fundamental principle of all the sciences—theological, metaphysical, moral, and natural. The Petrarchists adapt their theories to poetical tradition and to courtly elegance. To them, Neoplatonism is as exciting and congenial as Freudianism has been to twentieth-century poets. It is intellectually vital, socially fashionable, and quite poetical—especially since Neoplatonists cite poets who agree with them, and interpret others so that the agreement seems universal. Petrarchists, therefore, turn naturally to Neoplatonism, finding it central both to their contemporary world and to their poetic exemplars.

Because Donne is such a Petrarchist, I offer here a survey of Renaissance love theory. Since this theory has roots in Provençal poetry, and since Donne is sometimes thought to be a kind of stilnovist, I begin my survey early.

Courtly love theory—that is, doctrines in love poetry adapted to courtly tastes and manners—properly begins with the Provençal lyric.[3] For the student of late-medieval intellectual history, Provençal love theory is fascinating. It reflects a new interest in the individual and his spiritual potentialities; and it is related to such movements as scholasticism, Christian Neoplatonism, and, perhaps, Arabic Neoplatonism.[4] For the literary historian, however, Provençal poets and their imitators are important not for what they represent but for what they say. And their statements are fairly simple.

124

Epistemologically, Provençal poets say that the lover perceives, imagines, remembers, and desires his lady. Medically, they argue that the lady's glance sends into her lover's blood a spirit which causes pallor, trembling, heats, colds, and stammering. Socially and rhetorically, they develop a code of behavior and a method of amorous persuasion. Though their epistemology and medicine fascinate those modern critics who hanker after obscure ideas, it is their manners and rhetoric which are of chief importance to the Provençal lyric, to Andreas Capellanus, and to the European tradition of courtly love.

Provençal love theory must be seen as it functions within the lyric. Generally, each lyric is located at a stage of adulterous love: the poet respectfully but passionately discovers to his lady his hitherto undisclosed love; or, after she hears his declaration favorably, he joyfully declares that he serves her proudly; or he ecstatically announces that he has been profusely rewarded by her ultimate favors; or, with noble sorrow, he discloses that she has discourteously betrayed him. Within this context, the poet's emotions are intense, feudal, and idealized: burning like a moth in the flame of his lady's beauty and resurrected by her smile, he sings with joy of her sublime worth or with anguish of his hopeless desire. His reverence is reflected in his elegant, stylized language: he says that she is among other ladies like a rose among flowers. The lady's praises, too, are delicate and passionate: she is exalted for her eyes, her greeting, and her elegant bearing—for her breeding, above all, which is called "knowledge," "wisdom," and "understanding." Her sublimity is revealed primarily by her amazing effects upon her poet, and by his reverent tone. Thus, Provençal poetry combines propriety with intensity. Its technique is esoteric, relying on aureate language, peregrine comparisons, and difficult meters. It is both impeccably courteous and intensely passionate.

Courtly love theory is essentially an ideal of amorous conduct and rhetoric within a feudal society (Capellanus' *De amore*, for example, is chiefly composed of model speeches for each caste of lover). Provençal literature reflects a taste for subtlety—for complicated rules and obscure instances (as in the "courts of love," social gatherings which, as a pastime, dispute the proper course of conduct in difficult cases—often, probably, alluding to personal circumstances). In the lyric, however, the code of love is essentially a clear standard of propriety upon which the poet models himself, and to which he appeals when persuading, praising, or denouncing his lady (this last, generally, when she has been unfaithful). These are his principles: like contemporary courtiers, he accepts gentility as the highest social value; but he defines true gentility not by birth but by accomplishment and delicacy; he argues that love ennobles sentiments and inspires to worthy actions; and he concludes that since he loves so intensely as to be recreated by passion, he is worthy of his lady, no matter what her rank.

Upon this basis, the Provençal poet develops a feudal relationship between lady and lover: like a knight who serves a noble lord, the lover demonstrates his own nobility by his high-minded and worthy service; like the lord who accepts the worthy services of a noble knight, the lady is obligated to reward her servant.[5] For moderns, it is worth emphasizing that thus Provençal love theory establishes a mutual obligation between lover and lady. The Provençal poet is elaborately courteous in invoking his rights, since they are consequences of his gentility: he requests as grace what is his in equity, refuses to insult his lady even after she has betrayed him, and faithfully serves his lady without reward. Throughout, he reflects the luster of a proud and noble courtesy. But beneath that luster is the mutual obligation between feudal lord and servant: the lover repeatedly indicates what courtesy requires of his lady, and continually reminds her that the good servant *deserves* his reward.

Such is the code of courtly love—of adulterous propriety—which, passing into European literature, provides the basis in England for the lyrics of the courtly makers, and, in Italy, for the first, so-called Sicilian, school of courtly poets. Clearly, courtly love is a system of manners, not of metaphysics. Those of its lyrics which debate abstract questions are very simple: they either define love by a few general principles (love originates in sight, contemplation, and inordinate desire), or discuss difficult cases of love (such as whether love can arise from the mere report of an unseen lady).[6] In the thirteenth century, however, a change appears in the Provençal lyric. In response partly to non-literary impulses and partly to its own internal laws, to its continuous search for a *ne plus ultra* of sentimental refinement, the Provençal lyric turns with increasing frequency to such themes as eternal love for a dead lady, love which seeks no reward, and love of the Virgin Mary.[7] This change adumbrates the first truly philosophic school of the Romance love lyric, the *dolce stil novo*.

Although for scholars the *stil novo* lies under the shadow of the *Divina commedia*—which christened it, defined it, and realized its fullest poetic possibilities—it deserves to be considered in itself. So considered, it is characterized by its metaphysical definition of *fin' amors*. The stilnovists develop systematically the philosophic implications of the Provençal code of manners. Their philosophic bias is apparent even in their diction: such words as "conoscenza" and "insegnamento," which in earlier poets refer to breeding, here refer to scholastic learning. Combining Provençal elegance and passion with metaphysical learning and methodology, the stilnovists form one of the greatest schools of lyric poetry in the modern world.

Essentially, *fin' amors* presents two philosophic problems. The first is that while love ennobles, and only noble hearts love, the ontological relation between love and nobility is obscure. The stilnovists—particularly Guinizelli in "Al cor gentil"—provide the explanation. Nobility is merely the potentiality for love; love is the act, the Being of nobility: love and the gentle heart are one thing. At the sight of the lady, the potency for love is realized. Inevitably, the question of the lady's nature arises: what must she be to transform her lover's nobility from potency to act? Guinizelli does not answer this question,[8] though his lady is more exalted than earlier ladies. Dante, however, provides the answer: the lady must be a manifestation of God.

The second philosophical problem involved in *fin' amors* is that of love's relation to its effects. Provençal poets say that love causes nobility, and Guinizelli and Dante explain the mode of causality. Provençal poets also say that love causes trembling, pallor, burning, freezing, stammering, and death. They explain these effects physiologically, but psychologically the poet reconciles them to his general conception of love only by saying that love refines him as fire refines gold—presumably, through torment. Cavalcanti, however, explains these effects. He insists, against Guinizelli, that love is accidental—not essential—to the noble heart. He defines love as a psychological process culminating in so deep a meditation upon the lady, as to lead the soul to forget its own good, and thus to die to itself. From this state, Cavalcanti deduces the effects of love by means of faculty psychology. Like Guinizelli and Dante, Cavalcanti considers love as it results immediately from the perception of the lady. Where Dante concentrates upon ontology and the final cause, however, Cavalcanti concerns himself with psychology and efficient causes. The theory described here, and declared in "Donna me prega," colors the body of his lyrics, which are, characteristically, internal dramas among the faculties of the poet's soul, revealing his death and his suffering.[9]

In the *stil novo,* both the rules and the social nexus of *fin' amors* are discarded. Love poetry is concerned almost entirely with the effects of love upon the lover. This is not necessarily to say that stilnovist love is not sexual: even in Dante's *Vita nuova,* the lady who consoles Dante for Beatrice's death recalls those gracious ladies whose advances Provençal poets nobly reject. It is unclear whether stilnovist love is sexual. What is clear is that for the Provençals' adulterous situations, persuasive intentions, and feudal code, the stilnovists substitute psychology, ontology, and teleology to define the nature of the supreme lady, and of love as perception, apprehension, and desire.

Though he too locates love within the lover's soul, Petrarch initiates a Renaissance tendency to place rhetoric and morality above logic. His amorous philosophy, therefore, can be treated summarily. It has three strands: first, psychological analysis of the effects of love, in the manner of the stilnovists ("Quando giunge per gli occhi al cor profondo," for example); second, rudimentary Platonic allusions to the Idea of Laura's beauty (for example, in "In qual parte del ciel, in quale idea," "Per mirar Policleto a prova fiso," and "Movesi il vecchierel canuto e bianco"); and, third, echoes of traditional maxims which reflect upon the folly of desire and the vanity of life. In short, Petrarch has no systematic, logically elaborate metaphysic of love. He does, however, use many conceits—for example, amorous miracles, amorous resurrection, and the image on the heart—which later Petrarchists understand as fragments of a systematic theory of love.

At the end of the fifteenth century, a second truly philosophical period of amorous speculation begins. It appears chiefly in works of three kinds: annotated editions of Petrarch's *Canzoniere* (among them, Filelfo's, Vellutello's, Daniello's, Gesualdo's, Castelvetro's, and the notes of Chastiglione); published lectures upon individual Petrarchan lyrics (among them, Varchi's, Lucio Oradini's, Giovanni Cervoni da Colle's, Giovanbattista Gelli's, and Simon de la Barba da Pescia's—most of these first delivered in the Florentine Academy); and love treatises (by Ficino, Pico, Leone, Bembo, Speroni, Betussi, and Tullia of Aragon, for example). Large parts of the love treatises are concerned with cosmological and religious love—with the love between God and the universe, and that between God and man. Those parts are irrelevant here.

Essential to this body of speculative literature—though rarely noted by modern literary historians—is its methodology. The Neoplatonists assume that the Petrarchan clichés are literally true and philosophically important. They assume too that Petrarch agrees with both ancient and mediaeval philosophers. Three impulses motivate them: the Platonist's taste for esoteric truths revealed in myths; the humanist's search for universal truths in old literature; and the pedant's heavy-handed literalism. So motivated, Filelfo and Vellutello, for example, explain as natural philosophy Petrarch's assertions that his soul and body are separated ("Io mi rivolgo indietro a ciascun passo") and that he feeds on death ("Ben mi credea passar mio tempo omai," st. 4).[10] Even a rationalist like Mario Equicola, considering at length what poets say of love, treats them as authorities equal to physicians and metaphysicans. And the Neoplatonists base their philosophical systems on ingenious, literalizing explications of such poetic clichés as the burnings and freezings of lovers, their union, and the murderous cruelty of obdurate ladies.[11]

129

The methods by which Petrarch's statements were systematized in the Renaissance may be illustrated from Chastiglione's notes. In "Per fare una leggiadra sua vendetta," Petrarch says that when he saw his lady for the first time, his powers rushed to his heart to defend him from love, but failed to do so. Chastiglione notes that elsewhere Petrarch says that the way to the heart is through the eyes, and that therefore Petrarch's powers should have rushed to his eyes; he explains that Petrarch was attacked too suddenly for his powers to operate properly. Again, in "Perché la vita è breve," Petrarch says that only his lady understands his allusion. Chastiglione explains that Petrarch means what Plato says, that lovers understand each other without speaking. Again, in the same lyric Petrarch says that Laura's eyes "show heaven here on earth," and Chastiglione explains that Petrarch means what Plato says, that they diffuse the divine beauty of God. Thus Chastiglione illustrates the characteristic method of the Platonists: taking Petrarch's conceits to be philosophic statements, he reconciles them with each other, with Plato, and with other accepted philosophers, and so develops a systematic philosophy of love.

It is difficult to summarize Renaissance love theory, which is expressed in works as remote in time and taste as Ficino's and Tasso's. Nonetheless, three general features of Renaissance love theory may be marked. First, most theorists define love as "a desire for satisfaction, through union with that which is or appears to be good." [12] Their theories develop two aspects of this definition: they justify satisfaction by its final cause; and they discriminate among kinds of love according to whether their objects are, or merely seem to be, good.

Secondly, the theorists consider good to be equivalent with Being, so that they find love to be justified according to the degree in which it is a desire for that which Is. In practice, this means that they distinguish among levels of love by the extent of their materialism. Some theorists justify spiritual love by separating it entirely from sexual love, which they denounce; others accept sexuality as an attendant good; [13] many argue that physical love is good when it is limited to the senses of sight and hearing. But virtually all justify amorous enjoyment by its spiritual direction.

The third general feature of Neoplatonic literature is its agreement upon a collection of generalizations. Since their system is eclectic rather than deductive, the theorists usually accept all these generalizations, even where they seem incompatible. Virtually all these theories are expressed by Ficino.[14] For convenience, I list them in outline form:

I. The object of love:

    a. The object of love is divine beauty (which is said sometimes to inhere in, and sometimes to be merely suggested by, the lady);

    b. The object of love is the image of the lady; having once had that image fixed in his memory, the lover needs his lady's presence only because his eyes too desire her image;

    c. The purpose of love is to propagate beauty, or oneself, either through sex (Terrestial Venus), or through teaching (Celestial Venus);

    d. The purpose of love is to become one with the beloved;

    e. The purpose of love is to become one with that which is loved; since the ideal is what one loves, love ennobles the lover.

II. Amorous medicine:

    a. Love has astrological, physiological, and psychological causes;

    b. Among the causes are the infusion of blood from a glance, and temperamental likenesses (or differences);

    c. Among the symptoms of love are an interrupted sigh, pallor, trembling, solitary wandering, melancholy, sleeplessness, heat, and cold;

    d. Many of the signs of love appear simultaneously with their opposites, as weeping with smiling, joy with pain, hope with despair, and heats with colds;

    e. In this way and others, love miraculously transcends natural laws.

III. The state of the lover:

a. When one loves, he thinks only of his beloved, and not at all of himself; since thought is the only operation of the soul, to love is to die to oneself, by losing his soul;

b. When a beloved loves in return, she gives her lover's soul a home, and devotes her soul to him;

c. Therefore, if she refuses his love she is a murderess, but if she accepts it she resurrects him;

d. Because thought is the only function of the soul, and because lovers think alike, a pair of lovers is one-in-two;

e. Because each lover exists both in himself and in his beloved, a pair of lovers is four-in-one;

f. A love founded upon reason surpasses sensual love, because it transcends absence and the blows of fortune;

g. In the hope of becoming one with his beloved, the lover may repeatedly seek sexual union, but the body is incapable of permanent fusion; the soul, on the contrary, is capable of a truly hermaphroditic union, making two lovers one.

The subtle historian might systematize these principles further, but this list—though in a skeletal form—provides an acquaintance with the general current of Renaissance love theory.

The Renaissance love theorists echo the same authorities and each other. Nonetheless, they are engaged in a fruitful intellectual enterprise: by reinterpreting their literary and philosophic heritage, they seek to discover the ultimate meaning of secular life. Some of them, for example, are ascetics who ask the lover to turn to purely spiritual things once his awareness of them has been awakened by human love. Others isolate and emphasize the loveliest aspects of secular life, justifying the sentiments of human love by its divine elements. Since the issue between them is whether life on earth has any real value to the human soul, theirs is a vital debate about ultimate values.

Because the love theorists are eclectic and literary, they displease those modern critics whose tastes run to the doctrinaire logic

of the scholastics. For those, like T. S. Eliot, who consider Donne an
intellectual magpie, the happy confusion of Plato, Petrarch, Aristotle, Ovid, and Aquinas must seem desultory. But, as Douglas Bush
says, Renaissance love literature is far from contemptible.[15] It reflects a renewed intercourse between classical and Christian thought;
and it deals with important issues—theologically, with the relation
of love to understanding; and, morally, with the possibilities of fusing refined manners, delicate tastes, deep learning, and elevated intentions. Nor, despite a modern disregard for eclecticism, is the
Renaissance thinker confused; it is precisely because he is intellectually secure that he trusts himself to garner the truth from all past
literature, and from the Book of the Creatures; he is certain that
great literary thinkers have known eternal truths, and that he can
recognize them.

In Italian poetry there are, strictly speaking, two schools of
amatory philosophy: the *dolce stil novo,* which analyzes with scholastic logic the problems of *fin' amors;* and Renaissance Neoplatonism, which gathers esoteric doctrines from myth, metaphor, and
conceit. For half a century, many critics have accepted the idea that
Donne is essentially related to the *dolce stil novo:* Ezra Pound says
that Donne's verse can be understood only through that of Guido
Cavalcanti.[16] But in fact—as several scholarly studies have indicated
—it is Renaissance Neoplatonism which provides the context of
Donne's thought.[17]

The argument for Donne's relation to Cavalcanti rests on the
conception of a distinct form of language which combines thought
with passion. An emotional statement by Milton, Shelley, or Ten-
nyson, it is argued, is liable to be logically flaccid. But when Cavalcanti says "Love stays in that part where memory is," he means not
merely to connect love vaguely with memory, but to make a psychologically exact definition of the faculty—presumably, the sensory
memory—which loves. Similarly, when Donne says that love's "mysteries in soules doe grow," he makes the precise communication that
the union of lovers' souls is a mystery, incomprehensible to reason
but true, like the triune nature of God; and that, though its manifestations are in the body, its ground is the soul. Both Donne and

Cavalcanti, the argument goes, unite passion with logical accuracy, and thus belong essentially to the same school.

Even in its own terms, this argument breaks down immediately; for Cavalcanti means to assert every consequence that follows from his statements, but Donne does not. In saying that the lovers' souls are one, Donne does not imply that they see and hear the same things, for example. This difference, long noted, has led critics to say that, writing in the same mode as Cavalcanti, Donne disbelieves his philosophy.[18] The explanation lies instead in the fact that Donne does not write like Cavalcanti at all, that he belongs to a stage of Cavalcanti's tradition that is three centuries later and radically different. Postponing a consideration of Renaissance love theory in Donne, I shall digress here to consider Cavalcanti's lyrics, for they are at once little known to English readers and central to much critical discussion about Donne.

"Donna me prega, perch' eo voglio dire" is Guido's great abstract definition of love. Its tone is proudly elegant: courteously, Cavalcanti wants to write because a lady requests him to; aristocratically, he disclaims interest in any readers but those with refined knowledge. His is a world where elegant ladies discuss with respectful noblemen the subtleties of ethereal passions. Guido's purpose is to explain how the symptoms of desire—pallor, trembling, and death—result from a perception of the lady. His approach is systematic, considering in logical order love's location in the soul, its origin, virtue, powers, and so on. His method consists of translating Andreas into scholastic language:[19] that is, instead of saying that love wounds the lover's heart through his eyes, Guido systematically elaborates the epistemological passage of the image of the lady through sense, sensitive imagination, possible intellect, and memory. The result of Guido's method is to shift poetic concern from courtly manners to such scientific phenomena as the calmness of the possible intellect. Thus Guido fuses the aristocratic tone and poetic intensity of Provençal verse with a scientific method.

Most of Guido's lyrics are less general. They may be illustrated by "Perché non fuoro a me gli occhi dispenti":

Why were my eyes not quenched
 or removed, so that one should not have come through my sight
 to my mind in order to say:
 "Hearken whether you hear me in your heart"?
And a fear of new torments
 used to come to me then, so sharp and cruel
 that my soul cried: "Lady, help us
 so that the eyes and I remain not weeping!"
You have left them so, that Love comes
 to weep over them with pity,
 so much so that a profound voice is heard,
Saying: "You who feel great torment,
 behold this man, and you will see his heart
 in Death's grasp, carved to the shape of a cross."

Cavalcanti's art lies in the impersonality and supreme economy with which he reveals his intense passion. He achieves impersonality through a narrative based on analysis and abstraction: each aspect of his psyche is a person in an anguished drama (so that the image in the mind asks, with terrible understatement, whether its effects appear in the heart); and the pitiable state of the poet is revealed through various narrated outcries, and through the pity of personified Love. Furthermore, Cavalcanti's distance from his lyric is increased by his scientific accuracy: for example, in "came through my sight to my mind . . . in [my] heart," which means that the lady has been perceived sensuously, understood intellectually, and desired passionately. Then too, Cavalcanti's language is learned, noble, and almost biblically concentrated. Thus, he reveals his mortal passion while maintaining a pose of aristocratic quietude. In tone and art, "Perché non fuoro" is characteristic of Cavalcanti.

Whether one compares "Donne me prega" with "The Extasie" and "Aire and Angels," or "Perché non fuoro" with "The Canonization" and "The Funerall," he finds that the difference between Cavalcanti and Donne is absolute. Donne's indirectness and irony are remote from Cavalcanti's noble immediacy, Donne's sophistication and common sense from Cavalcanti's ethereal quietude, and Donne's hyperbole and conceit from Cavalcanti's scientific accuracy. Donne's premises are not those of *fin' amors;* and he has nothing

135

in common with Guido's ethereal passions and epistemological accuracy. Even in strictly logical terms, Donne's methods are not Cavalcanti's: for where Cavalcanti simply describes his sentiments in the language of a metaphysical psychology, the movement of Donne's poems is regularly deductive—and often rooted in Serafino's witty logic, a far cry from Aquinas' psychology. To read Donne as though he wrote in the mode of Cavalcanti is much the same as reading Ovid's *Metamorphoses* as a Roman *Paradise Lost.* My contentions are supported by analyses of Donne's philosophy in the next two chapters. For the nonce I leave them to discuss another modern critical notion, the belief that Donne is related to a different intellectual (though not philosophic) movement, that of anti-Petrarchism.

For many moderns, Petrarchism is a sort of Mrs. Grundyism. But it was not for the sixteenth-century reader. Petrarch wishes to spend one eternal night with Laura; and, according to Renaissance (though not modern) interpreters, he writes about the sight of Laura naked, her potential infidelity, and his own temporary but embarrassing sexual impotence [20]—and such themes appear in his imitators. Furthermore, Petrarch is not blind to feminine weaknesses: indeed, he states as a principle that no woman is both chaste and beautiful.[21] Again, Petrarch is not uniformly courteous: once, at least, he declares that if Laura expects him to die for her, she had best think again.[22] And, though the issue was debated, commentators often argue that Petrarch's love of Laura is not chaste.[23] For all these reasons, the notion that sexuality is anti-Petrarchan is as inconceivable as it is unfounded.

What the Italian anti-Petrarchists actually say is that the Petrarchists write words where Petrarch writes things; that they cover their sensual desires in a Neoplatonic guise; and that they praise their ladies falsely.[24] No one ever accused of naivety such Petrarchists as Serafino, Ariosto, and Aretino; but the anti-Petrarchists object to false rhetoric, overly delicate manners, and hypocritical declarations. That is, as nominalists (or, in literary terms, realists) they understand Neoplatonic idealizations of sentiment to be dishonest; and, as anti-Ciceronians, they suspect elevated rhetoric to be false.[25]

In intellectual history their importance lies in their contempt for aulic vapidity and Neoplatonic idealization.

From a properly historical viewpoint, there is clearly nothing anti-Petrarchan in Shakespeare's references to Marion's red nose or to greasy Joan: for only in parody was Petrarchism placed in the kitchen, among servants. Donne's position is less clear. "Elegie II: The Anagram" contains a passage which may imitate Berni's anti-Petrarchan "Chiome d'argento fine, irte e attorte"; [26] and "Loves Usury" is a sophisticated reversal of the Petrarchan theme of the aged lover begging release from love, on the ground of his long love service (Donne promises to submit to love in age, if he may have in youth the privilege of loveless promiscuity). Furthermore, Donne is no Ciceronian, and a Neoplatonist only in part. But he is far from the vulgarity of such anti-Petrarchists as Chaucer's Miller, who delights in the ill-success of Absalon's courtly wooing. And, unlike the anti-Petrarchists, he does not accuse the Petrarchists of hypocrisy.

Donne's attitude towards the idealizing Petrarchists is expressed in several places. In "To the Countesse of Huntington: That unripe side," he accuses the sighing lover of being lily-livered (1. 24), of teaching women disdain by revealing man's vulnerability (11. 35-36), and of believing naively that passion wins women's hearts, while the reverse is true (11. 51-56). In "Loves growth" (11. 11-12) he smiles at those who, having "no Mistresse but their Muse," think love to be "pure, and abstract." And in "The Extasie" (11. 21-23) he refers playfully to one who, through "good"—i.e., spiritual—love, has "growen all minde." Such passages show a kindly superiority to the inexperience and idealism of some poet-lovers—undoubtedly, to idealizing Petrarchists. But they do not show anti-Petrarchism in the sense of a programmatic attack upon literary and sentimental conventions.

Donne's references to Petrarchists suggest that he shares with the anti-Petrarchists a deep skepticism about sentimental idealization. Such skepticism does appear in his love poetry, but so do sentimental aspiration and Neoplatonic love theories. Perhaps the key to his feelings is a recurrent thought pattern: the emphatic assertion of an idealization of love, followed by its qualification by common sense. For example, in "A Valediction: forbidding mourning," Donne declares, with the Neoplatonists, that two lovers are absolutely and irrefragably one (like beaten gold); then, without abandoning his faith in love, he admits that they may be two—but two in perfect sympathy (the compasses). In "The Canonization," Donne declares with the Neoplatonists that lovers are resurrected after their deaths like the phoenix, and so immortal; then, admitting that they must in fact die, he asserts that they will die like saints. And in "The Anniversarie" Donne announces that the lovers' passion is absolutely eternal, as Neoplatonists say; then, admitting that they will die, he proclaims that they are nonetheless regal now, and destined to happiness hereafter.

The importance of this pattern in Donne's lyrics is great, for it signifies one of his finest achievements, the fusion of amorous exaltation with realism, common sense, and a broad, sophisticated awareness. It indicates, too, that Donne's lyric is constricted and distorted when it is made to seem merely anti-Petrarchan. Donne is immune to anti-Petrarchan criticism, for he does not create a world of myth and rhetoric. Neither does he falsify his desires, which are generally sexual and sometimes flagrantly libertine. (Although the French made a clear choice between Petrarchan and Anacreontic models, the libertines are *un*-Petrarchan, not *anti*-Petrarchan.) In short, Donne's lyric is not aulic or vapid. But neither is it a programmatic attack upon Petrarchism; for Donne's fundamental sympathies lie with those brave translunary things for which anti-Petrarchists have nothing but scorn.

Donne's love theory, then, is neither stilnovist nor anti-Petrarchan. But it is rooted in the tradition surveyed here.

X

Donne's Love Theory

There is today no settled critical opinion about Donne's philosophy. Some decades ago, Donne was thought to be a truly metaphysical poet. Then scholars demonstrated that he is not a mystic, that his knowledge of religious dogma is limited, and that his amorous theories are anticipated by Neoplatonists. Such discoveries have left Donne criticism in disarray. Some critics, finding Donne not to be St. Thomas, feel betrayed; others hail him as a carefree wit; and many maintain faith in the seriousness of his ideas without quite accounting for the new scholarly discoveries. The critical problem, then, is to discover the significance of Donne's thought in its time. To make that discovery, I shall first analyze Donne's use of Neoplatonic doctrine, and then define his general attitude to love.

Donne uses Neoplatonic theories to exalt love. "A Valediction: forbidding mourning," for example, is meant to console a lady upon parting (as its title indicates). Its first three stanzas elevate love by three sharp contrasts: that between the death of saints and the death of ordinary men; that between clergy and laity; and that between spheres and earth. Each contrast appeals to the lady to act with a dignity befitting her high love. And each expresses Donne's own love: its intensity (parting is death), holiness (its joys are sacred), and ethereal quality (it is translunary). By raising the lovers above ordinary men, then, Donne makes an emotional appeal, not a philosophic statement: indeed, philosophically it is inconceivable that the lovers should die (st. 1) and yet be translunary (st. 3). But the magnification of love here prepares for the philosophic arguments which follow.

In the final six stanzas of his lyric, Donne turns to philosophic proof. First he tells his lady that, since their love is so exalted, they do not need each other's physical presence—thus applying to their circumstances the Neoplatonic principle that, unlike "bestial" (i.e., purely sexual) love, spiritual love survives absence.[1] Then he proves that their love is indeed high by their ignorance of what they love— so invoking Ficino's theory that lovers, because their object is divine, do not know what it is they love.[2] Third, and most centrally, Donne claims with the Neoplatonists that lovers are one;[3] and because they are one, he insists, their parting will not really separate them. Thus, in "A Valediction: forbidding mourning," to comfort his lady upon parting, Donne establishes that their love is holy and immutable. He employs Neoplatonic doctrines to dignify his devotion by basing it upon ultimate principles, and to reinforce his consolation with philosophic proof.

"Elegie X: The Dreame" develops a Petrarchan theme, the lover's dream of sexual fulfillment. Donne addresses himself to the image of the lady engraved on his heart: he asks it to leave him, taking his heart too, so that, being abandoned to sense, he may enjoy sexual possession in a dream (in reality, his lady is chaste, and in any case real possession brings remorse); then Donne, changing his mind, invites the image to stay, declaring that he would rather be "Mad with much *heart,* then *ideott* with none." Donne's tone derives in part from his disillusioned belief that "true joyes at best are *dreame* enough," and from his preference, in a world of clouds, for the madness of love.[4] But it also derives in part from the glorious aura of four exalted Neoplatonic theories: the lady engraved on the poet's heart (1. 1); the image which is a truer object of love than the lady (1. 1—here emphasizing the sense that the world is merely a dream); the lover made noble by bearing the lady's image (1. 6); and love as a divine madness.[5] It is these theories which provide that note of heroic aspiration which, with Donne's disillusion, is the dialectic of the poem.

There are Neoplatonic doctrines throughout the *Songs and*

Sonets: for example, the kiss that mingles souls ("The Expiration," 1. 2), amorous resurrection ("The Canonization," st. 3), love's miraculous powers ("A Valediction: of my name, in the window," 11. 11-12), amorous union, and death from unrequited love. They generally function to elevate love. The point can be made through a study of "The Extasie."

The primary task of the expositor of "The Extasie"—as, indeed, of most of Donne's poems—is to discover its occasion. Apparently, "The Extasie" is intended to quiet the troubled emotions Donne's mistress feels upon being told that only asexual ("Neoplatonic") love is good.[6] In "The Extasie," Donne tenderly defends sexual love. He reminds his lady of their first, idyllic consummation; he recalls to her the exaltation of their motives then; and he stresses that in sex they did no more than manifest their spiritual union. Thus he reassures his lady of the propriety of their love.

Donne is concerned not only to reassure his lady, but also to refute her counsellor, and thereby to show their love to be justified in the eyes of the world. He therefore introduces into his lyric two bystanders. The first, whose appearance concludes the descriptive section of the poem, is a pure lover. Donne whimsically elaborates the ethereal, insubstantial quality of this lover—and, by implication, of his sort of love:

> If any, so by love refin'd,
> That he soules language understood,
> And by good love were growen all minde,
> Within convenient distance stood,
> He (though he knew not which soule spake,
> Because both meant, both spake the same)
> Might thence a new concoction take,
> And part farre purer then he came.

The second bystander appears at the conclusion of the dialogue of one. He is a lover "such as wee," capable of contemplating flesh:

> To 'our bodies turne wee then, that so
> Weake men on love reveal'd may looke;
> . . . .

> And if some lover, such as wee,
> Have heard this dialogue of one,
> Let him still marke us, he shall see
> Small change, when we'are to bodies gone.

Concluding his description of the ecstacy, Donne declares that he and his lady are purer than the "good" lover; concluding the dialogue of one, he announces that they need brook no criticism of their love. Thus Donne reassures his lady, and establishes the exalted nature of the love which has been criticized.

To elevate sexual love, Donne employs several Neoplatonic theories. For example, reminding his lady of the ecstasy they enjoyed before sexual consummation, he says:

> So to'entergraft our hands, as yet
> Was all the meanes to make us one,
> And pictures in our eyes to get
> Was all our propagation.

Union and propagation are the two purposes of Neoplatonic love:[7] here their joint presence indicates the completeness of the lovers' passion, while suggesting the inadequacy of the means they have so far used to fulfill it. Again, the idea of amorous ecstasy (or divorce of body from soul),[8] and the idea of amorous union—of a love which "interinaminates two soules" thereby creating an "abler soule"—are both Neoplatonic: they are both used here to establish the purely spiritual basis of the lovers' passion. Thus, to justify love upon the highest ground, Donne turns to Neoplatonic theory.

Indeed, not only in snatches but in its entirety the thought of "The Extasie" is anticipated by the tract writers. A. J. Smith has noted that many Neoplatonists defend sexual love [9] (and thereby refuted those who—presumably reacting to their students' naivety or embarrassment—say that Donne discovered sex). However, to my knowledge no analogues hitherto noted are so close to Donne as those to be found in Speroni and Equicola. For Donne's defense of sexual consummation rests on two grounds: the union of lover' souls; and the necessity of body and soul both in "That subtile knot which makes us man." The second of these arguments appears in Equicola.

In one place, Equicola considers as sexual perverts "the perfidious simulators who impudently declare that they love a beautiful lady, and yet desire no more than to see and hear her." [10] Then, in discoursing upon the mode of enjoying good things, he anticipates Donne:

> There are people who suffer from a new kind of madness. They seek to ignore the body's beauty, and to be kindled only by spiritual beauty, to be satisfied by sight and hearing alone, forgetting that human desire is fulfilled only when the mind has nothing more to desire, when it is totally satisfied: therefore to restrict desire to the eyes and ears is impossible, because love is both of soul and of body, and the operations of soul and body are mutually dependent. . . . The entire philosophy of Aristotle, prince of philosophers, shows the actions of the soul to be joined to those of the body, and those of the body to those of the soul, mingled and united: like wax imprinted on a seal, like sight in the eye's pupil, like matter and form, thus making one thing alone do body and soul combine to form man. . . . Wherefore we say that love is of both the soul and the senses. . . . And whoever speaks of loving only the soul of a beautiful, wise lady is far from the truth, and even further from it is he who speaks of loving only her bodily beauty. We conclude in all cases that to love truly is to love body and soul together, necessarily to love vigorously both the one and the other; and I affirm that in such love one may not be separated from the other. The lover seeks both sensual enjoyment, and to be loved in return. Therefore the lover wants two things: from his lady's soul, love; and from her body, the fruit of love, which fruit, if given by a soul which hates us, makes us angrier than sexual deprivation, for such a sexual consummation destroys our hope for mutual love. [11]

In justifying sexual love against "pure" lovers by man's dual nature, Equicola anticipates "The Extasie." (In arguing that love of the eyes and ears must proceed to sexual desire, he anticipates "Twickman garden"—see above, p. 87) Sperone Speroni anticipates Donne's other argument, the defense of sexual love as an aspect of amorous union:

> Perfect lovers . . . live in others, and die to themselves. Perfect love is like musical harmony or blended perfumes, mingling lovers so that they can be said to be neither two nor one, but two and one. Not content with seeing and hearing our beloved, we strive to satisfy all our senses. For it is from the senses that she passes to our mind, and with her,

subtly, the virtue of the thing which we contemplate as well as love (since we are not merely eyes and hands, but intellect and reason too). If she is such that the lover, contemplating her, delights in her, then the amorous Hermaphrodite is perfect. But in no other way can we form it, since only the senses are the way to the reason. Wherefore he is blind to love who does not care for sex but, as though he were a pure intelligence, seeks to satisfy his mind alone.[12]

These passages clarify "The Extasie." Like Equicola and Speroni, Donne is concerned to refute those who blindly argue that men should love as pure spirits do. (Donne, indeed, points out that even pure spirits operate through matter, and that each intelligence has its sphere.) Like the tract writers, Donne relies upon two principles, amorous union and the dual nature of man. His argument, however, is personal and reminiscent: the lady is reminded of their ecstasy, their union, and their motives (for example, "Wee see by this, it was not sexe,/ Wee see, we saw not what did move.") She is asked to remember the dialogue of one; and it is this dialogue—whose mere existence justifies their physical union—which defends sex. Thus, Donne colors his Neoplatonic doctrines with tender recollection. What is important here, however, is that in "The Extasie," as elsewhere, Donne exalts love through Neoplatonic theories.

Like his philosophic arguments, Donne's conceit operates in a Neoplatonic context. The primary mode of Donne's conceit is the extended consideration of love according to the principles of some other discipline, such as law ("Loves exchange"), physics ("The broken heart"), or religion. A primary aspect of Neoplatonic reasoning is a similar fusion of disciplines. For example, in *Della magia d'amore,* Guido Casoni da Serravalle attempts to prove, as his subtitle says, that "Love is a metaphysician, physicist, astrologist, musicologist, geometrician, arithmetician, grammarian, dialectician, rhetorician, poet, historian, lawyer," and master of virtually all other arts, sciences, and crafts. What Casoni does is to show that the generally accepted principles of love can be translated into the terms of each science. For example, he says that physics is the science of material changes, and that lovers change both by becoming two-in-one, and by dying and being resurrected. (To prove that lovers do so change, he cites various poets.) Then he analyzes amorous change in physical terms: extensively considering, for example, whether it is the lovers' essential or merely their corporal forms which change. When he considers motion, he shows that scientifically there are two kinds, the circular, which is eternal, and the rectilinear, which is mutable; and he says that both motions appear in love, since the lover's thoughts always circle about his lady, while his emotions change from joy to sorrow.[13] In short, he argues that the terms and principles of all sciences apply to love. He thereby provides a philosophic basis for Donne's conceit.

Donne's "A Valediction: of the booke" repeats Casoni's argument. It thus shows that Donne's conceit, far from being odd and perverse, is consistent with the most fashionable philosophy of his time. Donne reflects the continuous interplay in the Renaissance between Neoplatonic tracts and amatory poetry. Neoplatonists substantiate their theories by citing lyrical passages, and lyricists elevate their postures and sharpen their logic by referring to Neoplatonic theories. Donne is such a lyricist.

The Neoplatonic cast of several of his lyrics does not prove that Donne is a philosophical poet, however. The Neoplatonists provide him with a poetic procedure and a learned tone, but his lyrics are no more intended to be contributions to metaphysics than "The Waste Land" to archaeology, or "The Age of Anxiety" to psychology. Indeed, Donne's learning is less esoteric and more fashionable than that of Eliot and Auden, and need reflect no private researches, since such diluted Neoplatonism as his is characteristic of the Renaissance courtly lyric.

Nonetheless, whether because of the occasions which inspire him or because of his need to work each idea through, Donne develops a set of principles which appear repeatedly in his love poems, and which constitute a significant modification of Renaissance love theory. These principles are to be discovered in the corpus of his poetry. To define them, it is necessary first to distinguish between his two subjects: "bestial" (purely sexual) love, and "mixed" (sentimental) love.

Donne's poems of "bestial" love are most of the *Elegies* and such of the *Songs and Sonets* as "Communitie," "Womans Constancy," and "Confined Love." On the face of it, they would seem to be generally earlier than his other lyrics, and the biographical facts we have, though meager, tend to support such dating.[14] There is, however, no reason at all for assuming that Donne's licentious lyrics consistently pre-date those of exalted love: even the Petrarchan commentators recognize the psychological probability that a lover should fall back into a kind of love which he has repudiated, and that the lover of a noble lady should be tempted by less noble women. What is clear is that Donne is fairly constant to the Neoplatonic distinction between bestial and sentimental love.

Three aspects of Donne's purely sexual poems are noteworthy. The first is their flagrant promiscuity. In many Roman elegies, constancy is an involuntary sign of an irresistible passion. In courtly love, it is an essential rule, and a necessary element of the lover's nobility. For the Petrarchists, it is sometimes voluntary and sometimes fated, but always necessary to a love worthy of poetry. In this context, Donne's libertine attitude, like that of Ovid and the later Ronsard, is a striking display of amorous insouciance.

The second notable aspect of these poems is their argumentative and naturalistic bias. Donne attributes his promiscuity not to his own temperament, but to the nature of things. In *Elegie III, Elegie XVII*, "Communitie," and "Confined Love," he argues for promiscuity from the sexual behavior of animals, from the value of change in the universe, from the moral neutrality of women, and from women's physiological capabilities. (In "The Flea" and "The Primrose" he uses analogy—not proof—for the same purpose.) Such arguments, though merely witty and paradoxical, are recurrent, and clearly significant. Their philosophical importance, as Bredvold shows, is that they repudiate Natural Law (the theory that morality is a principle of the universe).[15] Where Neoplatonists elevate love by reference to Ideas, Donne methodically reduces love to an Idea-less thing.

The third noteworthy aspect of these poems is their calculating practicality. Though Donne's *Elegies* are generally thought to imitate Ovid, in this respect they are totally un-Ovidian. Ovid is, of course, eagerly amorous, gaily immoral, and shockingly unaware of the difference between a Roman matron and a Greek courtesan. But his is a sentimental love that keeps him awake at night, makes him jealous, and disturbs his reason; it is very different from Donne's.

The fourth elegy of the first book of the *Amores,* an elegy as close as any of Ovid to those of Donne, precisely shows Ovid's sentimentality. It is an address to Ovid's mistress, who is to come with her husband to a feast that Ovid will attend. Ovid asks her to come early, to mingle with the crowd, to make her husband drunk—to do several things which his eager sensuality suggests from a vague notion that something may come of them. Ovid's main concern is jealousy of the husband. He knows that the lady and her husband will lie together at the dinner; and he insists that she show in every way possible that her heart is with the poet. Finally, jealous lest her husband enjoy her person at home, Ovid asks his mistress to swear to him the next day, whether it be true or not, that she and her husband have slept separately.

Now, this elegy is pure Ovid—an effusion of sophisticated and sensual sentimentality. The poet speaks like a man who will hardly be able to resist touching his lady though her husband be present, and who says he knows not what. His schemes show that he knows the world, but they are not calculated, they have no clear issue— they are merely the demands of his jealous heart. Ovid is sophisticated—he wants his lady to lie to him. He is sexual—he does not pretend that his love is touched by spirituality. And he is unashamed —he is openly jealous of the lady's husband. But he is excited, bewildered, and impassioned.

Characteristically, Donne's *Elegies* are ostentatiously unsentimental. In *Elegie XI,* a slight thing, Donne maintains that he is sorry to have lost his mistress' bracelet only because the bracelet has monetary value. The originality here lies in the conception of an unsentimental lover. The same conception underlies the *Elegies* as a whole. In *Elegie I* Donne, having learned that he and his mistress have been discovered by her husband, consoles her with the thought that they can continue to meet, and that jealousy may kill her husband. In *Elegie IV* Donne, having been discovered by his lady's father, complains that all her escapades are laid on him. In *Elegie VII* Donne, deserted by his mistress, complains solely on the ground that his love-teachings will bear him no fruit, since he will have to find another, untutored, mistress. The *Elegies* do not follow the *Ars Amatoria:* Ovid advises flattery, but Donne outrages his mistress by his certainty that her motives are nasty, and that her conduct has been base. No more do the *Elegies* follow the *Amores.* Dryden says of the *Amores* that they portray the natural movements of the passions, and that their thoughts are "generally such as naturally arise from those disorderly motions of our spirits."[16] Nothing is clearer in Donne's *Elegies* than the fact that their thoughts are neither disordered nor natural consequences of the common passion of love; that they are flagrantly calculated, not wantonly sentimental.

Donne probably means to flaunt his wit and sophistication. But his insistence upon the baseness of his motives often seems instead to be despairing and disillusioned.[17] For it suggests a young man's struggle to adapt his aspirations to a satirically perceived world. Donne appears in fact, as he declares in "Love diet," consciously to transform his love to mere gallantry by reminding himself of the falsity of women. To judge women as Donne and Ovid do is to be faced with the alternatives of forgoing love, of admitting oneself to be helpless, of willfully deluding oneself, or of accommodating one's love to its object. Loving voluntarily, Ovid chooses to be deceived; but Donne suits his sentiments to what he considers the conditions of his love. He sometimes boasts of his cavalier attitude, sometimes scorns his mistress, and sometimes celebrates sex; he never forgets the finitude of his passion. As he says in "Love diet," he has plucked his buzzard love, pruning away illusion. And—unlike Gascoigne, who relegates the occasion and motives of his elegant rhetoric to prose addenda—he emphasizes the satiric elements of his circumstances, and the calculation of his motives.

There are, then, three aspects of Donne's purely sexual poems which are of primary significance: their promiscuity; their abstract, naturalistic arguments; and their insistence that Donne is without illusion. Virtually all Donne's love poems share with these their acceptance of sex, their abstract reasoning, their naturalistic bias, and their attempt at honest self-knowledge.

The same qualities appear in "Farewell to love" and "Loves Alchymie." These are ontologically the last of Donne's unsentimental love poems. (There is no reason to think that they must be chronologically last: the Petrarchan lover renounces his love repeatedly, and ineffectually.) "Farewell to love" describes the decay of love from all the senses to one, and then to "A kind of sorrowing dulnesse to the minde." "Loves Alchymie" asks, "Ends love in this, that my man, / Can be as happy' as I can; If he can / Endure the short scorne of a Bridegroomes play?" Appealing to no standard outside the naturalistic world of the *Elegies,* these poems appraise Donne's motives. "Ah cannot we," Donne asks regretfully in "Farewell to love," "As well as Cocks and Lyons jocund be, / After such pleasures?" In the *Elegies* critics feel Donne to be discontented, perhaps unwittingly; in "Farewell to love" and "Loves Alchymie," Donne explicitly recognizes his discontent with purely sexual love.

These poems announce one of Donne's major themes, the concern for amorous satisfaction. Like Donne, many Neoplatonists argue that purely sexual love is unsatisfying. But satisfaction is not their ultimate criterion of love's worth. For Neoplatonic tracts are generally ontological. They define the various objects of desire, placing them on the scale of Being; and they evaluate each kind of love according to the place of its object: their psychology consists merely of a pronouncement that a love of things low on the scale does or does not lead to a love of things higher. Donne's judgment of love, however, is introspective: he repeatedly asks what emotional satisfaction the lover is to find in love.

Donne's answers to this question are not always consistent; and since his lyrics cannot be dated, the inconsistencies cannot fairly be considered a development. There is, then, danger in systematizing his love theory—especially since his intentions are often casual and generally occasional. Nonetheless, the careful reader of Donne discovers several fairly constant basic principles.

In general, Donne denies that unreturned and asexual love are gratifying (see, for example, "Epistle to the Countesse of Hunting-

ton: That unripe side of earth," 11. 61-76, and "The Blossome").
He denies that purely sexual love is satisfying in "Loves Alchymie"
and "Farewell to love"; and he repeatedly denies that women's souls
are superior and glorious. If Donne is to be accounted a consistent
philosopher of love, then, it is necessary that he justify returned
love and do so upon other grounds than his lady's perfection, corporal or spiritual.

Donne does so. In "Negative love" and "Aire and Angels" he
announces that it is neither his mistress' body nor her soul which
he loves. This negative declaration is in itself a proof that love is
superior to other appetites. But generally Donne goes further: as in
"Aire and Angels," he accepts the Neoplatonic thesis [18] that the object of love is to be loved in return. That is, he accepts Equicola's
thesis (see p. 143 above) that love has two objects, sexual and spiritual union.

Donne develops this theory according to the principles of philosophic idealism. Love is amorous union. So long as lovers want nothing but each other, nothing else exists; so long as they have each
other, they have everything. Thus love does afford ultimate satisfaction; and it is justified without reference to the transcendence either
of the lady's worth, or of love's final cause. Donne's theory is that
a pair of lovers are complete in themselves: that they are a microcosm.

Donne, therefore, frequently uses the image of the microcosm.
The microcosm is man (or, in Donne, a pair of lovers) considered
as a little world. By philosophers and poets, the image is used to
dignify man: and so it is suited to an exaltation of lovers. But to
understand Donne's philosophy rather than his mere rhetoric, one
must consider the microcosm in relation to Being.

Being is primarily a concept of Platonic epistemology. Heraclitus says that nothing can be known, since only the eternal is knowable, and the world is in constant flux. Plato accepts the principle
that the secular world is not Real (i.e., of significance to the mind).
But he argues that there is a world of pure Being, eternal and
knowable, which man perceives or recollects through the world of
flux. Christian Neoplatonists adapt Plato's theory of Being to a con-

tempt for this world and a faith in the Christian afterlife. Concerned less with the mind than with the soul, they say that non-Being is matter, and Being soul. Aquinas accepts the principle that only what is eternal and knowable (ultimately, only God) is fully Real. But, following Aristotle rather than Plato, he denies the antithesis between matter and Reality. He says that form—the principle of eternal, knowable Reality—exists in matter, though imperfectly, and that the material world is the partially realized potentiality for form. He says that matter is Real insofar as it has form, and that it has form insofar as it is single or equally mixed (an inferior form of unity), and eternal.[19] In short, the Platonists argue that the secular world, being formless, lacks significance, and the scholastics that it has significance to the extent that it has form. Their views are important to the microcosm, because that image represents a kind of form.

The microcosm may be used Neoplatonically, as a system of analogies leading from the non-existent material world to Being; or it may be used Thomistically, as a demonstration that there is form in the world. For most Elizabethans, the difference is irrelevant. The microcosm is a moral, not an ontological concept in the beginning of Elyot's *The Governor* and in Ulysses' degree speech in *Troilus and Cressida*: it defines the moral duties of individual men. Donne, however, does not share the humanist's concern for a perfect society. In "Goodfriday, 1613. Riding Westward" and "A Hymn to Christ, at the Authors last going into Germany"—two very fine, characteristic poems—he uses the microcosm Neoplatonically, discovering eternal Christian verities in insignificant facts.

In his love poetry, however, Donne uses the microcosm to attribute Being to love. In "The good-morrow," for example, Donne refers to the philosophical theory that simple and perfectly mixed things are eternal, to show that the amorous microcosm has Being:

> My face in thine eye, thine in mine appeares,
> And true plain hearts doe in the faces rest,
> Where can we finde two better hemispheares
> Without sharpe North, without declining West?
> What ever dyes, was not mixt equally;

> If our two loves be one, or, thou and I
> Love so alike, that none doe slacken, none can die.

"The good-morrow" is the speech of a man newly and triumphantly aware that he is in love, and that his love is returned. Seeing himself reflected in his lady's eyes, and moved by a sense of their intimacy, the lover here considers that his picture on the convex eye of the lady is like the picture of half the world on a globe map; and that her picture on his eye completes the map of their little world. This thought, originating dramatically in the lover's jubilant sense of union and fulfillment, naturally leads to the idea that his world is better than the larger sphere. Here Donne's philosophic intention appears. For him "better" means more Real. Accepting the thesis of the Thomists that Reality is defined by eternity and proportion, he first establishes the proportion of their love (11. 3-4), and then its eternity (11. 5-7). Thus he proves the superior reality of his amorous microcosm.

Besides its Being, the microcosm expresses the isolation and the completeness of Donne's world. From his self-sufficient world of love, Donne magnanimously disdains "the Kings reall, or his stamped face" ("The Canonization"), "Late schoole boyes, and sowre prentices," and "all States, and all Princes," who do "but play us" ("The Sunne Rising"). To him, the only floods which count are those "wee two wept," the only chaos that which lovers grew "when we did show / Care to ought else" ("A nocturnall upon S. Lucies day"). The only real world is "this our Universe" where "Schooles might learne Sciences, Spheares Musick, Angels Verse" ("A Valediction: of the booke"). Donne's *Elegies* are full of fathers sniffing perfumes, mothers testing their daughters' bellies, whispering silks, and lecherous Frenchmen. But many of the *Songs and Sonets* are a withdrawal from the world of greedy, ambitious, battling men to the amorous microcosm.

Like the microcosm, Donne's religious imagery expresses the lovers' contempt for the world, and amorous withdrawal. Among the rest of men, even "graves have learn'd that woman-head / To be to more then one a Bed" ("The Relique"), while "Soldiers finde warres, and Lawyers find out still / Litigious men" ("The Canonization"). But the lovers are saints, secluded and pure. Indeed, it would be "prophanation of our joyes / To tell the layetie our love." Apart from vice and selfishness, the saintly lovers perform the rites of love in their amorous microcosm. Donne celebrates his love by contrasting it to the world at large.

Donne's primary justification of love, however, is based on the complete satisfaction it affords. The lovers are an entire world because they want nothing but each other. When they want other things, they are reduced from a world to two separate chaoses ("A nocturnall upon S. Lucies day"). But love "all love of other sights controules" ("The good-morrow"); and since nothing is but thinking makes it so, "the whole worlds soule" is contracted into their eyes, which do "all to [them] epitomize" ("The Canonization"). So long as the lovers care for nothing but their love, nothing else exists; having their love, they have the entire world. For, by eliminating all other desires, love "makes one little roome, an every where."

Such is Donne's philosophy of love. For if Donne is not a philosophic poet, he is intellectually dogged. When his premises are Ovidian, he follows them wherever they lead. When his premises are Neoplatonic, he follows them, too. His intention in his lyrics is almost always particular, and he is not entirely consistent. But the Neoplatonic terms of his verse, the logical cast of his mind, and his honesty lead him to develop what is surely no inconsiderable theory of love.

In terms of Renaissance philosophy Donne's achievement is almost magnificent. For the two most vital tendencies of Renaissance thought are subjectivism and naturalism: the Protestants, Neoplatonists, and Montaigne are concerned with what men think, more than with what they do; the astronomers, Machiavelli, and Bacon are concerned with what is, more than with what Is. Both philosophic idealism and naturalism appear in the love tracts,[20] but the Neoplatonist's concern for ontology and teleology prevents him from working out their implications. Donne, however, fully reconciles many Neoplatonic theories with both philosophic idealism and an exact observation of lovers as they are. His love theory is thus a real contribution to Renaissance thought.

Seeking as it does spiritual glory in a world which it condemns, and renouncing all satisfaction except that of solitary affection, it is less happy than theories which find divine reflections throughout the natural, social, and political world. But if Donne moderates Neoplatonic faith, he strengthens its emphasis upon observable fact. Certainly today Donne's theory remains one of the most appealing, and least trivial, of Renaissance justifications of love. It is not the least successful attempt to harmonize reason and observation with Neoplatonic glory.

XI

Donne's Neoplatonic Posture

$\mathcal{A}$morous Neoplatonism is fashionable in Italian courts in the sixteenth century, and at the English court under Charles I.[1] Only in a special society is it true, as Dryden claims, that metaphysics ought not to be addressed to ladies. In the Renaissance as in more modern times, the salon is the home of amorous philosophy.

Donne's philosophic posture is not, however, that of the salon, which is primarily an esoteric pose for expressing affected sentiments. In Speroni's "Dialogo d' amore," for example, after hearing that two lovers are one Tullia asks, "How then can the love between Tasso and me be so perfect, making us virtually a hermaphrodite, if he leaves me to follow the nobility of the prince?"[2] Tullia's is the manner of the salon: through a learned quibble she expresses the affected sentiment that Tasso would not leave her if he loved her. In "A Valediction: forbidding mourning," Donne, like Tullia, considers the possibility that lovers may be one although they part. But his Neoplatonism appeals to the fundamental principles which justify his emotions; it expresses his sense of union with his beloved. Thus Donne dignifies the Neoplatonic manner, raising it from witty flirtation to earnest thought and elevated passion. The richness of Donne's Neoplatonic manner can be more fully perceived in "The Canonization."

"The Canonization," like many Provençal poems,[3] answers a man who advises the poet to renounce his love. Donne treats the form with violent emphasis. Love has brought all worldly misfortunes upon him (he admits that the lovers may not be able to "live by love"). Nonetheless, when the subject is broached Donne breaks out, "For Godsake hold your tongue, and let me love." He angrily says that he might as well be chidden for gout or palsy as for love. He exclaims that he will tolerate being flouted for anything—"My five gray haires, or ruin'd fortune"—but not for love. And he scornfully tells his counsellor to busy himself somehow—"Take you a course, get you a place"—and not to meddle with Donne's love. In short, he meets the well-meant advice of a practical man with anger and scorn.

It is his counsellor's interference, not his character, which angers Donne in the first stanza. Nonetheless, that stanza suggests a contrast between Donne, who has lost the world for love, and his counsellor, whose interests are his estate, his talents, and court affairs. This contrast shapes the second stanza. Here, with exorbitant innocence, Donne declares that, though it has ruined him, his love has hurt no one else. "Alas, alas," he cries, "who's injur'd by my love?" His sighs, tears, colds, and heats—the elements of Petrarchan love—have caused no tempests, floods, winters, or plagues to trouble worldly men. As his conceits suggest, Donne's extravagant innocence is ironical. He is angry at base, worldly men who set themselves up as advisors to honest lovers—as the stanza's conclusion shows:

> Soldiers finde warres, and Lawyers finde out still
> Litigious men, which quarrels move,
> Though she and I do love.

Ficino says that love ends lawsuits, theft, homicide, and war.[4] Donne insinuates that worldly men exploit war and litigation; and he bitterly assures his advisor that there is no need to fear that Donne's love will end such profitable pursuits.

The final two stanzas defend the unworldliness of the lovers. They say that if the lovers cannot live by love, they will die for it; and that if they have no chronicles and tombs, they will be satisfied with sonnets and an urn (perhaps, as Horst S. Meller suggests, referring to the commonplace that Laura's ashes, in an urn, are immortalized by Petrarch's sonnets).[5] And they declare that, once dead, the lovers will be canonized and invoked, because in a raging world they alone knew the peace of true love. Thus Donne defends his love. His counsellor tells him that love is unwise: Donne scorns his wisdom and dedicates himself to a higher truth.

The key stanza of "The Canonization," the most discussed and the most puzzling, is the third. In the 1633 text, this reads:

> Call us what you will, wee are made such by love;
> Call her one, mee another flye,
> We'are Tapers too, and at our owne cost die,
> And wee in us find the' Eagle and the Dove,
> The Phoenix ridle hath more wit
> By us, we two being one, are it.
> So, to one neutrall thing both sexes fit.
> Wee dye and rise the same, and prove
> Mysterious by this love.

This stanza is central not only to "The Canonization," but also to the question of how sex functions in all Donne's lyrics. For many expositors assume that by "die" Donne virtually always refers to sexual consummation. Several scholars have denounced this view, arguing, in effect, that the Elizabethan "die," like the modern "make," has a sexual meaning only in a few, very clearly marked, instances. But this stanza seems to make sense only if "die" is sexual. And if Donne faces the contumely of fortune with the assertion that his orgasms make him glorious, he is as introverted as the New Critics think him to be. If the meaning of "die" is sexual here, it may be so anywhere in Donne.

The problem of interpretation is so acute as to have raised editorial questions. Grierson, who follows the 1633 text wherever he can,[6] makes no sense of it here; in line 7, therefore, he omits the comma after "so," and substitutes a comma for the period after "fit"—thereby suggesting a sexual meaning for "dye." Later editors —Hebel and Hudson, Shaaber, Hayward, and Bennett—follow Grierson. And Williamson's defense of the 1633 text is unconvincing.[7] He attributes line 7 to Donne's interlocutor, reading it as "If you are one, prove it by fitting both sexes to one thing." But line 7, unlike line 1 (which Williamson considers analogous), contains no syntactical indication that it is not the speech of the lover; and Donne's general practice does not admit of such unmarked inter- polations. As Williamson presumes, it would be desirable to find an acceptable reading of the 1633 text; but none has been found.

Furthermore, the stanza is full of obscure emblems. The moth in the flame, the eagle, the dove, and the phoenix are all frequent in emblem books, and some emblematic meanings seem relevant: for example, the eagle as virtue tired by wandering, or the dove as true love.[8] (One hitherto unnoted parallel is especially apt: Equicola says that the eagle and dove symbolize the marriage of Voluptuous- ness with Sorrow.[9]) But, because they lack clearly stated explica- tions, Donne's images are not truly emblematic.[10] And if they were, they would be fantastically ambiguous: the dove, for example, may be anything from Christian resurrection to marital fidelity, or from contemplation to an alchemical reaction.[11] Donne's images, then, strongly suggest emblems; yet neither their form nor their meaning is illuminated by emblem books.

The stanza presents still another problem. As they are usually interpreted,[12] lines 2 through 5 each refer to separate emblems: the moth in the flame; the burning taper; the eagle and dove; and the phoenix. According to this interpretation, lines 2 and 3 each present an emblem of self-destruction; and line 4 begins the lover's defense with a contrasting emblem. However, Donne's syntax does not con- form to such a reading. The "And" beginning line 4 suggests that line 3 and line 4 reinforce, not contradict, each other; the emphatic difference between "Call her" and "We'are" indicates that Donne's defense begins with line 3, not line 4. The stanza, then contains four problems: the meaning of "die"; the punctuation after "so" and "fit"; the meaning of moth, eagle, and phoenix; and the syntactical direction of lines 2-4. Upon the solution of these problems depend major critical issues—Donne's use of sex, the nature of his irony, and the emblematic quality of his images.

Its images suggest that Donne's stanza is Petrarchan. Most amorous emblems are derived from Petrarch and therefore have poetic analogues.[13] For example, Lederer refers Donne's line 4 to an emblem in which an eagle swooping down on a caged dove signifies future ill-fortune. Ultimately, this emblem may derive from the Provençal image of the falcon Love swooping down on the lover's heart;[14] its Petrarchan quality is indicated by its motto, which is a line by Petrarch, and by the virtually identical conceit of Tansillo's "Come augellin, ch' umane note finge." Similarly, all the images of Donne's stanza have Petrarchan parallels. They are structurally like Petrarchan conceits, without motto-like explications. And they take a clear meaning in the light of Petrarchan usage.

The Petrarchan analogues, some presented below, show Donne's stanza to rest on the contrast between moth in flame, and phoenix: a contrast traditionally employed to argue that love is life-giving, not destructive. They thereby indicate a probability that lines 2-3 are both about the moth in the flame: and so they are. For what Donne says is that his opponent may call the lovers moths burning in tapers, but, since each is the taper in which the other burns, it is not his opponent who will have to pay the candle. (In stanza 2, there is a similar insinuation that the man counsels Donne only because he is afraid that love may interfere with his affairs: and throughout Donne is bitter about the practicality of his advisor.) Line 4 continues the defense begun in line 3, declaring that from their point of view the lovers are not moths at all, but eagle and dove: from at least the time of the "Song of Solomon," the dove is a symbol of a beloved lady; and the eagle is a stock Petrarchan symbol of the high-minded lover whose eyes are eternally fixed on his beloved lady (see 11. 40-43 for the fixity of the lovers' gaze).[15] The stanza concludes with the assertion that the silly riddle of the phoenix makes sense when it is interpreted as referring to the lovers: for the phoenix is unique, sexless, and self-resurrecting, and so are the lovers. Thus, Donne denies that the lovers are moths to assert that they are the phoenix.

Stanza 3, then, is transitional. It begins angrily and defensively, saying that if the lovers are moths in flames, that is no business of anyone but themselves. Then it moves to a glorious statement of love's mysteries, establishing the ground for the final conceit of the poem, the lovers' canonization. The heart of the stanza is the assertion that the lovers are like the phoenix through their union

(1. 6); their sexual neutrality (1. 7); and their resurrection (1. 8). Each of these similarities assumes a Neoplatonic theory.

The first is the Neoplatonic commonplace that two lovers are one. The second is that, as Speroni says, their union is hermaphroditic:

> perfect love . . . perfectly ties and conjoins two lovers, so that, losing their individualities, they are both fused into one new being—just like Salmacis and Hermaphroditus. This miraculous union of two beings is referred to by our poets in various ways [here Speroni cites Petrarch]. . . . Thence, similarly, arise all those privileges of lovers, freed and different (as it is said) from all natural laws; and especially this one, that they live in others and die in themselves.[16]

Though the conception of the amorous hermaphrodite derives from Aristophanes' speech in Plato's *Symposium,* in the Renaissance its sense is spiritual rather than sexual. Its Renaissance meaning is made clear by Leone Ebreo, who thus explains why true amorous desire is increased, not satiated, by sexual fulfillment:

> such love is a desire for perfect union between lover and beloved, which union is impossible without total interpenetration. This is possible in souls, which are incorporeal: for pure spirits can interpenetrate, unite, and become one through mental means, which are most effective. But in separate bodies, which return to separate places, such union and penetration of the beloved increases the desire for union, for it cannot be perfectly achieved. And the mind, which *does* achieve an entire union with the beloved, leaving itself and becoming her, is left more desirous and anguished than before because it cannot have perfect bodily union.[17]

Expressing this theory through the image of the hermaphrodite, Guarino distinguishes true union from mere mixture: he says that the hermaphroditic fusion of lovers' souls is true union, and their sexual embraces, ending always in separation, a mere mixture.[18] Such analogues show Donne's second parallel of lovers to phoenix, to be Neoplatonic; and they also show his defense of love to be on higher grounds than that of the orgasm.

The third point that Donne makes is that lovers "dye and rise the same." This, too, is a Renaissance cliché. As Mario Equicola says, the Provençal poet conventionally asserts that the lover dies in his lady's radiance like a moth in a flame, and that he dies and is reborn a hundred times a day.[19] Pre-Petrarchan poets, inclined to peregrine comparison, early associate this conceit with the phoenix. Giovanni d'Arezzo, for example, says in "L' uscel fenice quando ven' al morire" that, like the phoenix, he dies and is recreated in the fire of his unfulfilled love. And in "Sicomo il parpaglion, ch' a tal natura," Jacopo da Lentini says that, foolishly ignoring the dangers of his lady's radiance, he draws near her like a moth to a flame; and that, being burnt in the sweet flame, he, like a phoenix, is brought back to life by his lady's beauty.[20] A similar conceit appears in Petrarch's "Come tal ora al caldo tempo sole," which Castelvetro refers to a sonnet of Dante da Maiano on the lover dying like a moth in a flame, and to a tercet of the more famous Dante on men as worms born to form angelic butterflies.[21] By the sixteenth century, the lover's phoenix-like death and rebirth is a commonplace of sentimental love poetry.[22]

The Neoplatonic philosophers explain this conceit. (Their concern with the lyric is clear in the many Neoplatonic explications of Petrarch, and in such a work as Casoni's, where several poets are cited to prove that lovers are indeed killed and resurrected.[23]) The great explanation is Ficino's. Ficino says that since thinking is the function of the soul, by thinking only of his beloved the lover dies to himself. He says that, however, when love is returned the lover is given his lady's soul instead of his own. And thus, he says, love is both death and resurrection.[24]

These Neoplatonic ideas, surely, are the heart of Donne's justification of love. They explain the 1633 punctuation of line 7. There is a comma after "so" because the word refers back to line 6: "by being one, we fit both sexes to one neutral thing." And there is a period after "fit" because the line is self-sufficient—one of three independent parallels between lovers and phoenix.

More important than the editorial problem, however, is the general tenor of the poem. Donne is given practical advice—told that his love is ruining his worldly prospects. He replies, in his first two stanzas, by scorning the practical values of his counsellor; in his third, by asserting that love recreates, not destroys, the lovers;

and, in his fourth and fifth stanzas—with a characteristic movement from Neoplatonism to realism and subjectivity—by declaring that if indeed the lovers cannot live by love, they will be glad to die for it, and that when they have died they will be worshipped as love's martyrs.

In adapting the Neoplatonic posture to such a dramatic context, and to a sense that the world oppresses true love, Donne is highly original. The quality of his originality may be highlighted by a review of some Petrarchan analogues. In "Qual più diversa e nova," for example, the phoenix appears in one of the many miraculous metamorphoses which Petrarch claims to have undergone through love. The conceit is used to elevate Petrarch's story, and to distinguish him from common men:

> Whatever most strange and unheard-of thing
>   ever existed in even the most uncanny regions,
>   that thing, if one judges rightly,
>   is most like me: to such a state have I come, Love.
> There where the day comes forth
>   there flies a bird that, unique and without consort,
>   from a willing death
>   is reborn, and recreated, entirely alive.
> Similarly alone is my desire,
>   and similarly on the summit
>   of its high thoughts it turns to the sun,
>   and similarly crumbles,
>   and similarly returns to its original condition;
>   it burns and dies, and retakes its body,
>   and then lives, a rival of the phoenix.

Petrarch elevates his love by showing its many mysterious parallels to the phoenix. Serafino uses the conceit of the lover's death and resurrection more prosaically. For example, in Sonnet 31, "Mercé, madonna, ahimé, ch' io son infermo," having fallen down at a dance, Serafino says that he was stricken dead by love; but he assures his lady that he will be on his feet in a minute, since love resurrects as well as kills. He uses the phoenix as an authoritative emblem supporting absurdly prosaic gallantry in Strambotto 106, "O morte: o la: soccorri: ecco che arrivo." [25]

Lover: Oh Death! *Death:* Yes? *L:* Help! *D:* Lo, I am here;
Why do you call? *L:* I burn. *D:* Who burns you? *L:* Love.
D: What can I do? *L:* Take my life.
D: Why, I kill you continually. *L:* Not me. *D:* Just ask your heart.
L: Heart! *Heart:* What is it? *L:* Are you dead? *H:* Sometimes dead,
   sometimes alive.
L: But what can you mean? *H:* Alas! *L:* Was a dead man ever reborn?
H: Only I. *L:* Then, Death, what can I do? Bit by bit,
like a phoenix I renew myself in the fire.

Some Petrarchists give the conceit a Neoplatonic bias. In the
first of two consecutive sonnets, Pamphilo Sasso, asking his lady
not to look at him, says that, since her beauty is too great for his
soul, her glance destroys him like a moth in a flame; in the second,
asking his lady to look at him, he says that even if he cannot com-
prehend all her beauty, her glance revivifies him like a phoenix in
the fire of love. G. B. Amalteo, praising his lady's eyes, says that
they make him a phoenix, burning him until he is dead to himself and resurrected in her. And V. Menni says that his lady's eyes,
which adorn the world and guide all men to the heavenly path, are
the sun,

> Et io fenice son, ch' al tuo bel raggio
> Rinasco e moro mille volte il giorno

> (And I am the phoenix, that in your beautiful ray
> die and am reborn a thousand times a day.)[26]

These poets associate the conceit of the phoenix with Neoplatonic
ideas—with divine Beauty, spiritual resurrection, and the Neoplatonic ladder. Their purpose, however, is panegyric, and their posture
that of extravagant adoration.

Perhaps the most precise analogue of Donne's stanza is Guarino's Madrigal 37, "Una farfalla cupida, e vagante." Guarino uses
the Neoplatonic conceit for elegant sentimentalizing. He treats it
as a catalyst to heroic and elegant folly, a reminder that causes him
to rededicate himself to his torment with fatuous ardor:

> My loving heart has been made
> a wandering moth, filled with desire,

that goes, as though in play,
dancing around the fire
of two lovely eyes, and so many, many times
does it fly away and back, and flee and return, and circle,
that in the beloved light
it will at last leave both its life and its wings.
But who sighs at that
sighs wrongly. Dear, fortunate ardor ["flame" and "passion"],
it will die a moth, and rise a phoenix.

As these analogues indicate, to prove that the lovers are superior to the counsels of reason (i.e., "mysterious," 1. 27), Donne cites three similarities between lover and phoenix: their unity; the sexlessness of their joint being; and their revivification. Each of these similarities involves a paradox, and thus elevates love through the conventional theme of "loves magique." [27] There is nothing novel in Donne's argument or in his imagery.

The greatness of "The Canonization" lies instead in its posture. For other poets, the Neoplatonic conceit is elegant: it elevates a story (Petrarch), magnifies a lady (Menni), or refines sentiments (Guarino). But in Donne it is a dramatically vital statement of principle. The beleaguered lover, his fortunes blighted and his mind troubled, turns in anger upon his advisor: spurning his counsel and scorning his values, he reveals his innermost beliefs—he declares his faith in love. Neoplatonism here takes on a fully dramatic value as a declaration of the principles by which lovers live in a hostile world. And the Neoplatonic posture provides Donne with a fine translunary flight—from bitter anger to a sublime statement of faith.

"The Canonization," then, shows what Donne's Neoplatonism contributes to his manner. "The Canonization" is a poem of complex motives, conflicting themes, and full vision. The lover is bitter, desperate, and dedicated; there is as much satire as panegyric in his tone, as much evil as good in his world. In such a poem, Neoplatonism resounds as it does not in the stylized, narrow world of the minor Petrarchists; and the Neoplatonic posture becomes truly heroic.

"The Canonization," too, shows the flexibility of Donne's Neoplatonic posture. Here he is a desperate man touched upon a sore spot. In "A Valediction: forbidding mourning," he is a tender lover consoling his dear lady, who weeps at their parting. In "The goodmorrow," he is a good, blunt fellow exalted by the discovery that he loves and is loved. In "The Sunne Rising," he is a joyful man awakening after a first night of love. In "The Extasie," he is a reasonable man calming his troubled lady. In all these poems, the basic situation is commonplace, the emotions ordinary: none is highly stylized and aristocratic. In each, the importance of the situation is purely subjective. And in each the realistic situation becomes incandescent, the commonplace lover transcendent, when he adopts a Neoplatonic posture.

A minor aspect of Donne's Neoplatonic manner, but one which deserves attention, is his confrontation of Neoplatonic theory with discordant facts. Throughout the sixteenth-century tracts, there is a disparity between high-flown theorizing, and clear-sighted observation of men and manners. Even Castiglione, who admires Bembo's Neoplatonic enthusiasm, adapts his theories to a workable standard of conduct.[28] Other tracts move from theological and cosmological theories to practical advice about courtship, marriage, and beauty aids.[29] Thus, the tracts frequently conjoin Neoplatonism with realistic observation.

Often the friction involved in this conjunction is made explicit. In Leone's tract, for example, the exalted effusions of Philo are repeatedly interrupted by his witty, amused, and well-inclined lady, who notes the ill-accord between Philo's theory and his gallant pretensions: asking, for example, why Philo courts her affection, when the object of love is an eternal Idea; or why, daydreaming, he failed to notice her, if she is the center of his thoughts.[30] Similarly, in Speroni's tract Tullia asks how it can be that lovers are one, if they leave each other. And in her own "Della infinità di amore," she asks Varchi how it can be that love is eternal, as Neoplatonists say, when she knows by experience that men are inconstant. (The interplay between the spirited, intelligent courtesan and the renowned logician is delightful. Varchi makes Tullia admit that the noun "love," unlike the verb "to love," does not change with time; and that all lovers profess their love to be eternal, while it is senseless to ask anyone not in love about his love. Varchi concludes that love is eternal, Tullia, with irony, that logic is indeed the hand of God.) Quibbling thus, the tracts often note disparities between Neoplatonic theory and observed fact.

Donne's themes are often similar. For example, "A Valediction: forbidding mourning" shows that lovers are one, although they part. "The Dissolution" shows that one lover may die and the other live, although they are one. And "The Anniversarie" shows that love is eternal although, as Christian dogma teaches, lovers die and are judged. Clearly, however, in these lyrics the Neoplatonic juxtaposition of theory with observation is not a quibble, but a fusion of exalted love with a broadly human awareness. This aspect of Donne's Neoplatonic posture may be seen in "Loves growth" and "Lovers infinitenesse."

In "Loves growth," Donne finds that, while theory makes love out to be infinite and unchanging, actually his love has grown. Naively, he is disturbed by his discovery:

> Me thinkes I lyed all winter, when I swore,
> My love was infinite, if spring make' it more.

With surprise, he finds that

> Love's not so pure, and abstract, as they use
> To say, which have no Mistresse but their Muse,
> But as all else, being elemented too,
> Love sometimes would contemplate, sometimes do.

(For this last line, cf. Speroni, pp. 143-44 above, who claims that we contemplate the lady as well as enjoy her sensually, since we are not all eyes and hands, but mind too.) Then, having stated the problem, Donne solves it. First he claims that his love has not really grown, but merely become more conspicuous. Finally, with a characteristic movement towards realism, he says that if it has grown, yet it will never diminish:

> And though each spring doe adde to love new heate,
> As princes doe in times of action get

> New taxes, and remit them not in peace,
> No winter shall abate the springs encrease.

As Donne's conclusion indicates, his real purpose is not to solve a Neoplatonic problem, but to declare his ever-growing, eternal love. His concern with the discrepancy between love's infinity and its growth is an element of posture. It has two functions. First, it highlights the purity of his love, which seems tainted even by love's increase. Second, it permits a gentle irony: the pretendedly naive discovery that mere theorists are wrong. This irony shows Donne to be reasonable, and so—like his final acceptance of the fact that love grows—it makes his confession of love more convincing. Thus, the Neoplatonic quibble, both in its sentimentality and in its irony, supports Donne's final statement of eternally growing love: it creates the posture of a reasonable but dedicated lover.

Neoplatonic questioning has a similar effect in "Lovers infinitenesse." Here Donne is concerned with the possibility of complete possession. Through elaborate argument, he shows that he can not legally claim all his lady's love; he says that, even if he could, he would not want a total love since his growing love requires growing rewards; and, in conclusion, he finds the solution to his problem not in possession, but in union:

> But wee will have a way more liberall,
> Then changing hearts, to joyne them, so wee shall
> Be one, and one anothers All.

In "Loves growth," Donne's Neoplatonic questioning is a pretense which emphasizes his devotion, permits an ironic excursion, and so establishes the posture of a common-sense lover. The legal quibbling in "Lovers infinitenesse" has a similar function. Donne is perfectly satisfied by his love. To show the infinity of his aspiration, he adopts the pose of a man troubled because he cannot have all his lady's love. Each difficulty reflects the needs of his jealous heart. And the final solution is an affectionate affirmation of the value of his love. It conforms to Neoplatonic theories: to amorous union, and love as the object of love. It conforms, too, to Donne's repeated statements that, in the amorous microcosm, lovers are "one anothers

All." But its primary function is to reveal to the lady Donne's faith in their love: the infinity of his needs, and the totality of his satisfaction.

In "Loves growth" and "Lovers infinitenesse," then, Donne makes Neoplatonic quibbles reflect a tenderness towards his lady, a broadly human awareness, and rich sentimentality. As in "The Canonization," "A Valediction; forbidding mourning," and elsewhere, he emphasizes his common sense through irony and a recognition of difficulties, and his emotions through a Neoplatonic posture.

Once or twice in his poems of sentimental love, as several times in his libertine lyrics, Donne concerns himself primarily with a general definition of love. "Aire and Angels" is such a poem, and it is interesting to see in it the interplay between philosophical questioning and extravagant manner:

> Twice or thrice had I loved thee,
> Before I knew thy face or name,
> So in a voice, so in a shapelesse flame,
> *Angells* affect us oft, and worship'd bee;
>   Still when, to where thou wert, I came,
> Some lovely glorious nothing I did see.
>   But since my soule, whose child love is,
> Takes limmes of flesh, and else could nothing doe,
>   More subtile then the parent is,
> Love must not be, but take a body too,
>   And therefore what thou wert, and who,
>   I bid Love aske, and now
> That it assume thy body, I allow,
> And fixe it selfe in thy lip, eye, and brow.
>
> Whilst thus to ballast love, I thought,
> And so more steddily to have gone,
> With wares which would sinke admiration,
> I saw, I had loves pinnace overfraught,
>   Ev'ry thy haire for love to worke upon
> Is much too much, some fitter must be sought;
>   For, nor in nothing, nor in things
> Extreme, and scatt'ring bright, can love inhere;
>   Then as an Angell, face, and wings

> Of aire, not pure as it, yet pure doth weare,
>   So thy love may be my loves spheare;
>   Just such disparitie
>   As is twixt Aire and Angells puritie,
> 'Twixt womens love, and mens will ever bee.

Essentially, "Aire and Angels" is a definition of the object of love.[31] It argues that the real object of love is neither the lady's body nor her soul, but her love. Donne's argument conforms to the Neoplatonic consensus that the object of love is union; to Ficino's declaration that love alone wants only itself in return;[32] and to Equicola's statement that the lover wants love from his lady's soul, and sexual satisfaction from her body (see p. 143 above). It also conforms to the principles Donne himself states elsewhere: lines 8-10 agree with lines 56-68 of "The Extasie" that love, like the soul, must take a body; and "Aire and Angels" in its entirety says, what Donne says often, that love is not admiration of beauty, either bodily or spiritual, but a union of hearts.

In "Aire and Angels," however, these principles are stated with a sharp sense of the lady's inadequacy. The interplay between Neoplatonism and skepticism is reflected in a delightful, and most characteristic, manner. In "Aire and Angels" as in "The Legacie," Donne assumes an attitude of overwhelming devotion, and begins a search. He encounters various difficulties in his search: he tries to love his lady as pure spirit, but finds her too intangible; he tries to love her body, but cannot really care for all of it; and he settles on her love as the object of his affections, though her love is less pure than his own. Throughout, he has nothing but praise for his lady: her pure spirit, lovely and glorious, works angelically; her bodily beauty, scattering bright, overwhelms admiration. But Donne's devotion is perpetually disappointed; and it is not really surprising when he finally concludes, with epigrammatic point, that woman's love is ever less pure than man's. This conclusion echoes the Renaissance cliché that the lover is more divine than the beloved;[33] but it also reveals Donne's disappointment.

As Donne's pretense of searching for the object of love indicates, the feeling behind "Aire and Angels" is a slight dissatisfaction with love, a sense that there ought really to be something else in it: a restlessness. That is, the balance between love's aspiration and its rewards is slightly different in "Aire and Angels" from what it is in "Lovers infinitenesse." Now, Donne's feeling, while easy to discuss, is most difficult to express. But Donne expresses it brilliantly in a fusion of breathless adoration with repeated, mildly disappointing, discoveries.

In "Aire and Angels," then, the Neoplatonic question of love's object—as in "Loves Growth" the question of its infinity—provides Donne with a mannered, elevated posture. And, through that posture, he precisely expresses one of the feelings which a common-sense lover may have.

Donne adapts the Neoplatonic manner to a variety of feelings, and to a reasonable analysis of emotional questions. A study of his Neoplatonic posture reveals two aspects of his greatness: the flexibility and mastery with which he develops stylized poses; and the richness with which he fuses a broadly human awareness with esoteric theories and exalted sentiments.

XII

Conclusion

The *Songs and Sonets* are elegant, extravagant, and fashionable. Their conceits are precious—death for love, pictures on hearts, floods of tears, and amorous union. Their method of deducing things from these conceits as from scientific principles is affected and sentimental. The *Songs and Sonets* reflect the elaborate manners, the sentimental affectation, and the neat wit of courtly Petrarchists.

Insofar as Donne is clever and courtly, he is a wit. He is also, however, a poet; and he dignifies the Petrarchan manner in three ways. First, he civilizes it. As Molière shows in various *précieux,* extravagant affectation often offends true elegance and good sense. In Donne, however, if nowhere else, it is rich, flexible, and poised. Its exaggerations are never fatuous or gauche. They are brilliantly suited to their social purposes.

Second, Donne makes the Petrarchan language significant. In that language, as developed by the *quattrocentisti,* tropes become facts, facts tropes, and everything leads to unexpected conclusions. But, for all their conclusions, the quattrocentists' lyrics do not go anywhere: they use six subtle arguments to prove that an artichoke is a symbol of love. Their elaborate and rigorous logic has no purpose outside of itself: Accolti writes about his lady's gift of an artichoke because a gift deserves a return; his poem is that return, and its logic shows only its author's cleverness. In Donne, however, the confusion between tropes and facts becomes a rich way of fusing sentiment with observation; and the extended Petrarchan conceit is made significant at every point.

Third, Donne makes the Petrarchan manner more conscious. For Bemboists, the lover must be naive; for witty Petrarchists, he must be affected. Their sophistication may appear in the narrative frame or social purpose of their lyrics, but these poets express simple emotions. By irony or dramatically defined enthusiasm, Donne incorporates a sophisticated awareness in his individual lyrics. Thus he transforms courtly wit to poetry, and fuses clever poise with serious statement.

Donne, then, modifies the techniques of the past and contributes to those of the future; he reflects and enriches his contemporary culture. In Petrarchism he finds a means of expressing his personality. Like the *symbolisme* attributed to him half a century ago, his Petrarchism has profound consequences for critical theory, poetical taste, and literary history.

Donne's use of Renaissance love conventions instances the rich originality which even rigid conventions admit. Modern critics often conceive of tradition as a cultural attic from which the poet may select esoteric doctrines and striking phrases. By writing greatly within a traditional context, Donne reveals that great poetry may be conventional.

He also shows that the thoughtful poet may accept the tastes and ideas of his time. Themselves in revolt against nineteenth-century values, modern critics are as suspicious of conformity as modern politicians of communism. At a hint that Donne inclines towards Petrarchism, they grow desperately casuistical: George Williamson, for example, perceives that Donne gives "the illusion of using Petrarchan conventions" and concludes that this is "the *coup de grâce* of his anti-Petrarchism." [1] However, in the Renaissance Petrarchism is vital both emotionally and philosophically.[2] Donne demonstrates its vitality; and he thereby reveals the great poet's dependence upon the culture of his time.

Furthermore, Donne's Petrarchan lyrics may remind critics of the importance of consonance in poetic imagery. Ignoring their conventional context, critics have found Donne's images to be discordant. Samuel Johnson, for example, appeals beyond Petrarchism to Universal Reason. But his Reason is in fact no more than a special taste for neoclassical urbanity.[3] Our reason does not reveal that a lady is like the moon and unlike the leg of a compass; and if reason falters, surely twentieth-century connotations are no guide to the Renaissance—when compasses, for example, had the aura of the modern microscope, not that of the ferula. Seen truly, the metaphysical conceit need not conjoin disparate things but may, indeed, compare a lady to the moon:

> O more then Moone,
> Draw not up seas to drowne me in thy spheare,
> Weepe me not dead, in thine armes.
> ("A Valediction: of weeping")

Especially in a Petrarchan context, Donne's conceits are not radical.

Donne's Petrarchism thereby suggests that (as Coleridge saw) it is the union—not the conjunction—of opposites which critics need study. Poets unify opposites in various ways. The mystic vision sees the world in a grain of sand. Denigrative irony yokes Cleopatra and her barge with a neurotic woman. Exaggerated emotions conceive a footman to be an eternal judge, and London Bridge a hell. Muscular transcendentalism declares that "Love has built his mansion in/ The place of excrement." And archetypal symbols show Teresias behind a fraudulent fortune-teller who sniffles. There are a host of special conventions—Petrarchism and Neoplatonism among them—each providing a mode of uniting that which, from an exoteric standpoint, appears disparate. Surely, the task of the literary critic is to find the particular mode of union in a poem.

Taking the opposite course, New Critics argue that poetry conjoins radically disparate things, so as to shock and thereby to broaden awareness. They see in the *Songs and Sonets* a senseless world where everything flies in the face of everything else. They are profoundly disturbed that a man with five gray hairs (query: a full head of hair beginning to turn gray?) should still enjoy sex, and that a lover should refer to saints, goddesses, and ecstasies. But surely their reactions are naive, as bald men will attest and popular songs reveal. Though his critics may find the world to be full of irreconcilability, Donne, after all, has a more unified sensibility.

Many critical questions remain. What, for example, is the relation between Donne's statements and reality: do they declare general propositions, reflect mental processes, or act, without either signifying or imitating? How does Donne indicate his situation, purpose, and attitude? Are there genres of lyric in the *Songs and Sonets* and, if so, what are they? What are the levels of style Donne employs, and what themes and images does he associate with each? I have treated some of these issues; I hope that other critics will resolve them.

However, Donne's Petrarchism does have clear implications for criticism. For the interpreter of Donne, it indicates the importance of the macroscopic questions; it emphasizes that the poetic context includes not merely isolated words, no matter how rich, but also statement, drama, gesture, and convention. For critics at large, it indicates the value of conventions, and the importance of unity. It suggests that poetry is the fruit of culture—not the indigestion which that fruit may provoke.

Properly understood, Donne's lyrics may also encourage a taste for confident poetry. Donne is not shaken by the knowledge that taxation is inequitable, or that courtiers take purgatives: despite these facts, he finds it easy to be tender to his lady and happy in his love. Some decades ago he was thought to be a hard-boiled romantic, wounded but defiant. In fact, however, Donne is not desperately cynical, fiercely truthful, or harshly amorous. He promises eternal love, heavenly reward, and peace transcending the world's hostility. He delights in fantasies: a dialogue of airborne souls overheard by a pure spirit transmuted by love; magical waters flowing from a petrified lover; an armlet maintaining the corpse of a man who died for love. He wages no war against women: his lyrics assume a masculine superiority too secure to need emphasis, and his epistles profess that polite subservience to ladies which is ashes to the mouth of many a modern critic. Though Donne is intelligent, he does not hate himself; though he is capable of anger and transcendence, he is well-bred; though he recognizes unpleasantness, he senses no universal decay. If an appreciation of Donne were to encourage a taste for similar poetry, surely some critics who praise his unified sensibility would be pleased.

Donne's Petrarchism bears upon critical practice and poetical taste. Historically, it must affect the concept of metaphysical poetry. Some decades ago, critics composed a dogma from the clichés of late-nineteenth-century appreciation—"complexity of feeling," "thought and passion," "dramatic realism," and "masculine wit" [4]—and from some new phrases, such as "radical image" and "the metaphysical shudder." Today their aesthetic slogans, never truly critical, are worn out. Essential similarities are no longer found among poets so diverse as Donne, Traherne, Godolphin, Crashaw, and Cowley. Crashaw is shown to be dissimilar to Donne by Austin Warren; Herbert is linked to an older tradition by Rosemund Tuve; [5] and no one can show that Traherne shares anything essential with Donne. Crashaw and Vaughan admired Herbert for dedicating his poems to God, and Donne knew Herbert's mother; but that no longer seems sufficient to establish the existence of a metaphysical school.

Properly, therefore, modern studies like Alvarez' seek the metaphysical style in secular poetry. They note that Sir Edward Herbert, Aurelian Townshend, Sir Francis Kynaston, Thomas Randolph, Thomas Stanley, William Habington, Sidney Godolphin, John Cleveland, Thomas Carew, and Abraham Cowley often echo or resemble Donne. [6] These are not, however, poets of magnificent passion, profound thoughts, unified sensibility, or the metaphysical shudder; and so it is necessary to redefine the metaphysical style. Donne's Petrarchism suggests an adequate definition. What these poets share is the logical, extended, often unsentimental, and sometimes libertine development of Petrarchan conceits—of love's wars, excommunicants, rebels, unions, and worlds. They share what Cleveland—himself a practitioner of the style—calls "the bastard Phrase" of "Beggars of the rhyming Trade": [7]

> Balm, Elixir, both the India's,
> Of Shrine, Saint, Sacrifice, and such as these,
> Expressions common as your mistresses.

These are the tropes, the "Tinsoyl'd Metaphors of Pelf," which Donne [8] makes available to the minor Stuart amorists, by adapting

175

them to new tones and purposes: to an elegant, sophisticated, and flexible manner. Once the sophisticated Petrarchism of Donne's love poetry is clear, the nature of amorous metaphysical poetry becomes clear as well.

The major movement in seventeenth-century English literature is from late-Renaissance to neoclassical.[9] In the earlier part of the century, under the influence of Italian and classical models, poets radically reshape traditional images, myths, and genres to new purposes. In the later part of the century, under the influence of French models, they become less bound to tradition, more direct, unaffected, and urbane. To express religious views, Milton (still a Renaissance figure) turns to biblical stories, classical genres, and Italian theories of epic language and form; but Dryden writes the directly expository *Religio Laici*. A similar change appears between the amatory lyrics of Donne and those of the "mob of gentlemen who wrote with ease" under King Charles;[10] between the religious lyrics of Donne and those of Traherne; and between the satires of Marston and those of Dryden.[11] It is a movement from complexity and stylization, from radically reinterpreted but rigorously maintained traditions, to simplicity and directness, to an ideal of courtly urbanity. The fortunes of metaphysical poetry reflect this movement. Donne's Petrarchism helps locate him within it as an Italianate, late-Renaissance poet.

Donne's Petrarchism places him in the Renaissance, as one of the last, and greatest, practitioners of an international style. It highlights his social poise, his witty grace, and his exalted theories. Hopefully, it may revive interest in the Renaissance lyric. Certainly, it should free Donne of the self-conscious unhappiness which has been foisted upon him, revealing him to be a witty, passionate, and thoroughly human poet.

appendix

A Note on the Translations and Texts

The translations in this book are my own. In making them, I have striven to be literal, clear, and faithful to the poetical (or, often, ridiculously prosaic) texture of the originals. Where these three aims seemed incompatible, I have sacrificed texture and balanced fidelity against clarity. In general, both for ease of reference and to give an idea of the movement of poems, I have separated my translations into lines: but though they look like verse, I know them to be prose.

The Italian originals are arranged alphabetically by author and first line. Since many of the poems I cite have been unedited for four centuries, the textual problems are enormous—though not really relevant to the points I make about Donne. My procedure has been silently to change type font, and correct obvious errors of spelling or spacing; to maintain the old spelling, except where a modern text uses "v" for older "u"; to be faithful to the texts I use, without collation; and to justify my translation only in three instances.

Unless otherwise noted, these are the texts I use: for John Donne, *The Poems,* ed. Sir Herbert Grierson (Oxford, 1933); for Giovanni Battista Guarino, *Rime* (Venice, 1598); for Petrarch [Francesco Petrarca], *Le rime,* ed. G. Carducci and S. Ferrari (Florence, 1957); for Serafino's sonnets, *Le rime,* ed. Mario Menghini (Bologna, 1894), I (the only volume ever published); for Serafino's other poems, *Opere . . . collette per Francesco Flavio* (Venice, 1502); and for Torquato Tasso, *Le rime,* ed. Angelo Solerti (Bologna, 1898), II.

Texts of Italian Poems

Antonio da S. Croce del Valdarno, Piero di: "Rispetto" * (Translation, p. 54).

> *Venir tipossa el diavolo allo letto*
> *da poi che io non viposso venir io*
> *et rompidi due chostole delpetto*
> *elaltre membra che tefatta idio*
> *et titiri permonti epervalli*
> *et spichati elchapo dalle spalle.*

Guarino: "Madonna inferma," Madrigal 56 (Translation, p. 89).

> *Langue al vostro languir l'anima mia:*
> *E dico, ah, forse à si cocente pena*
> *Sua ferità la mena.*
> *O anima d' Amor troppo rubella,*
> *Quanto meglio vi fora*
> *Provar quel caro ardor, che vi fa bella,*
> *Che quel che vi scolora?*
> *Perche non piace à la mia . . . , ch'io*
> *Arda del vostro foco, e voi del mio.*

Guarino: "Querela dell'amata," Madrigal 95 (Translation, p. 74).

> *Tu parti apena giunto*
> *Fuggitivo crudel. Fia mai quel giorno*

---

* *Biblioteca di letteratura popolare italiana*, I, ed. Severino Ferrari (Florence, 1882), p. 86.

Che fine al tuo partir ponga il ritorno?
Ò dolcissimo vago,
Se tu non fossi di vagar sì vago.
Almen ferma la fede,
Ne da me fugga il cor, se fugge il piede.

Guarino: "Risposta dell'amante," Madrigal 96 (Translation, p. 74).

Con voi sempre son io
Agitato, ma fermo;
E se'l meno v'involo, il più vi lasso.
Son simile al compasso,
Ch'un piede in voi quasi mio centro i' fermo,
L'altro patisce di . . . . i giri,
Ma non può far, che'ntorno à voi non giri.

Guarino: "Core in Farfalla," Madrigal 37 (Translation, pp. 163-64).

Una Farfalla cupida, e vagante
Fatt' è il mio cor amante;
Che và, quasi per gioco,
Scherzando intorno al foco
Di due begli occhi, e tante volte, e tante
Vola, e rivola, e fugge, e torna, e gira;
Che ne l'amato lume
Lascierà con la vita al fin le piume.
Ma chi di ciò sospira,
Sospira à torto. ardo caro, e felice
Morrà Farfalla, e sorgerà fenice.

Petrarch: 39 (Translation, pp. 43-44).

Io temo sí de' begli occhi l' assalto,
Ne' quali Amore e la mia morte alberga,
Ch' i' fuggo lor come fanciul la verga;
E gran tempo è ch' i' presi 'l primier salto.
Da ora inanzi faticoso od alto
Loco non fia dove 'l voler non s'erga,
Per non scontrar ch'i miei sensi disperga,
Lassando, come suol, me freddo smalto.

Dunque, s' a veder voi tardo mi volsi
Per non ravvicinarmi a chi mi strugge,
Fallir forse non fu di scusa indegno.
Piú dico, che 'l tornare a quel ch' uom fugge,
E 'l cor che di paura tanta sciolsi,
Fúr de la fede mia non leggier pegno.

Petrarch: 242 (Translation, p. 104).

Mira quel colle, o stanco mio cor vago:
Ivi lasciammo ier lei ch'alcun tempo ebbe
Qualche cura di noi e le ne 'ncrebbe,
Or vorria trar de li occhi nostri un lago.
Torna tu in là, ch'io d'esser sol m'appago;
Tenta se forse ancor tempo sarebbe
Da scemar nostro duol, che 'n fin qui crebbe,
O del mio mal participe e presago.—
Or tu c'hai posto te stesso in oblio
E parli al cor pur come e' fusse or teco,
Misero, e pien di pensier vani e sciocchi!
Ch'al dipartir dal tuo sommo desio
Tu te n'andasti, e'si rimase seco
E si nascose dentro a' suoi belli occhi.

Petrarch: 135, 11. 1-15 (Translation, p. 162).

Qual piú diversa e nova
Cosa fu mai in qualche stranio clima,
Quella, se ben s'estima,
Piú mi rasembra; a tal son giunto, Amore.
Là, onde il dí ven fore
Vola un augel, che sol, senza consorte,
Di volontaria morte
Rinasce e tutto a viver si rinova.
Cosí sol si ritrova
Lo mio voler, e cosí 'n su la cima
De' suoi alti pensieri al sol si volve,
E cosí si risolve
E cosí torna al suo stato di prima;

Arde e more, e riprende i nervi suoi,
E vive poi con la fenice a prova.

Petrarch: 298 (Translation, p. 100).

Quand' io mi volgo in dietro a mirar gli anni
    C'hanno, fuggendo, i miei penseri sparsi,
    E spento 'l foco ove agghiacciando io arsi,
    E finito il riposo pien d' affanni;
Rotta la fé de gli amorosi inganni,
    E sol due parti d' ogni mio ben farsi,
    L'una nel cielo e l'altra in terra starsi,
    E perduto il guadagno de' miei danni;
I' mi riscuoto, e trovomi sí nudo
    Ch' i' porto invidia ad ogni estrema sorte:
    Tal cordoglio e paura ho di me stesso!
O mia stella, o fortuna, o fato, o morte,
    O per me sempre dolce giorno e crudo,
    Come m'avete in basso stato messo!

Riccho Neapolitano, Antonio: "Ogni statuto che qua giu si lege" *
(Translation, pp. 55-56).

Ogni statuto che qua giu si lege
    Condamna ad morte quel che uccide et fura
    Et tu mhai morto, et non fai nulla cura
    Ne de sergenti, ne rector che rege
    Il cor mhai tolto non stimando lege
    De vulgo, de signor ò de natura
    Anti dimonstri non haver pagura
    Del ciel che guida questa valle et tege
    Ma sappi donna che non è finita
    In dio iusticia: ma nel fin martire
    Con pena harai si non mi porgi aita
    Pero ti voglii dogni fal pentire
    Et col tuo sguardo mi ritorna in vita
    Che giova il pentir di poi falire.

* *Opere . . . intitulata Fior de Delia,* revised (Venice, 1508), fol. c2[r].

Serafino: Strambotti [103, 104], L2^v (Translation, p. 57).

> *E se glie ver che lalma tormentare*
> *In quel loco se deve ove ha peccato*
> *Io dentro al corpo tuo spero habitare*
> *Poi che per crudel* moro damnato*
> *E con mia propria man voglio disfare:*
> *Quel falso cor: che a me si duro e stato*
> *Fin che te occidera per mia vendecta*
> *Chogni peccato alfin iustitia aspecta.*
>
> *E se glie ver chel spirto vada a torno*
> *Quando lalma dal corpo si diserra*
> *Sapii che te staro sempre dintorno*
> *Ne mai mi stancaro de farti guerra*
> *Tanto che ognhor biastimarai quel giorno*
> *Che non volesti contentarmi in terra*
> *Cosi spero alchun tempo possederte*
> *O vivo o morto in le mie man haverte.*

Serafino: Strambotto [106], L3^r (Translation, p. 163).

> *O morte: o la: soccorri: ecco che arrivo*
> *A che pur chiami? ardo: chi tarde? Amore*
> *Che faro io? fammi de vita privo:*
> *Tamazzo ognhor: me non: dimanda il core*
> *Cor mio: ch' ce: sei morto: hor morto or vivo*
> *Che dice aime: renasce uno hom che more?*
> *Sol io: che di poi morte a poco a poco*
> *Come phoenice me rinovo al foco.*

Serafino: Strambotto [101], L2^r (Translation, p. 56).

> *Sio per te moro e calo ne linferno*
> *Vendetta cridaran tutti i mei mali*
> *Di toi processi io ne faro un quinterno*
> *Dandolo in man delle furie infernali*
> *Tu serai condemnata in foco eterno*

---

* As it stands this should be translated "as a cruel man, I die damned." But the line is defective. It lacks a syllable; and the sequence of which this strambotto is a part makes clear that the sense is "by your cruelty," whatever the Italian text (probably "per crudeltà") may have been.

Et presto presto a me convien che cali
Et se alchun tempo vivi in festa e in canti
Lombra mia sempre ti stara davanti.

Serafino: Epistola V, "Tu sei disposto pur crudel lassarmi," 11. 97-112, F6^{r-v} (Translation, pp. 56-57).

Ma non serai si presto al tuo camino
Chel spirto mio verra seguendo lorma
Visibilmente sempre a te vicino
Sanguinolento: in quella propria forma
Che con la cruda man morte mi dei
Stia pur tuo corpo vigilante: o dorma
Non per farti alchun mal: chio non potrei
Ma perche un giorno del tuo error te penti
E che conoschi un di gli affanni mei
Odendomi ulular con crudi accenti
Lamentarmi di te non una volta
E rinfacciarti tutti i mei lamenti
E ben che lalma simplicetta e stolta
Sia fuor del corpo fatigoso e stancho
Non creder gia per questo sia disciolta
Che un vero amor per morte non vien manco.

Tasso: [446] 59, 11. 1-8 (Translation, pp. 77-78).

Amor, contra costei che 'n treccia e 'n gonna
S' arma e s' accampa e i suoi guerrieri accoglie,
Tra le schiere un desio ch' in noi s'indonna *
Guida in pensier ben mille ardite voglie:
Tutte le stelle in ciel d' invitta donna
Prometton l' amorose e care spoglie;
E fede e sofferenza e pronto schermo
Fanno a lei forza, e 'l suo destino è fermo.

* In accordance with Tasso's critical theories—which encourage the poet to use grammatical license, and to coin terms—this word is not properly Italian. Louise G. Clubb suggests that its license is grammatical: that it comes from "s'indonnire" ("to become a woman"). Sergio Baldi suggests that it is an Italianized form of *dominare* or *dominus*. I believe both senses to be present: the thought controls Tasso's mind, and it takes on the shape of a woman—perhaps suggesting that the lady herself is adolescent.

Tasso: [173] 44 (Translation, p. 89).

> *I begli occhi ove prima Amor m'apparse,*
>   *Ch'ivi quasi in suo ciel si gira e splende,*
>   *Fera nube m'adombra e mi contende*
>   *Quel dolce raggio ch'abbagliommi ed arse.*
> *Lasso! e quel freddo petto, ove destarse*
>   *Non può fiamma amorosa, or fiamma accende*
>   *Di rea febbre maligna, e no 'l difende*
>   *La neve e 'l gelo ond' egli suole armarse.*
> *Deh, perché non poss'io sí ardente foco*
>   *In sua vece soffrir per ch' ella poi*
>   *Breve favilla di mie fiamme senta?*
> *E ben sarebbe, Amor, diletto e gioco*
>   *Ogni altra face e parria fredda e spenta*
>   *A chi prova nel cor gli ardori tuoi.*

Tasso: 84 (Translation, pp. 83-84).

> *I freddi e muti pesci usati omai*
>   *D'arder qui sono e di parlar d'amore,*
>   *E tu, che 'l vento e l'onde acqueti, or sai*
>   *Come rara bellezza accenda il core,*
> *Poi ch'in voi lieti spiega i dolci rai*
>   *Il sol che fu di queste sponde onore,*
>   *Il chiaro sol cui piú dovete assai*
>   *Ch'a l'altro uscito del sen vostro fuore.*
> *Ché quegli, ingrato, a cui non ben sovviene*
>   *Com'è da voi nudrito e come accolto,*
>   *V'invola il meglio e lascia 'l salso e 'l greve;*
> *Ma questi con le luci alme e serene*
>   *V'affina e purga e rende il dolce e 'l leve,*
>   *Ed assai piú vi dà che non v'è tolto.*

Tasso: Canzone 20, "Perché la vita è breve," Stanza 3 * (Translation, p. 86).

> *E, se pur non si frange,*
>   *Più a dentro a' duri colpi il molle petto,*
>   *Non è virtù d'usbergo o d'arte maga;*

* *L'Aminta e rime scelte* (Milan, 1824).

186

Ma'l timoroso affetto
In selce par che mi trasmuti e cange.
Oh meraviglia! Amor la selce impiange;
Ma non avvien che da profonda piaga
Versi del sangue mio tepida stilla.
O mia fortuna, O fato, O stelle, O cielo,
Son di marmo e di gelo,
E'l marmo alle percosse arde e sfavilla.
Per la ferita intanto
(Sasselo Amor, che saettando apprilla)
Lagrime spargo, e'n lagrimoso canto
Di vostra lode fo canoro il pianto.

Tasso: 113, "Quel generoso mio guerriero interno," 11. 48-51, 58-60
(Translation, p. 77).

Quasi nuovo e gentil mostro si mira,
Per opra di natura o d'arte maga
Sé medesma e le voglie ancor trasforme
De l'alma nostra che per lei sospira.

. . . .
. . . e quanto è men feroce
Tanto più forte il sento,
E volontario d' danni miei consento.

Tasso: 105, "S'arma lo Sdegno, e'n lunga schiera e folta," 11. 9-14 (Translation, p. 77).

Bellezza ad arte incolta, atti soavi,
Finta pietà, sdegno tenace e duro
E querele e lusinghe in dolci accenti,
Ed accoglienze liete e meste e gravi
De la nemica mia l'arme già furo,
Or son trofei di que' guerrieri ardenti.

Tolomei, Claudio: "Chi non sa ben, com'una fiera Donna," 11. 13-15,
17-18, 25-36 * (Translation, pp. 85-86).

* *I fiori delle rime de' poeti illustri*, revised, ed. Girolamo Ruscelli (Venice,
1629), E6ᵛ—E7ʳ.

Ò *nova Circe, ò incantatrice Donna,*
  Che già m'intenerivi, or mi fai pietra,
  . . . s'io fatto voce, e pietra,

  . . . .
  Tu creduta sarai spietata Donna,
  In* nuda voce entro à sensibil pietra.

. . . .

Voi lagrime, che fuor di questa pietra
  Uscite giorno, e notte; à la mia Donna
  Gite, che'n volto mostra d'esser Donna,
  E dentro al duro petto è dura pietra.
  Poi piangendo le dite, ò altera Donna
  Spezzi il tuo cor pietà di lui, ch'è pietra.
Guardate ben, ch'innanzi à quella Donna
  Com'io per tempo ardir divenni pietra,
  Voi turbando il piacer de la mia Donna
  Non restiate cristallo, ò dura pietra.
  Dolce dunque parlate à quella pietra
  Aspra si che mai par non hebbe Donna.

---

* Apparently, this is a printer's error. I translate this as "Un' "; an alternative is "I'n' ": "*I* [in contrast to *you*, a pitiless lady] a bare voice within a feeling stone."

notes

Abbreviations

CL	Comparative Literature
ELH	Studies in English Literary History
HLQ	Huntington Library Quarterly
JEGP	Journal of English and Germanic Philology
JHI	Journal of the History of Ideas
MLN	Modern Language Notes
MLQ	Modern Language Quarterly
MLR	Modern Language Review
MP	Modern Philology
MS	Mediaeval Studies
N&Q	Notes and Queries
PMLA	Publications of the Modern Language Association
PQ	Philological Quarterly
RES	Review of English Studies
SRen	Studies in the Renaissance

Chapter I

1. A similarly varied set of analogues is offered, for example, by Helen Gardner, "Introduction," *The Metaphysical Poets* (Baltimore, 1963), reprinted from 1957.

2. In *The School of Donne* (London, 1961), Alfred Alvarez argues that Donne's style reflects the practical, learned, and sensible audience for whom he wrote. However, Alvarez offers no external evidence that Donne's audience was not always that for which he wrote verse compliments, funeral elegies, and fashionable sermons. Nor is the poetical community he posits apparent in a distinctive style: its supposed members simply do not write like Donne.

3. The first viewpoint is that of Samuel Johnson, the second that of Joseph A. Mazzeo, "Metaphysical Poetry and the Poetic of Correspondence," *JHI*, XIV (1953), 221-234; and "Universal Analogy and the Culture of the Renaissance," *JHI*, XV (1954), 299-304.

4. That readers in Donne's time would not have expected such symbolism seems clear from Madeleine Doran, "Some Renaissance 'Ovids,'" *Literature and Society,* ed. Bernice Slote (Lincoln, Nebraska, 1964), pp. 44-62.

5. For example, see Miss Doran, p. 49, on the various interpretations of the serpent. Similarly, though the phoenix symbolizes Christ's resurrection, ladies' beauty, and lovers' pangs, it is incredible that it implied that Christ is lady-like, or lovers Christ-like.

6. Rosemund Tuve, *Elizabethan and Metaphysical Imagery* (Chicago, 1947); *A Reading of George Herbert* (Chicago, 1952).

7. Maurice W. Kelley, *This Great Argument* (Princeton, 1941), pp. 106-115, shows that Milton disallows invoking the Holy Spirit. Nonetheless, the invocations in *Paradise Lost* seem addressed to the Holy Spirit as Kelley shows Milton to define it: that which regenerates, adds to the comprehension of spiritual things, and teaches and enlightens the Gospel. Clearly, what is essential here is the epic form, which demands an invocation.

8. That Donne is a Petrarchist is a cliché of Italian criticism: see, for example, Peter Borghesi, *Petrarch and his Influence on English Literature* (Bologna, 1906), p. 87; Carlo Segre, *Relazioni letterarie fra Italia e Inghilterra* (Florence, 1911), pp. 157-158; Antonio Cecchini, *Serafino Aquilano e la lirica inglese del '500* (Aquila, 1935), p. 149; Paul Van Tieghem, *Précis d' histoire littéraire de l'Europe* (Paris, 1925), pp. 22-25; and Mario Praz, "John Donne e la poesia del suo tempo," *Machiavelli in Inghilterra* (Rome, 1942), pp. 219-237.

The idea has also been enunciated by Clay Hunt, *Donne's Poetry* (New Haven, 1954); Alfred H. Upham, *The French Influence in English Literature from the Accession of Elizabeth to the Restoration* (New York, 1908), pp. 177-185; Frederick B. Artz, *From the Renaissance to Romanticism* (Chicago, 1962), pp. 37-38; Raymond M. Alden, "The Lyrical Conceits of the 'Metaphysical Poets,' " *SP*, XVII (1920), 183-198; and even Sir Herbert J. C. Grierson, *The First Half of the Seventeenth Century* (New York, 1906), pp. 155-158.

9. See Mario Vinciguerra, *Interpretazione del petrarchismo* (Turin, 1926).

10. On the Petrarchan tradition, see Ernest H. Wilkins, "A General Survey of Renaissance Petrarchism," *CL*, II (1950), 327-339. For an extended definition of some varieties of Petrarchism, see for example Joseph Vianey, *Le pétrarquisme en France au XVIe siècle* (Montpellier, 1909); Luigi Baldacci, *Il petrarchismo italiano nel cinquecento* (Milan, 1957); and W. Theodor Elwert, "Il Bembo imitatore," *Studi di letteratura veneziana:* Civiltà veneziana studi 5 (Venice, 1958), pp. 111-145.

11. The differences between Marino and Donne are noted by Frank J. Warnke, "Marino and the English Metaphysicals," *SRen*, II (1955), 160-175. Donne's style is considered to be Ramistic by Rosemund Tuve, "Imagery and Logic: Ramus and Metaphysical Poetics," *JHI*, III (1942), 374-400. But on the absolute clash between metaphysical and Ramistic sermon styles, see Perry Miller, *The New England Mind: The Seventeenth Century* (New York, 1939), pp. 331-362. Miss Tuve's thesis is that Ramus promotes argumentative imagery. But she seems to misunderstand Ramus, who means not to make images logical, but to consider everything in a speech, images included, to be persuasive in purpose, and only in that sense "arguments." See Miller, and Father Walter J. Ong, *Ramus: Method, and the Decay of Dialogue* (Cambridge, Mass., 1958), pp. 66, 104-105, 116, *et passim*. The theory that Donne's conceit reflects universal analogy is defended by Mazzeo.

12. For Gongorism, see Joseph G. Fucilla, "Pedro de Padilla and the Current

of the Italian Quattrocentist Preciosity in Spain," *PQ*, IX (1930), 225-238; for *préciosité*, Vianey.

13. See Evelyn M. Simpson, "Donne's Spanish Authors," *MLR*, XLIII (1948), 185; Geoffrey Keynes, *A Bibliography of Dr. John Donne* (Cambridge, Eng., 1958), 3rd ed., pp. 205-206; and, on the compass image, Mario Praz, *Secentismo e Marinismo in Inghilterra* (Florence, 1925), p. 109, n. 1, and Don Cameron Allen, "Donne's Compass Figure," *MLN*, LXXI (1956), 256-257. On Donne's Italianate love theory, see, for example, Merritt Y. Hughes, "The Lineage of 'The Extasie,'" *MLR*, XXVII (1932), 1-5.

Chapter II

1. The nature of the neoclassical attack is evident in one of the earliest Petrarchan replies, Angelo Colotio's sixteenth-century introduction to Serafino's works, reprinted in *Rime*, ed. Mario Menghini (Bologna, 1894) I, 25-28—see ch. iv below. The sixteenth-century attacks from realists and vulgarians are described by Arturo Graf, "Petrarchismo ed antipetrarchismo," *Attraverso il cinquecento*, ed. Giovanni Chiantore (Turin, 1926), pp. 3-70.

2. "English Poetry: Time and Man," *Prefaces to English Literature* (New York, 1965), p. 71.

3. For the intimate relation between neoclassicism and anti-Petrarchism in France, see Claude Pichois, "Autour de Pétrarque: un épisode de la bataille romantique en France (1822)," *Petrarca e il petrarchismo: Atti del terzo congresso dell'Associazione internazionale per gli studi di lingua a letteratura italiana* (Bologna, 1961), pp. 265-276 (hereafter cited as *Petrarca e il petrarchismo*). For anti-Italianism as an element of French neoclassicism, see Arthur Tilley, *The Literature of the French Renaissance* (Cambridge, Eng.), II, 312-313; and, in France and England, "The Anti-Italian Tendency in the Eighteenth Century," A. F. B. Clark, *Boileau and the French Classical Critics in England (1660-1830)* (Paris, 1925), pp. 337-360. As Clark's evidence shows, anti-Italianism in England waxes and wanes with the neoclassical movement.

Furthermore, the Italians like the metaphysicals are attacked for pedantry, conceits, and a lack of urbanity. On p. 341, Clark quotes Addison's statement, in *Spectator* 5, that the "finest writers among the modern Italians express themselves in such florid form of words and such tedious circumlocutions as are used by none but pedants in our own country: and at the same time fill their writings with such poor imaginations and conceits, as our youths are ashamed of before they have been two years at the university." He also quotes Addison, *Spec.* 279, on the "mixed wit" of the Italians: "Virgil has none of those little points and puerilities . . . of Ovid . . . none of those mixed embellishments of Tasso. Everything is just and natural." And, on pp. 341-342, he cites Shaftesbury's *Characteristics*: "The Italian authors . . . may be reckoned no better than the corruptors of true learning and erudition; and can indeed be relished by those alone whose education has unfortunately denied them the familiarity of the noble ancients and the practice of a better and more natural taste." Fundamentally, then, the Italians are seen to have the same faults as the metaphysicals: puerile wit, affectation, and a lack of a true, natural manner.

4. For example, by Hallett Smith, "The Art of Sir Thomas Wyatt," *HLQ*, IX

(1946), 323-355, and J. W. Lever, *The Elizabethan Love Sonnet* (London, 1956), pp. 1-35.

5. In *Astrophel and Stella* 1, "Loving in truth," Sidney is told by his Muse to "look in thy heart and write." She does not mean that sincere poetry is best, but that Stella's picture, engraved on his heart, will inspire him—see William A. Ringler's notes in *Poems of Sir Philip Sidney* (Oxford, 1962). It is also, however, a Petrarchan cliché that the poet writes not for fame, but to unburden his heart.

For the lover's independence, see D.G. Rees, "Wyatt and Petrarch," *MLR*, LII (1957), 389-391: Wyatt's manly declaration here is faithful to his Petrarchan original. Thus, critics of both Wyatt and Sidney are learning to lay aside Romantic principles, and to read Petrarchan poetry on its own terms.

6. W. Theodor Elwert, "Il Bembo imitatore," *Studi di letteratura veneziana* (Venice, 1958), Civiltà veneziana studi 5; Ferruccio Ulivi, *L'imitazione nella poetica del rinascimento* (Milan, 1959), pp. 46-47, *et passim;* Giulio Marzot, "Il tramite del petrarchismo del rinascimento al barocco," *Studi petrarcheschi*, VI (1956), 123-175; Dámaso Alonso, "La poesia del Petrarca e il petrarchismo (Mondo estetico della pluralità)," *Lettere italiane*, XI (1959), 277-319; Baldacci, *Il petrarchismo italiano nel cinquecento;* Mario Vinciguerra, *Interpretazione del petrarchismo* (Turin, 1926).

7. Benedetto Croce, "La lirica cinquecentesca," *Poesia popolare e poesia d'arte: Studi sulla poesia italiana dal tre al cinquecento* (Bari, 1957), pp. 341-441. On Chariteo, see Flora (n. 8 below); and G. Getto, "Sulla poesia del Cariteo," *Giornale storico della letteratura italiana*, CXXIII (1946), 53-68.

8. Thomas G. Bergin, introduction to *Lyric Poetry of the Italian Renaissance: An Anthology with Verse Translations,* ed. L. R. Lind (New Haven, 1954), pp. xxiii-xxiv. Francesco Flora, *Storia della letteratura italiana: Edizione minore,* II (Verona, 1954), 12-14. Flora also notes that there is no more reason to be prejudiced against imitation in Petrarchan poetry, than in Virgilian poetry (176); and has, as well, a fine appreciation of the much-maligned *quattrocentisti* (I, 244).

9. See Jean Boutière and A.-H. Schutz, intro. and notes, *Biographies des troubadours: textes provençaux des XIIIe et XIVe siècles,* "Introduction," pp. xii-xiv, xv-xvii, *et passim.*

10. The pervasiveness of Latinate echoes in the *Canzoniere* can be surmised from Pierre de Nolhac, *Pétrarque et l'humanisme,* I : Bibliothèque littéraire de la renaissance, I (Paris, 1907), 163-212; and Umberto Bosco, *Francesco Petrarca* (Bari, 1961), pp. 128-155. See also the notes to *Rime.*

11. See Nicola Scarano, "Fonti provenzali e italiane della lirica petrarchescha," *Studi di filologia romanza,* VIII (1901), 250-360; Giuseppe Guido Ferrero, *Petrarca minore* (Turin, 1942), extracted from *Annali della Facoltà di magistero della r. università di Torino,* I (1942). How Petrarch transforms his Provençal sources—generally, by a greater spirituality—is discussed by Giuseppe Guido Ferrero, *Petrarca e i trovatori* (Turin, 1959?).

12. *Petrarca* (Turin, 1946).

13. From the sixteenth-century commentators to the modern critics, skilled readers have recognized Petrarch to be a master of the unadorned, simple style: see, for example, Umberto Bosco, "Il linguaggio lirico del Petrarca tra Dante e il Bembo," *Petrarca e il petrarchismo,* pp. 121-132. There is interesting confirmation in linguistic

analysis, as shown by Emilio Bigi in the same volume, *"La rima del Petrarca,"* pp. 135-145.

14. *I sonetti, le canzoni, et i triomphi di M. Laura in risposta di M. Franchesco Petrarcha per le sue rime in vita, et dopo la morte di lei. Pervenuti alle mani del Magnifico M. Stephano Colonna* (colophon: Venice, 1552). *Olimpia d'amore . . . Rime piacevoli, & honeste, le quali ogni giovane potrà accomodare al suo senso* (Bologna, n.d.). *Il Petrarca spirituale di frate Hieronimo Malipiero Venetiano, dell' ordine de minori d'osservanza* (Venice, 1567).

Chapter III

1. In the last fifteen years, the idea that Donne parodies Petrarchism has become old-fashioned, and his manly realism received less stress. But other explanations of his departures from Elizabethan poetical practices have been egregiously weak. For example, J. B. Leishman, *The Monarch of Wit* (London, 1951), considering many of Donne's lyrics to be unemotional displays of academic wit, reduces them to mere bagatelles. John Buxton, *Elizabethan Taste* (London, 1963), pp. 317-338, claims that, in contrast to *Poly-Olbion,* Donne's lyrics are private verses, overturning decorum for the amusement of a coterie. He too, then, reduces Donne's lyrics to bagatelles; and he fails to explain their difference from Elizabethan lyrics—which, clearly, are more pertinent than epics and geographical allegories. Because such theories deny importance to the *Songs and Sonets,* Donne's manly realism still explains his un-Elizabethan decorum to those who admire his verses—for example, Alfred Alvarez, *The School of Donne* (London, 1961).

2. Only by ignoring these facts could one seek Wyatt's essential spirit in purely English manliness, or Early-Tudor rudeness; but many critics do—for example, Sir E. K. Chambers, *Sir Thomas Wyatt and Some Collected Studies* (London, 1933), p. 126; and Lever, *The Elizabethan Love Sonnet,* p. 22.

3. A list of Wyatt's clearly humanistic works appears in Hyder E. Rollins, ed., *Tottel's Miscellany (1557-1587)* (Cambridge, Mass., 1929), II, 76-77. Rollins' conclusion that Wyatt is not a humanist results from his ignoring the original elements in his translations, failing to recognize Petrarch as a humanistic model, and slighting the significance of Wyatt's imitations in satire and psalm of Alamanni, a vernacular humanist of great continental repute.

In "Sir Thomas Wyatt: Classical Philosophy and English Humanism," *HLQ,* XXV (1962), 79-96, and in *Sir Thomas Wyatt and His Background* (Stanford, 1964), pp. 79-110, Patricia Thomson reveals the Christian humanism of Wyatt's translation *Quyete of Mynde.* She fails, however, to perceive that his love poetry too is humanistic.

4. In ll. 17-23 of "A spending hand," Wyatt departs from his model, Horace, *Satires,* II, 5, to say that to live for pleasure is to live like a swine. In ll. 77-79 of "My mothers maydes," he turns part of Horace's proof that today's pleasures should be grasped (*Carmina,* II, 16, ll. 9-11) to a proof that passion should be controlled. In l. 6 of "Myne owne John Poynz," he transforms Alamanni's promise to temper his sorrow (*Satira* X, l. 6) to a declaration that he will rein his passions. The resemblances to Neo-Stoicism here and in his echoes of Persius are not accidental. For

Wyatt translates Seneca ("Stond who so list upon the Slipper toppe") and professes a love for him (in "Ffarewell Love and all thy lawes for ever"). And his dominant theme is that the virtuous man is above ill fortune.

5. For Wyatt's sources, see Rollins, II; Sergio Baldi, *La poesia di Sir Thomas Wyatt* (Florence, 1953), pp. 218-237; and Ruth Hughey, ed., *The Arundel Harington Manuscript of Tudor Poetry* (Colombus Ohio, 1960), II. No longer adequate is A. K. Foxwell, *A Study of Sir Thomas Wyatt's Poems* (London, 1911), pp. 76-78, 147-152.

6. These ways, as scholars generally define them, are denunciations of the lady, clamorous demands for sexual reward, and omissions of descriptions of feminine and rural beauty—see, for example, Baldi, pp. 165-180; Lever, pp. 22-35; Patricia Thomson, "Wyatt and the Petrarchan Commentators," *RES,* n.s. X (1959), 231-233; and Rudolf Gottfried, "Sir Thomas Wyatt and Pietro Bembo," *N&Q,* n.s. I (1954), 278-280.

Wyatt's departures from Petrarch were once thought of as primarily translator's inaccuracies: for example, by Emma Chini, "Il sorgere del petrarchismo in Inghilterra e la poesia di Sir Thomas Wyatt," *Civiltà moderna,* VI (1934), 206-209, and Peter Borghesi, *Petrarch and His Influence on English Literature,* p. 45. More recently, they have been explained as effects of spiritual grossness: for example, by Patricia Thomson, "The First English Petrarchans," *HLQ,* XXII (1959), 94-96, and Ruth Hughey, II, 132, *et passim.* But clearly it is impossible that a successful ambassador to European Renaissance courts should be rude out of ignorance that Petrarch is polite, or from a sheer want of breeding.

Wyatt's un-Petrarchan features have also been attributed to the influence of the school of Serafino—for example, by Baldi, pp. 191-199; Cecchini, *Serafino Aquilano e la lirica inglese del '500,* p. 64; John M. Berdan, *Early Tudor Poetry* (New York, 1931), pp. 467, 472-476; and Mario Praz, "Petrarchismo," *Enciclopedia italiana di scienze, lettere, e d'arte* (Rome, 1935-43), XXVII. But Wyatt's transformations of Petrarch cannot be traced to Serafino in detail, and their general method is entirely different from his: Wyatt imitates particular poems, while Serafino freely applies the Petrarchan vocabulary to his own themes and situations.

7. Similarly, in his satires Wyatt imitates Alamanni and Horace, finding there techniques for treating the contrast between happy moderation and unhappy ambition, and adapting them to the contrast between oppressed virtue and triumphant vice—see my "Wyatt's Petrarchism: An Instance of Creative Imitation in the Renaissance" in *HLQ,* XXIX (1965), 1-15.

8. For example, in "I have sought long with stedfastnes" he ingenuously asks for justice because a lady has refused his proferred love without adequate cause:

> Ffor fansy rueleth, tho right say nay,
>
>> Even as the goodeman kyst his kowe;
>
> None othre reason can ye lay
>
> But as who saieth, I reke not how.

9. For Wyatt as for the Stoics, Fortune leads not to religious meditation but to magnanimous resolutions. It personifies the world's disregard of merit:

> Yf fortune then lyst for to lowre,
>
>> What vaylyth Right?
>
> ("It was my choyse, yt was no chaunce").

10. Baldi, p. 17 and n. 20, relates Wyatt's poem to a token from Anne Boleyn; in his list of sources, he says that only the hart and collar are from Petrarch. Miss Thomson notes that the commentators of Petrarch suggest the hunt and various interpretations of "Cesare" (but not Wyat's interpretation). She finds, however, that Wyatt's attitude to his lady and to love—which are, after all, his most characteristic notes—are not anticipated by the commentators (*RES*, n.s. X, 231-233).

11. An entirely possible misunderstanding; the phrase is difficult enough to require paraphrase ("farmi felice") by Lodovico Castelvetro, *Le rime del Petrarca brevemente sposte* (Basilea, 1582).

12. For the comments of "E. K." (repeated by William Webbe) and of Gabriel Harvey, see Buxton, pp. 233-234. Harvey's marginal comment on Gascoigne's inconstancy refers both to his life and to his poetry.

13. Because of protests against its scandalous content, Gascoigne had to change the setting of his novel to Italy in its second edition. He was in financial difficulties when his novel was first printed, and may have wanted the money that an exposé would bring. For the evidence, though not for its interpretation, see C. T. Prouty, *George Gascoigne* (New York, 1946), pp. 189-194; and, on Gascoigne's finances at the time, pp. 45-56.

14. Dante Alighieri, *De vulgari eloquentia,* ed. and comment by Aristide Marigo, 3rd ed. rev. Pier Giorgio Ricci (Florence, 1957), pp. 172-177.

15. I cite Gascoigne's works from *The Complete Works,* ed. John W. Cunliffe (Cambridge, Eng., 1907), 2 vols.

16. Gascoigne's location of love in the liver is especially suggestive; for, unlike the heart, the center of perception and affection, the liver is the seat of the natural soul—of growth, digestion, and excretion. See, for example, Helkiah Crooke, *Microcosmographi: A Description of the Body of Man* (London, 1615), pp. 410, 513, 517-518; John Banister, *The Historie of Man* (London, 1578), fol. 98; Robert Burton, *The Anatomy of Melancholy,* ed. Floyd Dell and Paul Jordan-Smith (New York, 1926), pp. 128-129, 131, 133, and 149-150. In pp. 658-659, Burton may mean that sexual desire resides in the liver, and sentimental love in the brain.

Gascoigne indicates that love is sex not only by locating it in the liver, but also by attributing to it the stages that he does: in courtly love, the sight of the lady precedes the kindling of love's heat.

17. Many critics have taken Gascoigne's lyrics as parodies of Petrarchism. For example, in *George Gascoigne,* p. 214, and in the "Notes" to *George Gascoigne's "A Hundreth Sundrie Flowres"* (Columbia, Missouri, 1942), C. T. Prouty notes that in *Works,* I, 11, Gascoigne says that his "The arraig[n]ment of a Lover" and "The Divorce of a Lover" are written "in jeast." However, Gascoigne (who in any case mentions only two poems) is using "in jeast" to mean "not literally true"—as he does in the instance cited by the *NED,* sense 3, where "in jest" means "idle tales." Gascoigne has been neither arraigned nor divorced. He ridicules those who misunderstand "the sense of the figurative speeches," taking them for "sad earnest"; he reminds the reader that pastorals are not always written by shepherds and that Churchyard is not a sexton. He wants his reader not to be "Parrot like," but to understand "the meaning of the Authour." Far from mocking the sophisticated Petrarchan convention, Gascoigne finds it necessary to explain the most basic element of literary sophistication, the difference between figurative and literal language.

18. In his "Notes," Prouty says that "harde favoured" means "well favoured." The *NED* gives no authority for any interpretation besides "ugly" or "harsh-featured," and neither does Prouty. Reading the poem as a praise of ugliness removes the necessity for an unsupported and improbable interpretation of the phrase—see my "Donne's 'The Anagram': Sources and Analogues," *HLQ*, XXVIII (1964), 79-82.

19. As Carducci and Ferrari note, though Petrarch is excusing himself for having avoided a friend who lived near Laura, many Renaissance commentators understand him to be excusing himself to Laura herself. Thus, Petrarch's own lyrics were often read to be as preposterously gallant as Gascoigne's.

20. My conception of Petrarchan imitation owes much to two seminal studies, Hallett Smith's "The Art of Sir Thomas Wyatt," *HLQ*, IX (1946), 323-355, and J. W. Lever's *The Elizabethan Love Sonnet*.

Chapter IV

1. Donne's use of genres needs further study. O. B. Hardison, *The Enduring Monument* (Chapel Hill, 1962), pp. 95-102, argues that the Renaissance love lyric is essentially praise of the lady; but this theory is adequate only to some lyrics. It ignores the introspective strand in Petrarchism; and it dilutes Hardison's significant definition of the Renaissance poem of praise—a definition which, to be meaningful, must include the use of amplifying rhetoric and magnifying diction. Louis L. Martz, in *The Poetry of Meditation* (New Haven, 1954), says that Donne sometimes writes in a contemplative genre. But Martz often defines that genre so loosely that it becomes a useless critical tool—as is forcibly shown by George Williamson, "The Design of Donne's *Anniversaries*," *MP*, LX (1962-63), 183-191.

Donne's satires accord with Elizabethan critical theory. His elegies are defined by their meter and, less surely, by their subjects—a definition fitting better with classical practice than with Renaissance theory. Donne's various "anniversaries," "epicedes," and "obsequies" suggest an entirely unclassical conception of genre. And it is remarkable that he thought "The Progresse of the Soule" (on metempsychosis) to be an epic—as Don Cameron Allen shows him to have done in "The Double Journey of John Donne," *A Tribute to G. F. Taylor,* ed. Arnold Williams (Richmond, Va., 1952), pp. 83-99. In general, Donne seems to write as courtier rather than *vates*, and to be simply careless of genre.

2. Walsh's comment may be found in George Williamson, *The Proper Wit of Poetry* (Chicago, 1961), p. 110. As critics generally recognize and Williamson says (p. 111), Walsh's view is important to Dryden.

3. The comments of Warton and the anonymous author of *Dialogue on Taste* (1762) appear in Arthur H. Nethercot, "The Term 'Metaphysical Poets' Before Johnson," *MLN*, XXXVII (1922), 15-16. Pope—who praises Donne for his satires, but not for his lyrics—attacks Crashaw for imitating Petrarch: see Nethercot, "The Reputation of the 'Metaphysical Poets' During the Age of Pope," *PQ*, IV (1925), 168-169.

4. Samuel Johnson, "Edmund Waller," *Lives of the English Poets* (London, 1925), I, 170. That Johnson is thinking of the metaphysical poets is especially clear in "He seldom fetches an amorous sentiment from the depths of science; . . . he writes to common degrees of knowledge; and is free at least from philosophical

pedantry, unless perhaps the end of a song *To the sun* may be excepted, in which he is too much a Copernican" (168-169).

5. Important documents of early-seventeenth-century criticism by Dudley North are printed in L.A. Beaurline, "Dudley North's Criticism of Metaphysical Poetry," *HLQ*, XXV (1962), 299-313.

6. From the "Apologia di Angelo Colotio . . . al magnifico Sylvio Piccolhomini s. et benefactore," in *Le rime di Serafino*, ed. Mario Menghini, I, 24-25.

7. Quoted by Claude Pichois, "Autour de Pétrarque: un épisode de la bataille romantique en France (1822)," *Petrarca e il petrarchismo*, pp. 270-272.

8. For example, by Grierson, "Introduction," *Poems*, II, xxxvii-xxxix.

9. See my "Donne and the Greek Anthology," *N&Q*, X (1963), 57-58.

10. According to Sir Herbert Grierson, "Introduction," *The Poems of John Donne* (London, 1933), p. xx, some few songs of Donne are Petrarchan complaints against the obduracy of the lady: "The Relique," "The Dampe," "Twicknam garden," "A nocturnall upon S. Lucies day," "The Blossome," and "The Primrose." Considering Donne's use of Petrarchan motives alien to his natural vein, Grierson explains that he wrote these poems to compliment Lady Magdalen Herbert.

For the improbability of Grierson's explanation, see H. W. Garrod, "Donne and Mrs. Herbert," *RES*, XXI (1945), 38-42; and Grierson's earlier comments in "Introduction," *The Poems of John Donne* (London, 1912), II, xx-xxv. More important, however, is the critical inadequacy of Grierson's list. It is inaccurate in what it includes: "The Primrose," though possibly addressed to a particular lady, is probably a merely general commentary on love (see Jeanes-Jacques Denonain, *Thèmes et formes de la poésie "métaphysique"* [Paris, 1956], p. 127 ff.); "A nocturnall" is explicitly about a lady who returned the poet's love; and "The Relique" is no complaint, but an exaltation of lover and lady for the purity of their mutual affection. Grierson's list is misleading, furthermore, in that it omits "The Apparition," "The Will," "The broken heart," "The Funerall," and other lyrics which are indeed complaints against "a lady whom he reproaches, not for fickleness or sensuality or a half-hearted reluctance to yield to love, but for a too impeccable coldness." And, finally, Grierson identifies Petrarchism with the love complaint: a simplification as mistaken as identifying the epic style with the catalogue of ships.

11. For example, the initiation of love in "The good-morrow"; the amorous complaint in "Twicknam garden"; the complaint at parting in "The Expiration"; the remonstrance against Love in "Loves exchange"; the elegy for a beloved lady in "A nocturnall upon S. Lucies day"; the renunciation of love in "Farewell to love"; the expression of sorrow at the lady's illness in "A Feaver"; the dream in "The Dreame"; the token in "A Jeat Ring sent"; the amorous anniversary in "The Anniversarie"; and the definition of love in "Negative love."

12. Death for love appears, for example, in "The Dampe" and "The Expiration"; sun-darkening ladies in "The Sunne Rising," 1. 15, and "The Baite," st. 4; pictures on hearts in "Witchcraft by a picture," 11. 13-14, and "The broken heart," 11. 29-32; a ship of love in "Aire and Angels," st. 2; floods of tears in "A nocturnall," 11. 22-24, and "The Canonization," 11. 11-12; and miraculous ladies in "Loves exchange," st. 5, and the last line of "The Relique."

13. Though its title is often taken literally by modern critics, the first of the *Songs and Sonets*, "The good-morrow," is about the lovers' souls awakening to love.

"Farewell to love," which is the last renunciation of love, is not really the last poem of the collection. But of the three poems which follow it, "A Lecture upon the Shadow" can be read as a moralization upon the course of love made after love's renunciation; "Sonnet. The Token" is a sonnet, and "Selfe Love" a fragment. Thus, given the common Renaissance practice of printing sonnets and fragments separately, the *Songs and Sonets* correspond to the Petrarchan pattern: beginning with the initiation of love, going through a variety of complaints, celebrations, and conscientious doubts, and concluding with a renunciation of love.

14. In the *Chronicle of the Kings of England*, quoted by J. William Hebel and Hoyt H. Hudson, eds., *Poetry of the English Renaissance, 1509-1660* (New York, 1947), p. 986.

15. For example, Giovan Antonio Tagliente, *Opera amorosa, che insegna a componer lettere et a rispondere a persone damor ferite, o ver in amor viventi in thoscha lingua composta con piacer non poco e diletto di tutti gli amanti, laqual si chiama il Rifugio di amanti, o vero componimento di parlamenti* (Venice, 1527); and Girolamo Parabosco, *Delle lettere amorose* (Milan, 1558).

16. *Biblioteca di letteratura popolare italiana*, I, ed. Severino Ferrari (Florence, 1882), p. 86.

17. For the convention of poetic death, see Mario Equicola, *Libro di natura d'amore* (Venice, 1536), fols. 183^v-184^r, 185^r, *et passim*. This cliché underlies Rosalind's "Men have died from time to time and worms have eaten them, but not for love," in *AYLI*, IV, i, 107-108.

18. For example, in Stram. 88, "Quando la morte harra di me vittoria"; Stram. 89, "Quando sero portato in sepoltura"; Son. 30, "Cresi venire al ballo."

19. *Rimatori napoletani del quattrocento*, ed. Mario Mandalari (Caserta, 1885), p. 48, "Se tu aucidi et averamie morto," and pp. 12-15, "Per certo se troppo dura." On the punishment of reluctant ladies, see William Allen Neilson, "The Purgatory of Cruel Beauties: A Note on the Sources of the 8th Novel of the 5th Day of the *Decameron*," *Romania*, XXIX (1900), 85-93. Beatrice refers to such punishment when she talks of virgins leading apes in hell in *Much Ado*, II, i, 42-52.

20. By Luigi Tonelli, *L' amore nella poesia e nel pensiero del rinascimento* (Florence, 1933), pp. 61-62. Chariteo's sonnet is printed in *Lirici cortigiani del '400*, ed. Alessandro Tortoreto (Milan, 1942). For its popularity, see Tortoreto's comment, and also Vianey, *Le pétrarquisme en France au XVIe siècle*, p. 198.

More like "The Apparition" is Antonio Riccho's "Prendi crudel dela mia debil musa," *Opere . . . intitulata Fior de Delia* (Venice, 1508), e4^r. Here Riccho (or, Ricco) declares that he is about to die from the torments of unfulfilled love; and, warningly, he says, "Know, ungrateful lady, that if you were deprived/ Of all pity of amorous sort/ Yet I hope for justice below, on the other side./ Because, when that god [Love] is angry/ At a soul that follows evil,/ He punishes it in the Tartarean kingdom." (". . . sappi ingrata che se fosti priva/ Dogni pieta con amoroso segno/ Spero giustitia giu ne laltra riva/ Perho che advien, che quando prende sdegno/ Quel Dio dunalma, che nel mal procliva/ Ne fa vendetta nel tartareo regno.")

21. Donne's suspicion that his lady may prove unchaste is far from unconventional. Sexual jealousy, a standard Provençal theme, is common in Neapolitan court poetry (see for example *Rimatori*, pp. 38-39, 147) and in late Renaissance Petrarch-

ism—among Tasso's clichés about love are the statements that hate follows love, and that jealousy is a sign of ardent love (*Conclusioni amorose* 12 and 46). Renaissance courtiers, more sophisticated than college freshmen, would not find in Donne an amazing discovery that women might be unchaste, but a fine display of exacerbated sentiment.

22. *Delle rime piacevoli del Berni, Casa, Mauro, Varchi, Dolce, et d' altri auttori, liquali sopra varii soggetti capricciosi hanno mostrato la bellezza de gl'ingegni loro. Libro primo* (Venice, 1603), fols. d9ᵛ-d10ʳ.

23. See Marcel Françon, "Un motif de la poésie amoureuse au xviᵉ siècle," *PMLA*, LVI (1941), 307-336; D.C. Allen, "Latin Literature," *MLQ*, II (1941), 419; and Anteo Meozzi, *Il petrarchismo europeo: secolo xvi* (Pisa, 1934), p. 21.

Chapter V

1. There is an analogue to "The Funerall" in Serafino. Donne says "That subtile wreath of haire, which crowns my arme;/ The mystery, the signe." In "Quel cerchio d' or ch'ognun mi vede al braccio," Serafino says, "That golden circlet which everyone sees on my arm/ Is a sign." The similarity is clear in the light of the conventional use of "gold" to refer to a lady's hair, and of Donne's mention, in "The Relique," of a "Bracelet of bright hair." However, I suggest that Serafino illustrates the linguistic methods of Donne—not necessarily that he provides his material.

2. Though the witty Petrarchists are not philosophical poets, they inherit philosophical terms, themes, and arguments. For example, see the fusion of Christianity with courtly Neoplatonism in Guarino's Son. 100, "Questa terrena, ed infiammata cura," and Tasso's 113, "Quel generoso mio guerriero interno."

3. Petrarch 23, "Nel dolce tempo de la prima etade," 11. 12-13; Serafino, Stram. 167, "Quanti occelletti el di faccio dolenti"; Petrarch 119, "Una donna piú bella assai che 'l sole," 11. 1-2; Tasso 84, "I freddi e muti pesci usati omai"; Petrarch 23, "Nel dolce tempo," 1. 27; Guarino, Mad. 2, "Vien da l' onde o dal cielo?"

4. For the general influence of the witty Petrarchists, see Ernest H. Wilkins, "A General Survey of Renaissance Petrarchism," *CL*, II (1950), 327-339; for their especial popularity in Donne's time, see Joseph G. Fucilla, "A Rhetorical Pattern in Renaissance and Baroque Poetry," *SRen*, III (1956), 47-48.

5. Petrarch 23, "Nel dolce tempo," 1. 80, *et passim;* Serafino, Son. 30, "Quel nimico mortal de la natura" (not merely the statue has been petrified: the mountains are heaps of men she has turned to stone); Petrarch 134, "Pace non trovo e non ho da far guerra," and Petrarch 76, "Amor con sue promesse lusingando"; Accolti, "A Dorothea Spannocchi: Le cathene che stan con nuova sorte"; Petrarch 75, "I begli occhi, ond' i' fui percosso in guisa"; Serafino, Stram. 122, "Ben par chel fragil vetro amor non sente." For Bernardo Accolti Aretino, I use the sonnets printed at the end of *Commedia* (Florence, 1513).

6. Antonio Tebaldeo, Son. 134, "Serei corso al tuo dolce e gentil loco" (see also 133-136); Serafino, Son. 61, "Quello epitafio, el qual tu brami molto"; Accolti, "Dun Carciophono, Tu dai fuoco a chi arde in pena e lucto."

7. Son. 30, "Cresi venire al ballo, e venni al laccio."

8. Sons. 27, and 75, "Nel celeste balcone, ove sovente," "Quale spirto celeste

in un momento"; and Son. 33, "Eterno imperator d'homini e dei," in *Rime,* ed. Erasmo Pèrcopo (Naples, 1892).

9. "Castel da crudel oste assediato," quoted by Alessandro d'Ancona, *Pagina sparse* (Florence, 1914), p. 211; Stram. 99-104; Stram. 89, "Quando sero portato in Sepoltura," *et passim.* For other interesting parallels to Donne's conceit about tears and sighs, see Stram. 167, "Ah lasso a quante fier la sete toglio" and Stram. 168, "Quanti occelletti el di faccio dolenti"; in the first of these Serafino waters thirsty flocks with tears, and in the second he calcines birds with hot sighs.

10. Pamphilo Sasso, *Opera* (Venice, 1500), Sons. 338-342; on Serafino's influence, see Cecchini, *Serafino Aquilano e la lirica inglese del '500,* Janet G. Scott, *Les sonnets élisabéthains* (Paris, 1929), pp. 303-332, and Mary A. Scott, "Elizabethan Translations from the Italian . . . II. Translations of Poetry, Plays, and Metrical Romances," *PMLA,* IV (1896), 389-398. For Serafino's influence upon préciosité, see Vianey, *Le pétrarquisme en France au XVIe siècle;* on Gongorism, see Joseph G. Fucilla, "Pedro de Padilla and the Current of the Italian Quattrocentist Preciosity in Spain," *PQ, IX* (1930), 225-238.

11. Pages 68-69, 125-126, 268; Vianey calls Serafino the poet of the ring.

12. Serafino, Son. 2, "O falso Anello impresa alta e superba" (*Rime,* 1502) takes the ring as an emblem of his lady's false cruelty—though probably meaning only that she was obdurate and attractive, while Donne means that his lady was false.

13. For another lady who loves a poet because he reflects her picture, see Donne, *Elegy X: The Dreame,* 11. 1-5:

> she,
>
> Whose faire impression in my faithfull heart,
>
> Makes mee her *Medall,* and makes her love mee,
>
> As Kings do coynes, to which their stamps impart
>
> The value: . . .

14. In stanza 9, heatedly fancying his lady's corruption, Donne turns to Ovid for his images. His doing so suggests that he found Petrarchism expressive of sentiments and fantasies, but not adaptable to satiric pictures of manners.

15. On the phoenix poems of Serafino, Guarino, and Donne, see below, pp. 155-65. The debate or contest between Love and Death is a familiar theme of Renaissance emblems, lyrics, and painting.

16. Mario Praz considers this poem relevant to Donne. In *Secentismo e marinismo,* p. 109, n. 1, he compares it to 11. 25-28 of "Song: Sweetest love, I do not goe":

> When thou sigh'st, thou sigh'st not winde,
>
> But sigh'st my soule away,
>
> When thou weep'st, unkindly kinde,
>
> My lifes blood doth decay.

The analogue I give seems to me closer, but my argument applies equally to either of Donne's passages.

17. For example, in the frontispiece of *Whitney's "Choice of Emblems,"* ed. Henry Green (London, 1866). See also Josef Lederer, "John Donne and the Emblematic Practice," *RES,* XXII (1946), 196-197, and Rosemary Freeman, *English Emblem Books* (London, 1948), pp. 146-147. There is, however, no validity in the assumption that all surviving references to compasses and circles bear on Donne's

poem. There are a vast number of such references even in love poems, as a reader of the *Arabian Nights* must know. The most comprehensive survey of them is probably John Freccero, "Donne's 'Valediction: Forbidding Mourning,'" *ELH*, XXX (1963), 335-376. Such references prove only that the conjunction of love with compasses is not strikingly original and not in itself worth concentrated attention. When one looks for similar treatments of the image, Guarino's is surely closer to Donne's than are any other compasses scholars have discovered. An argument might be made for the lyric reprinted by Peter J. Seng, "Donne's Compass Image," *N&Q*, V (1958), 214-215; this lyric seems, however, to imitate Donne, and in any event its method is clearly emblematic, and very different from Donne's. Praz and D. C. Allen cite Guarino's Mad. 96 as Donne's source.

18. The two-in-oneness of lovers is a commonplace in Italian literature from Jacopo da Lentini's "Uno disio d'amore sovente," 11. 16-17, to Tasso's *Conclusioni amorose*, 36. One of its most famous statements is that of Marsilio Ficino, *Convivio*, Sp. II, ch. viii. Ficino here suggests both Donne and medieval Romance wit by his subtlety, and by some of his images—especially amorous rebirth, and the picture on the heart.

It is a cliché of the Petrarchan lyric and a commonplace of Renaissance amorous philosophy that spiritual love transcends absence. For example, Pico della Mirandola proves the superiority of the second stage of love, love for a body in imagination, by its persistence despite absence: *Dell' amore celeste e divino, Canzone di Girolamo Benivieni, Fiorentino, col comento del conte Gio: Pico Mirandolano* (Luca, 1731), p. 127.

19. Here I follow the modern editors—Hebel and Hudson, Bennett, Hayward, and Shaaber, for example. Grierson, though noting "Naked" as a well-authorized variant, prints "In that."

20. Son. 195, *Opere* . . . Vol. IV: *L'Aminta e rime scelte* (Milan, 1824).

21. The assimilation of Petrarchism to Alexandrianism is itself a characteristic of witty Petrarchism—see James Hutton, *The Greek Anthology in Italy to the Year 1800*, Cornell Studies in English, XXIII (Ithaca, N.Y., 1935), pp. 45-47, 56.

22. *Contrary Music* (Madison, 1963), pp. 39-40, *et passim*.

23. Lederer, *RES*, XXII, 196-197; Freeman, pp. 148-149.

24. On the Petrarchan origin of most amorous emblems, see Mario Praz, "Petrarca e gli emblematisti," *Ricerche anglo-italiane* (Rome, 1944), pp. 311-319.

25. For example by Frank J. Warnke, "Marino and the English Metaphysicals," *SRen*, II (1955), 160-175, and Laura Pettogello, "A Current Misconception Concerning the Influence of Marino's Poetry on Crashaw's," *MLR*, LII (1957), 321-328.

Chapter VI

1. Baroque criticism sometimes illuminates Donne. For example, Tesauro attacks Petrarch for the chastity of his style, and defends the conjunction of opposites as a play of intelligence between ceremony and meditation—see Ezio Raimondi, "Un esercizio petrarchesco di Emmanuele Tesauro," *Petrarca e il petrarchismo*, pp. 277-288.

That Donne's religious poetry is baroque seems implicit in Martz, *The Poetry of Meditation*, which learnedly argues that this poetry derives from the meditative techniques of the Counter-Reformation. But Martz fails to distinguish Counter-Reformation from earlier meditative techniques. In fact, Donne's religious poetry is often like Petrarch's: for example, compare *Holy Sonnets* I, 11. 6-14, and XIX, 11. 9-14, to "I' vo pensando, e nel penser m' assale," 11. 1-18, 73-75, 91-92, and 134-136. In general, Donne is concerned more with introspection than with scenes from Christ's life, more with abstraction than pictorialization; and therefore he shares more with Petrarch than with Southwell, Marino, or Crashaw.

2. Probably no better attempt along these lines will be made than Frank J. Warnke, *European Metaphysical Poetry: Elizabethan Club, Series 2* (New Haven, 1961). Yet Warnke's general definition describes Shelley as well as it does Donne, equating as it does the baroque with an acute interaction between sensible knowledge and spiritual reality.

3. For Serafino and the Spanish baroque, see Joseph G. Fucilla, "Pedro de Padilla and the Current of the Italian Quattrocentist Preciosity in Spain," *PQ,* IX (1930), 225-238; for Serafino and *préciosité,* Vianey, *Le pétrarquisme en France au XVIᵉ siècle.*

4. The distinction between metaphysical and baroque is wisely explained by Helen C. White, "Southwell: Metaphysical and Baroque," *MP,* LXI (1964), 159-168.

5. Rosemond Tuve, *Elizabethan and Metaphysical Imagery,* argues that Donne uses the same three levels of style as the Elizabethans, only in different places and combinations. The essence of the Elizabethan theory of decorum, however, is the separation of the styles, and the limitations of their employment. By violating this separation and limitation, Donne disregards the theory of the three styles. There is, of course, no reason for a modern critic not to use the three levels of style as part of his own critical apparatus. But from a historical point of view, it seems clear that Donne uses an entirely different poetic—as Ruth Wallerstein argues in *Seventeenth-Century Poetic* (Madison, 1950).

6. For example, see Andrea Capellano, *Trattato d'amore,* ed. Salvatore Battaglia (Rome, 1947), ch. iii (pp. 12-13); and the list of Romance uses provided by G. A. Cesaro, *Le origini della poesia lirica e la poesia siciliana sotto gli svevi* (Milan, 1924), 2nd ed., p. 389.

7. The canzone is said to be the most solemn of all Petrarch's in *Il Petrarca con nuove spositione* (Lyone, 1564), a stylistically sensitive commentary. Its psychological content is recognized by all the commentators. Filelfo, *Trionfi e sonetti . . . correti . . . per me Hieronymo Centone Paduano* (Venice, 1492), interprets the canzone as a detailed narrative about a particular incident in which Petrarch made advances to Laura: an interpretation mistaken but interesting, insofar as it makes clear, by contrast, the extremely indefinite quality of Tasso's psychology.

8. *I fiori delle rime de' poeti illustri,* ed. Girolamo Ruscelli (Venice, 1579), fols. 54ᵛ-55ᵛ. This anthology is central to the change of taste in the mid-century: the rejection of Bembo's stylistic chastity, and the beginnings of the new extravagance.

9. *Opere* (Milan, 1824), IV.

10. For example, Leone Ebreo, *Dialoghi d'amore,* ed. Santino Caramella (Bari, 1929), pp. 48-49, and Ficino, *Convivio,* I, 3. (Ficino says that the love of eyes, ears, and mind is the *only* true love; Leone says merely that it is the *best* love, because

insatiable.) See also Giuseppe Betussi, "Il raverta," *Trattati d'amore del cinquecento,* ed. Giuseppe Zonta (Bari, 1912), p. 12.

11. There is a remote resemblance between Donne's passage and 11. 3-8 of one of Serafino's ring sonnets, "O falso Anello impresa alta e superba": "Sol degno fusti tu del suo bel seno/ Serpe crudel che stai fra i fiori e lherba/ Et per exemplo suo mia man te serba/ Che in dolce aspecto angelico e sereno/ Gionge rinchiuso a me mortal veneno/ De fuor pietosa: e dentro al core acerba." ("Only you were fit for her lovely breast, cruel serpent who art among flowers and grass; and it is as her analogue that my hand wears you, for she keeps poison, mortal to me, hidden beneath her sweet, angelic, serene aspect—she is piteous on the surface, but within, bitter at the heart.")

Chapter VII

1. In passionate celebrations of love like "The Extasie," Donne's insistence that he and his lady are composed of both body and soul is a striking example of such acceptance.

2. Critics who insist upon Donne's conjunction of opposites are usually concerned to fuse Johnson's discussion of his conceit with at least one more modern view. The first—culminating in the now discredited Hugh l'Anson Fausset, *John Donne: A Study in Discord* (London, 1924)—is that Donne's personality is a unique and amazing amalgam of incompatible character traits. The second—represented by W. J. Courthope, *A History of English Poetry* (London, 1903), III, 103-117, 147-168 —is that Donne reflects the chaos of a time when medieval and modern intellectual impulses meet. (Today, it is recognized that the Renaissance is a discrete and harmonious—though intermediary—period of intellectual history: see, for example, Paul O. Kristeller, *Studies in Renaissance Thought and Letters* [Rome, 1956].) The third is the theory that Donne's is a poetry of irony and dissonance—a view adequately refuted by Rosemond Tuve's *Elizabethan and Metaphysical Imagery.*

3. The most commonly met argument here is that Donne conjoins libertinism with satiric melancholy. But in fact Donne's libertine lyrics are gay—as their imitations by Suckling, Cowley, and others suggest. And where Donne's lyrics are satiric, far from being libertine they show his life to be pure, secluded, and dedicated: see also *Satyre I,* 11. 2-4, 47-48, and *Satyre IV,* 11. 67-68. Possible exceptions are "Loves diet," "Loves Alchymie," and "Farewell to love": and the latter two should not be read without consideration of the Petrarchan theme of the renunciation of love.

4. For individualistic Petrarchism, see, for example, the lyrics of Michelangelo.

5. Surely, it is an exaggeration to argue that Petrarch's *Canzoniere* is a verse equivalent of Augustine's *Confessions,* as does Nicolae Iliescu, *Il canzoniere petrarchesco e Sant' Agostino* (Rome, 1962). But all serious Italian critics recognize Petrarch's lyrics to be a psychologically and metaphysically significant study of his own motives, and of man's place in the universe. See, for example, Umberto Bosco, *Petrarca* (Turin, 1946).

6. A Christian realist is one who is aware of the human condition, and considers that it signifies man's need of God. In Donne's religious writings, death has such significance, and so it may in his lyrics—see "The Anniversarie," for example.

Similarly, note Donne's insistence, in his amatory as in his religious writings, that man is composed of both body and soul.

7. Petrarch's interiorization stands out especially in contrast to the poets he imitates—see Ferrero, *Petrarca e i trovatori.*

8. Courtly Petrarchists, of course, write about dinners, balls, gifts, tourneys, and statues in the garden. It is worth noting, here, that concrete occasions and facts are essential to Jonson's epigrams, too.

9. There are other ways of treating the death of a beloved. In Jonson's epitaphs, for example, there is the repeated impulse to cite the objective reason for the beloved's importance, and the universal reasons for mourners to be consoled. In Dante's *Vita Nuova,* on the other hand, there is the attempt not to recall general principles and thereby moderate grief, but to make grief a general principle: when strangers arrive in Florence, Dante explains to them the desolation that has befallen the town with Beatrice's death, in "Deh peregrini che pensosi andate."

10. What is meant by "affective rhetoric" may be seen in a comparison. In "A nocturnall upon S. Lucies day," Donne says,

> . . . I am by her death, (which word wrongs her)
> Of the first nothing, the Elixer grown.

Then he proves that he is nothing, through various logical arguments. In "Gli occhi di ch' io parlai sí caldamente," Petrarch says, "The eyes of which I spoke so warmly,/ And the arms and the hands and the feet and the face/ . . . Are a bit of powder that feels nothing./ And yet I live." Both poets say that the lady is dead, and the lover left in despair. But Petrarch develops the statement emotionally, recalling his lady's glories; Donne develops the statement conceitedly, proving that the hyperbole of his nothingness is literally true.

11. Inexplicably, critics have disagreed about the meaning of this poem. That the lady is in fact dead I take to be clear in 1. 28, "I am by her death"; that she was beloved is clear, for example, in 1. 13, where Donne attributes the change in him which her death has caused, to love's alchemy.

12. For the vigil, see 1.44; for the time of day, 11. 1, 45.

13. Ll. 10-12, 37-43. The sorrowful lover's address to those lovers who are joyful in the spring—a Provençal form—is suggested by these lines.

14. See n. 10, above.

15. Among sixteenth-century Neoplatonists, this is a medical and metaphysical principle: see, for example, the comments of Vellutello, Castelvetro, and Filelfo upon Petrarch's "Piovommi amare lagrime dal viso." All take medically Petrarch's statement that, when Laura leaves, his soul goes too; Castelvetro says that the separation of his soul from his body is a death, and generally called a death by the Neoplatonists, though it is not true death.

16. Mario Praz considers this a possible source of "The Blossome" in *Secentismo e marinismo in Inghilterra,* p. 34, n. 2. Since the conceit of the separated heart is a commonplace, Praz' suggestion has little authority.

17. In "Quel vago, dolce, caro, onesto sguardo," Petrarch reproaches his intellect because, though otherwise quick as a leopard, it failed to predict Laura's death. The self-knowledge here resembles that in "The Blossome," where Donne tells his heart that it loves to be subtle to plague itself.

18. Castelvetro says that it is commonly (though wrongly) believed that Petrarch's "Mira quel colle" is a dialogue between Petrarch, who wants to go, and his heart, who wants to stay. Such a belief would emphasize the parallels between Petrarch's sonnet and "The Blossome."

Chapter VIII

1. There is a widespread belief that, as an anti-Petrarchist and a Senecan prose stylist, Donne must prefer experience to general maxims. But Donne is not an anti-Petrarchist (see pp. 136-38, above); and the Senecan style, especially for seventeenth-century divines, is a means of declaring traditional moral truths—see Don Cameron Allen, "Style and Certitude," *ELH*, XI (1948), 167-175. Donne's generalizations are tied to experience—as are those of Petrach, another Senecan, Allen notes. But Donne is not self-conscious about the uniqueness of his experience; and he does not give it particular spatial and temporal limits. It is virtually impossible, for example, to guess which lyric of Donne refers to town experiences, and which to the country.

2. The symbolistic biases of critics in the tradition of Eliot, and of their interpretations of Donne, are brilliantly characterized by Frank Kermode, *The Romantic Image* (New York, 1957).

3. Donne's resonant sense of morality and the vanity of things reflects the moral clichés of his time. His love theory is Neoplatonic (see Chs. x and xi below), and his religious doctrine is entirely conformable to that of the seventeenth-century High Church—see William R. Mueller, *John Donne: Preacher* (Princeton, 1962), an adequate statement of the current scholarly consensus.

4. Critics in the tradition of Eliot interpret Donne's conjunction of opposites as an attempt to order experience, but such a use of the *discordia concors* is purely Romantic—see René Wellek, *A History of Modern Criticism: 1750-1950* (New Haven, 1955), I, 2-3; for Romantic developments of the theory, see Wellek, II, 4-20, 40-45, *et passim*.

Furthermore, many modern critics define Donne precisely by the effort which Wellek considers peculiar to Romanticism, "the great endeavor to overcome the split between subject and object, the self and the world, the conscious and the unconscious" through "the implications of imagination [and] symbol"—*Concepts of Criticism* (New Haven, 1963), p. 220. (Wellek adds to symbol "myth, and organic nature"; but it remains true that the theory of imagination often attributed to Donne is purely Romantic.)

5. This objection to modern historical interpretations of Donne is raised by Arnold Stein, *John Donne's Lyrics* (Minneapolis, 1962), pp. 3-5. Fundamentally, of course, his argument defends critical laissez-faire against any and all historical results.

6. See Aldo Capasso, *Studi sul Tasso minore*: Studi e ritratti, Collezione di monografie letterarie diretta da Achille Pellizzari, XVIII (Genoa, 1940), pp. 111-356.

7. For the well-known scientific principle that love transcends natural laws (for example, by mixing heats with colds, and by resurrecting dead men), see Petrarch's "Io mi rivolgo indietro a ciascun passo," and "Quando giunse a Simon l'alto concetto," with the comments by Sebastiano Fausto da Longiano (Venice, 1532), Francesco Filelfo *(Trionfi e sonetti . . .)*. See also st. 4 of Petrarch's "Ben mi credea

passar mio tempo omai" with the various commentaries, including that of Allessandro Vellutello (n.p., 1528).

8. There are critics who argue that Donne is underbred on principle, doggedly coarse so as to prove that life is earnest. These critics say that Donne substitutes the rhythms of speech for those of song, and so rebels against Spenserianism. However, the rhythmical characteristics of Spenser and Lyly—aural units of equal length, whose equality is emphasized by parallelism, alliteration, and assonance; and metrical regularity—are not those of lyrics set to music. Furthermore, two of Donne's lyrics are called "Song," and several have surviving seventeenth-century musical settings—see André Souris, John Cutts, *Poèmes de Donne, Herbert, et Crashaw* (Paris, 1961).

But the question of song is peripheral. More central is that of dramatic and lyric reading. The dramatic reader is conscious of accent within phrases, and of crescendo and diminuendo within periods; the lyric reader, of accent within metrical feet, and of crescendo and diminuendo within lines. Donne deserves a lyrical reading.

9. Although it cannot be made out well enough to be reprinted, according to John Cutts there is a musical setting of "The Apparition."

Chapter IX

1. Twentieth-century critics often argue that it is medieval, but only when concerned more with the state of contemporary society than with Donne's meaning: see Kermode, *The Romantic Image,* pp. 144-147, *et passim.* Donne's religious ideas, once thought to be medieval (see, for example, M. P. Ramsay, *Les doctrines médiévales chez Donne* [Oxford, 1916]), are now generally understood to be of the Renaissance —see, for example, Mueller, *John Donne: Preacher.* And Donne's "vast medieval learning" in theology has turned out to be a familiarity with Renaissance commonplace books—see Don Cameron Allen, "Dean Donne Sets his Text," *ELH,* X (1943).

2. As it is, for example, by Merritt Y. Hughes, "The Lineage of *The Extasie,*" *MLR,* XXVII (1932), 1-5, and "Some of Donne's 'Ecstacies,' " *PMLA,* LXXV (1960), 509-518; Frank A. Doggett, "Donne's Platonism," *Sewanee Review,* XLII (1934), 274-292; and A. J. Smith, "The Metaphysic of Love," *RES,* n.s., IX (1958), 362-375.

3. Provençal studies are much embattled. English-speaking scholars especially have crusaded under the banners of two strange gods: Irony, which makes changelings of many a plain remark; and Implication, which promotes intellectual background and emotional nuance to the place of poetry's primary, explicit meaning. The view I present is that of most European scholars—for example, Etienne Gilson, "Appendix IV: Saint Bernard and Courtly Love," *The Mystical Theology of St. Bernard,* trans. A. H. C. Dounes (New York, 1940), pp. 170-197; and Alfred Jeanroy, *Histoire sommaire de la poésie occitane* (Toulouse, 1945), *La poésie lyrique des troubadours* (2 vols.; Toulouse, 1934), and elsewhere. The same general view pervades Italian studies of the early Italian lyric.

4. Its Neoplatonic idealization is stressed by Mario Casella, "Poesia e storia: I. Il più antico trovatore; II. Jaufre Rudel," *Archivo storico italiano,* XCVI (1938), 3-63, 153-199; its Arabic parallels by Father A. J. Denomy, C. S. B., "An Inquiry into the Origins of Courtly Love," *MS,* VI (1944), 175-260, and *"Fin' Amors:* the

Pure Love of the Troubadours, its Amorality and Possible Source," *MS*, VII (1945), 139-207.

5. Though some modern critics of English literature think that Provençal love service is servile and self-abasing, see J. Anglade, "La conception de l'amour chez les troubadours," *Mercure de France*, LXI (1906), 321-331; and Silvio Pellegrini, "Intorno al vassallaggio d'amore nei primi trovatori," *Cultura neolatina: Bollettino dell' Istituto di lingue e letterature romanze*, IV (1944-45), 21-36.

6. There is a most illuminating set of epistolatory lyrics by Jacopo Mostacci, Pier della Vigna, and Jacopo da Lentini. In "Sollicitando un poco meo savire," Mostacci says that though people are amorous, love, being invisible, must be non-existent; and he asks for replies. Della Vigna, in "Pero ch' amore no se po' vedire," replies that love, like magnetism, shows its presence by its effects. Lentini, in "Amore è un desio che ven da core," misses the point entirely: thinking that the question is whether love can arise without visual perception of the lady, he answers that the truest love cannot. This sequence of lyrics—thought to be an important philosophic discussion by Bruno Nardi, *Dante e la cultura medievale* (Bari, 1949), pp. 1-4, 9-15— illustrates the intellectual limitations of courtly love poets. (Just possibly Lentini's sonnet does not really belong to this sequence and the confusion belongs to his medieval and modern editors; in any case the discussion is subtle and shallow.)

7. See Cesare de Lollis, "Dolce stil novo e 'noel dig de nova maestria,' " *Studi medievali*, I (1904-05), 5-23.

8. Traditionally, critics have interpreted Neoplatonically "Al cor gentil," st. 6, where Guinizelli says that, when God reproaches him for having adored his lady, he will cite in his defense her angelic appearance. But since a personal God here condemns human love, there is obviously no Neoplatonic theory expressed in the passage.

9. The best studies of Cavalcanti are Guido Favati, "La canzone d'amore del Cavalcanti," *Letterature moderne*, III (1952), 422-453, and his brilliant "Tecnica ed arte nella poesia cavalcaniana," *Studi petrarcheschi*, III (1950), 117-144; and J. E. Shaw, *Guido Cavalcanti's Theory of Love* (Toronto, 1949).

10. Filelfo, *Trionfi e sonetti; Il Petrarcha . . . d'Alessandro Vellutello* (Venice, 1528).

11. Though he acknowledges classical rather than Petrarchan sources, see for example Marsilio Ficino, *Sopra lo amore o ver' convito di Platone* (Florence, 1544), Sp. VI, ch. ix, pp. 152-155; Sp. II, ch. viii, pp. 46-47; and Sp. II, ch. viii, pp. 45-46.

12. See for example Leone Ebreo, *Dialoghi d' amore*, pp. 6, 50; Pico della Mirandola, *Dell' amore celeste e divino*, pp. 34-38, 71-73; and Giuseppe Betussi, "Il raverta: 1544," *Trattati d'amore del cinquecento*, ed. Giuseppe Zonta (Bari, 1912), p. 8.

13. Some divergences of opinion are noted by A. J. Smith, op. cit. Ficino provides an interesting example: in Sp. I, ch. iii, he says that love and coitus are contradictories; in Sp. II, ch. vii, that both terrestial and celestial Venus are honorable; in Sp. II, ch. ix, that the only sense compatible with love is sight; in Sp. IV, ch. iv, that the soul must discard the body; in Sp. VI, ch. vi, that love may be contemplative, practical, or voluptuous; in Sp. VI, ch. xvii, that bodily love is proper, so long as it does not lose its spiritual cast; in Sp. VII, ch. i, that sensuous love leads to the Idea; and in Sp. VII, ch. xv, that true love goes from bodily to spiritual beauty, and

that false love goes from sight to touch. Generally, theorists contradict each other, varying between Pico's asceticism and Equicola's Epicureanism. Most value love according to its degree of spirituality: see, for example, Benivieni, St. VII, p. 7; Pico, pp. 115-129; and Equicola, fols. 79-81. But many insist that love must be sexual: for example, Giacomo Guidoccio, *Dialogo d'amore* (Padua, 1589), a6^r, says that it is sophistry to deny that sex is important to lovers.

14. The only one which is not—listed by me as III, g—is to be found in Giambattista Guarini (Guarino), *Compendio della poesia tragicomica*, ed. Gioachino Brognoligo (Bari, 1914), pp. 224-225, and Sperone Speroni, *Dialogi* (reprinted . . . and corrected) (Venice, 1543), a5^r-v.

15. *The Renaissance and English Humanism* (London, 1939), pp. 72-73.

16. *ABC of Reading* (New Haven, 1934), pp. 59, 77, 128-129.

17. Besides the works listed in n. 3 above, see Helen Gardner, "The Argument about 'The Ecstasy,' " *Elizabethan and Jacobean Studies Presented to F. P. Wilson* (Oxford, 1959), pp. 279-306, for Leone's influence in two poems of Donne.

18. This viewpoint, suggested by the argument of Grierson, *Poems of John Donne* (Oxford, 1912), II, xxxiv-xxxv, is made fully explicit by Praz, *Secentismo e marinismo in Inghilterra*, pp. 99-102.

19. Shaw stresses the Neoplatonic rather than the scholastic parallels. Bruno Nardi, "L'averroismo del 'primo amico' di Dante," in his *Dante e la cultura medievale*, pp. 93-129, claims that the calmness of intellect Cavalcanti speaks of reveals that he is an Averroist, but both Shaw and Favati explain Guido in a manner more suitable to the text, and more compatible with Christianity.

20. Petrarch, "A qualunque animale," 11. 31-33, and Filelfo's commentary on "Quando giunge per gli occhi" and "Nel dolce tempo de la prima etade."

21. "Due gran nemiche inseme erano aggiunte" declares that chastity and beauty are incompatible; cf. Donne, "Goe and catche," 11. 16-18. See also Petrarch's suspicions in "Se 'l dolce sguardo di costei m' ancide," with the commentary of Vellutello, *Il Petrarcha* (1528).

22. "Io non fu' d'amar voi lassato unqu'anco."

23. Filelfo understands Petrarch to be writing about a basely sexual affair—see n. 21, above. More common is the view that Petrarch, at least in early life, is moved by a love that is sexual and concupiscent, though unfulfilled: see, for example, Giovam Battista Gelli, "Lettione seconda . . . Sopra un sonetto di M. Francesco Petrarcha," *Tutte le lettioni* (Florence, 1551), d1^r-f8^r; and *Il Petrarca nuovamente ridotto alla vera lettione. Con un nuovo discorso sopra la qualità del suo amore* (Venice, 1607), b6^r-b12^v. Giovanni Cervoni da Colle, *Sopra il sonetto del Petrarca, "Amor, fortuna, e la mia mente schiva"* (Florence, 1560), a7^r, says that Petrarch's love of Laura is sexual, as appears in their quarrels and other signs of sexual affairs. In Malipiero's *Il Petrarca spirituale*, a2^r-b4^r, Petrarch's ghost says that it is silly to allegorize Laura, since his subject is concupiscence.

24. See Francesco Flamini, *Il cinquecento* (Milan, n.d.), 5th ed., pp. 203-206. Studies of anti-Petrarchism, mostly anecdotal, are also found in Benedetto Croce, *Poesia popolare e poesia d'arte* (Barri, 1957), pp. 341-343; Andrea Sorrentino, *Francesco Berni* (Florence, n.d.), pp. 164-174; and Arturo Graf, "Petrarchismo e antipetrarchismo," *Attraverso il cinquecento* (Turin, 1888), pp. 3-70. Equicola sum-

marizes Battista della Alberti's anti-Petrarchan remarks in *Libro di natura d'amore* (Venice, 1531), fols. 28^r-29^v.

25. Anti-Petrarchism is defined as anti-Platonism and anti-Ciceronianism by Baldacci, *Il petrarchismo italiano nel cinquecento*, pp. 39-43, 165-179.

26. To imitate an anti-Petrarchan poem is not necessarily to be an anti-Petrarchist: Sidney, though a Petrarchist, imitates this same poem of Berni. For a fuller discussion, see my "Donne's 'The Anagram': Sources and Analogues," *HLQ*, XXVIII (1964), 79-82.

Chapter X

1. The justification of this theory is the idea that the soul, unlike the body, is above place—see Marsilio Ficino, *Commentaire sur le "Banquet" de Platon*, ed. and trans. Raymond Marcel (Paris, 1956), Sp. VI, ch. xvi, 233. The theory is a commonplace—see, for example, Pico della Mirandola, *Dell' amore celeste e divino*, p. 127.

2. Sp. V, ch. viii; Sp. II, ch. vi, pp. 152-153. See also the summary of Bembo's views in Mario Equicola, *Libro di natura d' amore*, fols. 33^v-35^v.

3. This Neoplatonic commonplace is found, for example, in Ficino, Sp. II, ch. viii, p. 157; Guido Casoni da Serravalle, *Della magia d'amore* (Venice, 1592), fols. d1^v-d2^r; Sperone Speroni, *Dialogi*, fols. a5^{r-v}; Leone Ebreo, *Dialoghi d'amore*, pp. 44-50; and throughout the tracts and Petrarchan commentaries. Equicola, fol. 73^r, most relevantly notes that for pseudo-Dionysius and the theologians love is a unitive virtue, and a desire for union. The two-in-oneness of lovers is a commonplace in love poetry, from Jacopo da Lentini's "Uno disio d'amore sovente," 11. 16-17, to Tasso's *Conclusioni amorose*, 36.

4. Cf. Samuel Daniel, "Still let me sleep, embracing clouds in vain,/ And never wake to feel the day's disdain"—where "disdain," however, is the coldness of his mistress in reality.

5. Again, these are commonplaces. For the engraven image, see, for example, Ficino, Sp. II, ch. viii, pp. 157-158, Sp. VI, ch. ix, p. 214, and Casoni, fols. d1 $^{r-v}$; for the image as a truer object of love than the lady herself, see the discussion of Neoplatonic analogues in Helen Gardner, "The Argument about 'The Ecstasy,'" *Elizabethan and Jacobean Studies Presented to F. P. Wilson*, pp. 286-290; and also Ficino, Sp. VI, ch. x, p. 222; on the image making the lover like what he loves, see for example Ficino, Sp. VII, ch. viii, pp. 252-253; on love as a divine madness, Ficino, Sp. VII, ch. xiv, pp. 258-260, Leone, pp. 53, 57-58, 23-25, and Casoni, fols. c1^{r-v}.

6. My interpretation is basically at odds with that of Pierre Legouis, who states his view most fully in *Donne the Craftsman* (Paris, 1928), pp. 61-68, and reaffirms it in his introduction to Donne's *Poèmes choisis* (Paris, 1955), p. 29. In "Donne's *Extasie*, contra Legouis," *PQ*, XV (1936), 247-253, George Potter establishes the possibility of disagreeing with Legouis; but no one has refuted him.

Legouis argues that "The Extasie" is a drama of seduction, a sophistic appeal to the lady which slyly indicates to the reader Donne's actual intention, sexual consummation. Legouis, however, ignores the fact that the action of the poem is placed in the past, and that it is the narrator who attributes the defense of love to both lovers. Now, the narrator, as opposed to the lover, has no motive for untruthfulness according to Legouis, and yet it is the narrator whose honesty he suspects: so that Legouis' basic premise is absurd.

Further, his particular arguments are defective. Legouis considers the sweating hands of the lovers to be a sort of obscene wink to the reader, since Renaissance psychologists think hot hands to be a sign of a lecherous temperament (*Donne the Craftsman*, pp. 62-63). Now, I am not sure that Legouis recognizes the difference between a lecherous temperament and a lustful desire; but in any event the theory applies only to naturally hot hands. Anyone's hands could be heated by being clasped, as the lovers' are; hence, Legouis' interpretation is unwarranted. Furthermore, what lines 5-12 say is that the lovers' hands were united by sweat, their eyes by a glance; and that they had yet used no other means to become one, or to propagate. Here the pictures in the lovers' eyes represent propagation, the hands spiritual union. And, most damaging to Legouis' interpretation, Donne indicates that the lovers intend to use further means of propagation: he is certainly not furtive. Thus Legouis' argument from the sweating hands, the keystone of his interpretation, is completely invalid.

Legouis says further that Donne reveals his cynical intentions to the reader by contradicting himself in ll. 33-48 (pp. 65-66). But these lines explain how it is that the lovers, who had thought their aim to be sex, now know better. The explanation may be defective; but the facts to be explained clearly contradict Legouis' idea that the lover intends by his explanation to seduce his lady—after all, till now she had thought her own motives to be sexual. Thus, Legouis' interpretation may be laid to rest.

7. In Sp. II, ch. vii, Sp. VI, ch. v, and elsewhere, Ficino distinguishes Celestial Venus as contemplation, and Terrestial Venus as propagation. Leone, however, clearly identifies contemplation with union (*Dialoghi d'amore*, pp. 36-41, *et passim*); hence the distinction between union and propagation as the ends of divine and vulgar love, respectively, becomes a commonplace.

8. See especially the articles by Hughes, listed in ch. viii, n. 3.

9. "The Metaphysic of Love," *RES*, n.s., IX (1958), 362-375; also, see Hughes.

10. (Venice, 1536), fol. 199^r.

11. Ibid., fols. 206^r-207^r. The thirteenth of Francesco Contarini's *Amorose proposte* (Venice, 1601) declares it impossible to love either body or soul separately.

12. Fols. a5^r-a7^r.

13. Fols. d1^v-e1^v, e4^{r-v}.

14. Though Walton has been discredited, it seems clear that Donne's youth was not chaste, that he married for love, and that he afterwards repented of his youthful loves.

15. To Bredvold, they show that Donne, unlike Hooker and Elyot, believes man to be an amoral part of an amoral universe. See Louis I. Bredvold, "The Naturalism of Donne in Relation to Some Renaissance Traditions," *JEGP*, XXII (1923), 475-476, *et passim*. Ornstein replies that Donne believes morality to be a principle of reason, if not of nature. See Robert Ornstein, "Donne, Montaigne, and Natural Law," *JEGP*, LV (1956), 213-229. In either case, Donne rejects the notion that the universe operates on moral principles.

16. "Preface Concerning Ovid's Epistles" to *Translations from Ovid's Epistles,*

in *Poetical Works,* notes by Rev. Joseph Warton, Rev. John Warton, and others (London, 1851), p. 334.

17. Grierson, *Poems of John Donne* (Oxford, 1912), II, xl, says that Donne imitates Ovid, but that his imitation is more a matter of wit and less of the soul; Praz, *Secentismo e marinismo in Inghilterra,* p. 18, says that Donne is tormented in the Latin world of the *Elegies,* reflecting his disappointments in love.

18. See, for example, Ficino, Sp. V, ch. viii, p. 193.

19. For Plato and Heraclitus, see Robin Léon, *Greek Thought and the Origins of the Scientific Spirit* (New York, 1928), pp. 185-186; and Karl R. Popper, *Conjectures and Refutations* (New York, 1962), pp. 143-153, 75-93. For the Augustinian attribution of non-Being to matter, see Etienne Gilson, *Philosophy of St. Bonaventura,* trans. D. I. Trethorvan (New York, 1938), pp. 204-237. On Aquinas, see ibid., pp. 159-161, and Gilson's *La philosophie au moyen age* (Paris, 1947), pp. 525-541.

20. For subjectivism (the stress on man's will) and naturalism in Renaissance Neoplatonism, see Giuseppe Saitta, *Il pensiero italiano nell' umanesimo e nel rinascimento: I. L'umanesimo* (Bologna, 1949), pp. 515-516, 557 ff., *et passim;* and also his *La teoria dell' amore e l'educazione nel rinascimento* (Bologna, 1947).

Chapter XI

1. On Caroline Neoplatonism, coteries, and *vers de société,* see Upham, *The French Influence in English Literature from the Accession of Elizabeth to the Restoration,* pp. 308-364. No valid study of the "secular metaphysical poets" can ignore Upham.

2. Sperone Speroni, *Dialogi,* fol. a8ʳ.

3. Mario Equicola, *Libro di natura d'amore,* fols. 131ᵛ-132ʳ, notes that Provençal poets often say that when their friends tell them to renounce their fruitless love, they refuse.

4. *Commentaire sur le "Banquet" de Platon,* Sp. V, ch. ix, p. 194.

5. *LTLS,* LXIV (April 22, 1965), 320. Meller notes that in Giolito's *Il Petrarcha,* there is an impress of an urn with Petrarch and Laura engraved on it, and a phoenix—the printer's emblem—close above. Below, there is a sonnet declaring that Petrarch's verse made Laura immortal. In *LTLS,* LXIV (May 13, 1965), 376, A. J. Smith responds that the essential thing about Donne's lyric is the sexual pun on "die" in the third stanza—a view I dispute in the text.

6. *Poems of John Donne* (Oxford, 1912), II, cxiv—cxxi. Grierson's emendation—retained in his 1929 edition—is supported by good MSS. But George Williamson, "Textual Difficulties in the Interpretation of Donne's Poetry," *MP,* XXXVIII (1940-41), 3-72, agrees with Grierson that the 1633 text is to be followed wherever the sense permits. Sir E. K. Chambers, reviewing Grierson's edition in *MLR,* IX (1914), 270, attacks Grierson's argument but agrees that 1633 is in fact the best text.

7. Williamson, *MP,* XXXVIII, 45-46.

8. See Josef Lederer, "John Donne and the Emblematic Practice," *RES,* XXII (1946), 194-195; and D. Philippi Picinelli, *Mundus Symbolicus* (Cologne, 1694).

9. Fol. 44ᵛ.

10. On the differences between Donne's conceits and emblems, see Freeman, *English Emblem Books,* pp. 148-149, *et passim.*

11. Besides the interpretations provided by Picinelli, see Edgar H. Duncan, "Donne's Alchemical Figures," *ELH,* IX (1942), 270-271. Since it is of the essence of hermetic philosophy to translate all sorts of difficult literary and philosophical passages into alchemical theory, the mere fact that Donne's symbols appear *in* alchemical treatises is no indication at all that they derive *from* them.

12. For example, by Williamson, *MP,* XXXVIII, 45-46.

13. On the Petrarchan origin of amorous emblems, see Mario Praz, "Petrarca e gli emblematisti," *Ricerche anglo-italiane* (Rome, 1944), pp. 303-319. Lederer (*RES,* XXII, 185) attributes the similarities between Donne and the Petrarchists to the Alexandrian derivation of both emblem and Petrarchan conceit. But he does not show either that Donne draws upon the emblem rather than upon Petrarchan lyrics, or that the emblem itself uses Greek rather than Italian sources.

14. For this image, see Francesco Flamini, *La lirica toscana del rinascimento* (Pisa, 1891), pp. 438-440; and Watson, *Hec.* 67, "When *Cupid* is content to keepe the skies."

15. For the eagle who stares fixedly at the sun, and so represents the lover whose eyes are fixed on his lady, see, for example, Petrarch 19, "Sono animali al mondo di sí altera," with the note, and Serafino, Son. I, "L'acquila che col sguardo affisa el sole" (cf. Watson, *Hec.* 78, "What scowling cloudes"). The closest parallel to Donne's line I know is Serafino's *Epistola* V, ll. 38-39: "Ma haria ben facto el mio constante amore: /Laquile e le colombe insemi amice," "But my constant love surely would have joined the eagle and the dove as friends." Donne may well have found a symbolic significance in this pun of l'Aquilano ("The Eagle-ite"). But the image is far from unique—for example, in "Ma petite columbelle," Ronsard says that he holds his lady as an eagle clasps a trembling dove.

16. Speroni, *Dialogi,* a5^{r-v}. This passage precedes that quoted on pp. 143-44, above. That Donne twice parallels Speroni suggests influence.

17. *Dialoghi d'amore,* p. 56.

18. *Il pastor fido e Il compendio della poesia tragicomica,* ed. G. Bragnoligo (Bari, 1914), pp. 224-225.

19. Equicola, fols. 183^v-184^r, 185^r. Cf. Speroni, quoted above, pp. 143-44.

20. These sonnets are printed in Fausto Montanari, *Studi sul canzoniere del Petrarca* (Rome, 1958), pp. 79 and 83.

21. Lodovico Castelvetro, *Le rime del Petrarca brevemente sposte.*

22. See, for example, Jean Festugière, *La philosophie de l'amour de Marsile Ficin et son influence sur la littérature française au XVIe siècle* (Paris, 1941), pp. 96-98, 110, 116, *et passim;* and Watson, *Hec.* 44, 56, 57, 91, and *Tears* 40.

Though the phoenix image is sometimes used with a sexual meaning, it is primarily the symbol of holy mysteries, such as the union of the Virgin Mary with Jesus (see Henry Green, *Shakespeare and the Emblem Writers* [London, 1870], pp. 383-384). Donne's own use of the phoenix to represent the consummation of a marriage in the epithalamion "Haile Bishop Valentine" reveals his intention of exalting both the married couple and the miracle of marriage; he considers sexual consummation as merely one element of spiritual union and rebirth. See also the exaltation implied by the phoenix symbol in a similar epithalamion, "Ecco luce amorosa," *Biblioteca di letteratura popolare italiana,* I, 184-185.

23. Guido Casoni da Serravalle, *Della magia d'amore,* fols. d3^v-e1^r. For the

importance of Petrarch to the tracts—greater than that of Plato—see Luigi Tonelli, *L'amore nella poesia e nel pensiero del rinascimento* (Florence, 1933), pp. 280 ff.

24. *Commentaire*, Sp. II, ch. viii, pp. 155-158. Ficino's Platonic casuistry here is especially suggestive of Donne.

Sometimes, Neoplatonists use amorous death to mean a submission of soul to sense—for example, Alessandro Farra, "Discorso de miracoli d'amore," *Trè discorsi* (Pavia, 1564), a7^r-cl^v. But more often by amorous death they mean a transcendence of the body—see Farra, c2^r-c6^v. It is in the light of this meaning of "death" that the Neoplatonists read Petrarch (see Farra, c2^r-c6^v) and other love poets—see, for example, Gianbatista Gello (Gelli), *Espositione d' un sonetto platonico, fatto sopra il primo effetto d'amore che e il separare l' anima dal corpo de l'amante, dove si tratta de la immortalita de l' anima secondo Aristotle, e secondo Platone* (Florence, 1549).

A sensual poet like Antonio Riccho adapts Ficino's argument. In "Horsu Madonna ogni vergogna scaza," he says that his lady's refusal kills him, and that she ought to return him to life by yielding her body to him.

25. Cf. Watson *Hec.* 22, "When werte thou borne sweet *Love?* who was thy sire?"

26. Pamphilo Sasso, Son. 68 and 69, "Non mi guardar che dreto a quel splendor" and "Guardame che la acerba e ria ferita," *Opera*; Amalteo, "Se de' begli occhi il Sole," st. 3, *I fiori della rime de' poeti illustri* (Venice, 1579), fol. 145^r; and Menni, "Occhi, non occhi già, ma viva luce," quoted by Fucilla, *PQ*, IX, 235.

27. For amorous union, cf. "The Extasie," 11. 33-48, which also note the difference between an amorous union and the lovers who compose it; and for amorous miracles, "A Valediction: of my name, in the window," st. 2—Donne's claim to be mysterious is much like Petrarch's claim that his tranformation into the phoenix is marvellous, and Ficino's demonstration that the lovers' rebirth, being double where their death is single, is miraculous.

28. See Tonelli, p. 287.

29. Among the more practical Neoplatonic guides to love are Francesco Sansovino, *Ragionamento d' amore* (1535) and Bartolomeo Gottifredi, *Specchio d' amore* (1547), both edited by Giuseppe Zonta, *Trattati d'amore del cinquecento* (Bari, 1912); and Guidoccio, *Dialogo d'amore*, which combines Neoplatonic theories like the divine furor of love with practical advice, such as to choose a lady who is not too good-looking so as to avoid jealousy.

30. Leone, pp. 197-199, 171-173.

31. By making the last couplet central, critics create difficulties. Joan Bennett, "The Love Poetry of John Donne: A Reply to Mr. C. S. Lewis," *Seventeenth Century Studies Presented to Sir Herbert Grierson* (Oxford, 1938), pp. 99-102, tries to show that there is no denigration of women in this couplet. She says that Donne argues that woman's love is just impure enough to keep man's soul bound to the earth; and that the reader must ignore irrelevant connotations of "puritie." But Donne's lyric is not a discussion of what holds his soul to the earth. He says that it is his love, not his soul, which is enveloped by his lady's love ("my loves spheare") after distinguishing love from the soul, its parent. He claims to have loved this particular lady, not the infinite, before he knew her ("Twice or thrice had I loved thee"). In short, he is not saying that love is a vague desire which fixes on a lady, but that the object of his love of this lady is her love of him.

On the other hand, Mrs. Bennett is surely right in defending the rich emotionalism of the lyric against those who claim it to be a mere epigram, or emotional *discordia concors,* solely on the basis of the wit in the final couplet.

32. *Commentaire,* Sp. V, ch. viii, p. 193.

33. Leone, pp. 230-231, and Pico—see Eugenio Garin, *Giovanni Pico della Mirandola* (Florence, 1937), p. 210—agree that the lover is the more divine. Ficino, Sp. VI, ch. xiii, p. 182, repeats Plato's dictum that soul is weak in women, and that therefore celestial lovers turn to boys. (He thinks of education, not pederasty.) Francesco Cattani da Diacceto, "Panegirico all' amore," *I tre libri d' amore* (Venice, 1561), L1r-L3r, says that the lover is full of divinity, and that the beloved will be punished after death if she fails to worship him. Furthermore, the "courts of love" debated whether men or women love more truly. Thus, Donne is far from alone in proclaiming the superiority of masculine love.

Chapter XII

1. *The Proper Wit of Poetry* (Chicago, 1961), p. 42.

2. Donne's fusion of thought with passion has been considered revolutionary; but from its beginnings Romance love literature shows such a fusion. Though the moral integrity of Andreas is exaggerated by D. W. Robertson, Jr. in "The Subject of the *De Amore* of Andreas Capellanus," *MP,* L (1953), 145-161, Andreas clearly shows a concern with philosophy and morality that has no parallel in Ovid. The *dolce stil novo* is both passionate and scholastic. And Petrarchism is the philosophical lyric of the Renaissance—witness Petrarch's Augustinianism and Michelangelo's Platonism.

3. As René Wellek says in *A History of Modern Criticism,* I, 99, Johnson expresses a dislike for all special tastes from a viewpoint which is itself one of the most special in the history of criticism.

4. For nineteenth-century adumbrations of virtually all the clichés used to define metaphysical poetry by Eliot and his followers, see Joseph E. Duncan, *The Revival of Metaphysical Poetry* (Minneapolis, 1959), especially pp. 113-126. On pp. 113-115, Duncan properly notes that by the time of Grierson's edition, virtually all of Eliot's ideas were standard.

5. *Richard Crashaw* (University, La., 1939), pp. 91-92, 98-114, *et passim; A Reading of George Herbert* (Chicago, 1952).

6. For example, Habington in "Against them who lay unchastity to the sex of Women" (cf. "Song: Goe and catche"); Townsend in the martial imagery of "To the Countesse of Salisbury: Victorious beauty, though your eyes" (cf. "The Dampe"); Stanley in "La Belle Confidante" (cf. "A Valediction: forbidding mourning"); and Randolph in "Upon his Picture: When age hath made me" (cf. *Elegie V: His Picture*).

7. Cleveland's "The Hecatomb to his Mistress," cited by Williamson, p. 74.

8. Williamson seems entirely innocent of the knowledge that these tropes are Donne's. But see "Both the' India's of spice and Myne," "The Sunne Rising," 1. 17; "a fast balme," "The Extasie," 1. 6; "the Elixir grown," "A nocturnall," 1. 29; and the various religious images in "The Canonization," "The Relique," "A Valediction: forbidding mourning," and throughout Donne's lyrics.

9. There is an excellent discussion of this change by R. C. Bald, ed., *Seventeenth Century Poetry* (New York, 1957), pp. 11-34.

10. Suckling, for example, is regularly more easy and conversational than Donne. Compare, "Oh! for some honest Lovers ghost" with "Loves Deitie"; "Out upon it, I have lov'd" with "Womans constancy"; "Song: No, no, fair heretic" with "Loves growth"; or the image of the microcosm in "Loves World" with that in "The Dissolution."

11. For funeral poems, see Ruth Wallerstein, *Studies in Seventeenth-Century Poetic*.

selected bibliography

Primary Italian Works

Accolti, Bernardo. *Commedia.* Florence, 1513.

Alunno de Ferrara, Francesco. *Le osservationi . . . sopra il Petrarca . . . con . . . dechiarationi delle voci, e de luoghi difficili con le regole et osservationi delle particelle, et delle altre voci a i luoghi loro per ordine di alphabeto collocate.* 2 vols. Venice, 1550.

Bembo, Pietro. *Gli asolani.* Venice, 1546.

————. *Prose.* Ed. C. Dionisotti. Turin, 1931.

Berni, Francesco. *Delle rime piacevoli del Berni, Casa, Mauro, Varchi, Dolce, et d'altri auttori, liquali sopra varrii soggetti capricciosi hanno mostrato la bellezza de gl' ingegni loro, Libro primo.* Venice, 1603.

Betussi, Giuseppe. "Il raverta." Ed. Giuseppe Zonta, *in Trattati d'amore del cinquecento.* Bari, 1912.

Biblioteca di letteratura popolare italiana, I. Ed. Severino Ferrari. Florence, 1882.

Capellano, Andrea. *Trattato d'amore . . . con due traduzioni toscane inedite del sec. xiv.* Ed. Salvatore Battaglia. Rome, 1947.

Casoni da Serravalle, Guido. *Della magia d'amore.* Venice, 1592.

Castelvetro, Lodovico. *Le rime del Petrarca brevemente sposte.* Basilea, 1582.

Castiglione, Baldesar. *Il libro del cortegiano.* Ed. Vittorio Cian. Florence, n.d.

Cattani da Diacceto, Francesco. *I tre libri d'amore.* Venice, 1561.

Cavalcanti, Guido. *Rime.* Ed. Guido Favati. Milan, 1957.

Cei, Francesco. *Sonecti, capituli, canzone, sextine, stanze, ed strambocti.* Florence, 1514.

Cervoni da Colle, Giovanni. *Sopra il sonetto del Petrarca "Amor, fortuna, e la mia mente schiva."* Florence, 1560.

Chariteo (Cariteo). See Gareth, Benedetto.

Chastiglione, Giovambatista da. *I luoghi difficili del Petrarcha nuovamente dichiarati.* Venice, 1532.

Colonna, Stephano. *I sonetti, le canzoni, et i triomphi di M. Laura in risposta di M. Franchesco Petrarcha per le sue rime in vita, et dopo la morte di lei. Pervenuti alle mani del . . .* Venice, 1552.

Colotio, Angelo. "Apologia . . . al magnifico Sylvio Piccolhomini s. et benefactore," in *Le rime di Serafino de' Ciminelli dall' Aquila.* Ed. Mario Menghini. Vol. I. Bologna, 1894.

Contarini, Francesco. *Amorose proposte*. Venice, 1601.

Daniello da Lucca, Bernardino. *Sonetti, canzoni, e triomphi di Messer Francesco Petrarcha con la spositione di* . . . Venice, 1541.

Dante Alighieri. *Le opere minori:* II. *Rime*. Ed. G. L. Passerini. Florence, 1923.

———. *Rime della "Vita nuova" e della giovinezza*. Ed. M. Barbi and F. Maggini. Florence, 1956.

———. *De vulgari eloquentia*. Ed. and trans. Aristide Marigo. Florence, 1957.

Dolce, Lodovico. *Modi affigurati e voci scelte et eleganti della volgar lingua*. Venice, 1564.

———. *Il Petrarca nuovamente revisto* . . . *con* . . . *indici del Dolce utilissimi di tutti i concetti, e delle parole, che nel poeta si trovano. E di piu con una breve, e particolare spositione di tutte le rime*. Venice, 1557.

Equicola, Mario. *Libro di natura d'amore*. Venice, 1531.

———. *Libro di natura d'amore*. Venice, 1536.

Farra, Alessandro. "Discorso de miracoli d'amore," in *Trè discorsi*. Pavia, 1564.

Fausto da Longiano, Sebastiano. *Il Petrarcha col commento di* . . . *con rimario et epiteti in ordine d'alphabeto*. Venice, 1532.

Ficino, Marsilio. *Commentaire sur le "Banquet" de Platon*. Ed. and trans. Raymond Marcel. Paris, 1956.

———. *Sopra lo amore o ver' convito di Platone*. Florence, 1544.

Filelfo, Francesco. *Trionfi e sonetti di Misser Francescho Petrarcha correti e castigati per me Hieronymo Centone Paduano*. Venice, 1492.

I fiori delle rime de' poeti illustri. Ed. Girolamo Ruscelli. Venice, 1579.

Gareth, Benedetto. *Le rime di* . . . *detto il Chariteo*. Ed. Erasmo Pèrcapo. 2 vols. Naples, 1892.

Gelli, Giovam Battista (Gello, Gianbatista). *Tutte le lettioni di* . . . Florence, 1551.

———. *Espositione d'un sonetto platonico, fatto sopra il primo effetto d'amore che e il separare l'anima dal corpo de l'amante, dove si tratta de la immortalita de l'anima secondo Aristotle, e secondo Platone*. Florence, 1549.

Gesualdo, Giovanni Andrea. *Il Petrarcha colla spozitione di* . . . Venice, 1533.

Gottifredi, Bartolomeo. "Specchio d'amore" (1547). Ed. Giuseppe Zonta, in *Trattati d'amore del cinquecento*. Bari, 1912.

Guarini, Giambattista (Guarino, Giovanni Battista). *Compendio della poesia tragicomica*. Ed. Gioachino Brognoligo. Bari, 1914.

———. *Rime*. Venice, 1598.

Guidoccio, Giacomo. *Dialogo d' amore*. Padua, 1589.

Lanfranco Parmegiano. *Il Petrarcha* . . . *con alcune annotationi, et un pieno vocabulario del medesimo, sopra tutte le voci, che nel libro si contengono, bisognose di dichiaratione, d'avvertimento, e di regola, et con uno utilissimo rimario* . . . *et un raccolto de tutti gli epiteti usati dall' autore*. Venice, 1554.

Leone Ebreo. *Dialoghi d'amore*. Ed. Santino Caramella. Bari, 1929.

Liburnio, Nicolo. *Le tre fontane* . . . *sopra la grammatica, et eloquenza di Dante, Petrarcha, et Boccaccio*. Venice, 1526.

Lirici cortigiani del '400. Ed. Alessandro Tortoreto. Milan, 1942.

Lirici del cinquecento. Ed. Luigi Baldacci. Florence, 1957.

Malipiero Venetiano, Frate Hieronimo. *Il Petrarca spirituale*. Venice, 1567.

Bibliography

Minturno, Antonio. *Ragione d'alcune cose segnate nella canzone d'Annibal Caro, "Venite al' ombra de gran gigli d'oro."* N.p., n.d.

Olimpia d'amore . . . *Rime piacevoli, e honeste, le quali ogni giovane potrà accomodare al suo senso.* Bologna, n.d.

Oradini, Lucio. *Due lezzioni.* Florence, 1550.

Parabosco, Girolamo. *Delle lettere amorose.* Milan, 1558.

Petrarca, Francesco. *Le rime.* Ed. G. Carducci and S. Ferrari. Florence, 1957.

Il Petrarca con nuove spositione. Lyone, 1564.

Il Petrarca nuovamente ridotto alla vera lettione. Con un nuovo discorso sopra la qualità del suo amore. Venice, 1607.

Pico della Mirandola, Giovanni. *Dell' amore celeste e divino, Canzone di Girolamo Benivieni, Fiorentino, col comento del conte Gio: Pico Mirandolano.* Luca, 1731.

La poesia lirica del duecento. Ed. Carlo Salinari. Turin, 1951.

Riccho Neapolitano, Antonio (Ricco). *Opere* . . . *intitulata Fior de Delia,* revised. Venice, 1508.

Rimatori del dolce stil novo. Ed. L. di Benedetto. Turin, 1944.

Rimatori napoletani del quattrocento. Ed. Mario Mandalari. Caserta, 1885.

Rime di diversi illustri signori napoletani, e d'altri nobiliss. ingegni. Libro Quinto. Venice, 1552.

Delle rime di diversi nobili huomini et eccellenti poeti nel lingua thoscana, nuovamente ristampate. Libro secondo. Venice, 1548.

Rime diverse di molti eccellentiss. auttori, con nuova additione. Libro primo. Venice, 1546.

Sansovino, Francesco. "Ragionamento d'amore" (1535). Ed. Giuseppe Zonta, in *Trattati d'amore del cinquecento.* Bari, 1912.

Sasso, Pamphilo. *Opera.* Venice, 1500.

Serafino dall' Aquila. *Opere* . . . *collette per Francesco Flavio.* Venice, 1502.

―――. *Le rime di Serafino de' Ciminelli dall' Aquila.* Vol. I. Ed. Mario Menghini. Bologna, 1894.

Simon de la Barba da Pescia. *Nuova spositione del sonetto che comincia "In nobil sangue vita humile, e' queta." Nela quale si dichiara la vera nobilità di Madonna Laura.* Florence, 1554.

Speroni, Sperone. *Dialogi.* Venice, 1543.

Tagliente, Giovan Antonio. *Opera amorosa, che insegna a componer lettere et a rispondere a persone damor ferite, o ver in amor viventi in thoscha lingua composta con piacer non poco e diletto di tutti gli amanti, laqual si chiama il Rifugio di amanti, o vero componimento di parlamenti.* Venice, 1527.

Tasso, Torquato. *La Gerusalemme liberata.* Ed. Piero Nardi. Verona, 1956.

―――. *Opere, IV: L'Aminta e rime scelte.* Milan, 1824.

―――. *Le prose diverse,* II. Ed. Cesare Guasti. Florence, 1825.

―――. *Le rime.* Ed. Angelo Solerti. Vol. II. Bologna, 1898.

Tebaldeo, Antonio. *L'opere d'amore.* Venice, 1550.

Tullia d'Aragona. "Dialogo della infinità di amore" (1547). Ed. Giuseppe Zonta, in *Trattati d'amore del cinquecento.* Bari, 1912.

Varchi, Benedetto. *Lezione,* in *Opuscoli inediti or rari di classici o approvati scrittori.* Vol. I. Florence, 1845.

Vellutello, Allessandro. *Il Petrarcha con l'espostione d'* . . . Venice, 1528.

index

Many of the entries in this index are classified under the following headings: Critics, Renaissance; Love poets, Italian; Love prose writers, Italian; and Major conceits, poetic and philosophical. The three other main areas with which the index is concerned—Donne's lyrics, my own critical concepts, and contemporary scholars—did not seem to call for special notice.

Handwritten note in top margin: HOBO

Donald L. Guss is associate professor of English at Wayne State University. *John Donne, Petrarchist* grew out of discoveries made during his study of Renaissance materials virtually unknown to English-speaking scholars.

Barbara Woodward edited the manuscript. The book was designed by Richard Kinney. The typeface for the text is Linotype Granjon originally designed about 1580 and redesigned by G. W. Jones for Linotype in 1924. The display face is Libra designed by S. H. De Roos for Amsterdam in 1938.

The book is printed on Warren's Olde Style white wove paper and bound in Bancroft's Arrestox B over boards. Manufactured in the United States of America.